Untamed

Untamed

*The Psychology of
Marvel's Wolverine*

SUZANA E. FLORES

Foreword by PAUL JENKINS

McFarland & Company, Inc., Publishers
Jefferson, North Carolina

Library of Congress Cataloguing-in-Publication Data

Names: Flores, Suzana E., 1973– author. | Jenkins, Paul, 1965– writer of foreword.
Title: Untamed : the psychology of Marvel's Wolverine / Suzana E. Flores ; foreword by Paul Jenkins.
Description: Jefferson, North Carolina : McFarland & Company, Inc., Publishers, 2018. | Includes bibliographical references and index.
Identifiers: LCCN 2018024726 | ISBN 9781476674421 (softcover : acid free paper) ∞
Subjects: LCSH: Wolverine (Fictitious character) | X-Men (Fictitious characters) | Marvel Comics Group.
Classification: LCC PN6728.W5984 F57 2018 | DDC 741.5/973—dc23
LC record available at https://lccn.loc.gov/2018024726

British Library cataloguing data are available

ISBN (print) 978-1-4766-7442-1
ISBN (ebook) 978-1-4766-3319-0

Front cover images © 2018 iStock

Printed in the United States of America

McFarland & Company, Inc., Publishers
 Box 611, Jefferson, North Carolina 28640
 www.mcfarlandpub.com

To the creators: Roy Thomas, Len Wein, John Romita, Sr., and Herb Trimpe—"muchas gracias" for creating one of the most inspirational comic book characters of all time.

To Hugh Jackman for capturing the complex persona of Wolverine like no other, and for bringing him to life on the big screen.

To the billions (yes, that's with a "B") of Wolverine fans around the globe—an emotional "thank you" for the passionate personal investment you've found so compelling in the modern mythology of Marvel.

And to one of those fans in particular, my friend Al Padilla—thank you for your support and encouragement and for standing by my side no matter what.

A profoundly heartfelt thank you is offered to the late Len Wein and Herb Trimpe, who devoted their lives to Wolverine. Len and Herb—your vision and influence has secured Wolverine's place in the pantheon of mythology for all time.

Wolverine embodies suffering more than other X-Men because he is built to withstand it; to survive it; to endure it. Logan has natural aggression tempered by the extraordinary humanity he so desperately tries to hide. He's always trying to keep the beast in check. I think this is what makes him so interesting. Logan represents very real themes of trauma and resiliency. And what keeps him going is his search for answers. He wants to know more about himself; to evolve— which is what we all do. If I could say one thing to Logan, I'd tell him to chill; to take it easy. Everything's going to be okay. Logan's a little crazy, but then again, so are we.

—Len Wein, legendary comic book writer
and co-creator of Wolverine

Table of Contents

Acknowledgments

First and foremost, I would like to thank my agent, friend and greatest advocate, Elizabeth Kracht. Your wisdom, support and enthusiasm have been valuable beyond measure.

Thanks are also extended to Wolverine's legendary godfathers: Roy Thomas (who conceptualized the character), Len Wein (who wrote the character), John Romita, Sr. (who first designed the character's look), and Herb Trimpe (the first artist to draw him for publication). Although I speak for myself here, I am certain that I also speak for the billions of Marvel fans worldwide when I once again say "thank you" for the vision and creativity you have crafted and shared.

Listing every Wolverine illustrator and writer who has contributed to and inspired the character's development and evolution would be nearly impossible. However, each of them has invested an inestimable slice of their talents, their skills, and indeed their own selves to this character. I admire their immense talent and would like to thank them all.

Thank you to Hugh Jackman for his holistic, humanistic, and horrific portrayal of a wounded antihero with generational mythology within his grasp.

To the Wolverine creators, writers, and illustrators who agreed to be interviewed for this book—Roy Thomas, Len Wein, John Romita, Sr., Joe Rubinstein, John Romita, Jr., Adam Kubert, Tom DeFalco, and Paul Jenkins.

To Virginia Romita for giving me the courage to share my pain and my truth—proudly and without apology.

To Patricia Trimpe (wife of the late Herb Trimpe)—I thank you for sharing the inspiration behind the vision of the Wolverine character.

To Chandler Rice and Sharon Richardson of Desert Wind Enterprises—this work would not have been possible without you. The best fortune of my life was meeting you at the Great American Comic Con: Las Vegas. Thank you for connecting me to Len Wein, Joe Rubinstein, and John Romita, Sr. and Jr., among others. Thank you also for your guidance, your support, your amazing sense of humor that kept me going on this project, and your friendship.

Thanks to J. David Spurlock and John Cimino (The Mego Stretch Hulk) for your assistance and insight into the creative inspiration behind Wolverine.

An immense thank you to Janet Poggendorf for your amazing talent with copyediting, as well as your immeasurable support and patience as we tackled this work together. I could not have done this without you. Thank you especially for your brilliant contributions to the X-Men chapter. I do believe that this chapter welded our friendship together for life, because we both know all too well that "Magneto *was* right!"

Thank you to the mental health clinicians who shared their insights and suggestions for this work either through interviews or via consultations: Dr. Clive Hazell, Dr. Lisa Gaudet, Dr. Vijay K. Jain, Dr. Jon McCaine, Larry Yarbrough, Max Stoltenberg, Roumen Bezergianov, Ed Ottesen, Tehrina Billi, Joel Terry, and Janelle Otero.

Thanks to Dr. Eric Snyder for consultation on genetic mutations and for clarifying that all of us are mutants in one way or another!

A most outsized thank you to Doug Kline, comic book enthusiast and author of *The San Diego Comic Con Survival Guide*, and to Elliott Serrano, comic book writer and geek culture expert (a.k.a. Chicago's "King of Geeks"). I am eternally grateful for your expertise in imparting the wit, wisdom, and melodramas of comic book history and for providing many hours of consultation and support as you helped me navigate more than 40 years of *Wolverine* and *X-Men* comic book history.

A magnificent hat tip and emotional low bow to fellow authors and friends who reviewed my work and offered invaluable feedback and suggestions: Joe Clifford, Danny Gardner, Garrett Box, Charles Lemoine, Jonathan Maberry, Jill Sherer Murray, and Peter Hogenkamp.

To comic book fans who offered ideas and recommendations—Gene Lewis, Enrico Mowatt, Bert Branson, David Loh, Steven Serrano, E.P. McFarlin, Aaron Gabbard, Rob Fritzsche, Lynn Patterson, Lyndsay Wagoner, Jason Howell, Zachary Smith, Brenden Smith, and others—a profound "muchas gracias!"

Thank you to Joe Garcia, Larry Yarbrough, Gerald Newport, and Joseph de la Rosa, who contributed their insights as military personnel and first responders. As you know, Logan also served in the military and faced danger every day—just as you have. You are all heroes. Thank you for your service.

Thank you to Ben Millard for providing much-needed IT and emotional support during a writing crisis, and to Tara Goodyear for her remarkable copyediting work.

To my parents, Jose Mario and Rosa Flores, my aunt Elena Segura, and all my family members whom I love eternally—thank you for being my greatest cheerleaders. Thank you for your love and reassurance, and for putting up with me as I spent too many hours working on this book and far too much time away from you.

To Al and Nicole Padilla—thank you for believing in this book, for believing in me, and for believing that I was the one to write it. After all that you have done for me, you are more than friends; you are family.

Thanks are likewise extended to my dear friends who always have my back and who offered their assistance through either reading certain chapters or offering emotional support along this journey: Derrick Ryce and Nellie Tehrani, Niranjani and Dr. Narayan Prabhakar, Dr. Robert Bright and Luc Bouchard, Robert Wray and David Jensen, Dr. Ruth Yoash-Gantz and Dr. Frank Gantz, Patti Vasquez, Cortney and David McCormick, Dr. Leslie Waite, Joe Neal, Roberta Grasseschi and Christopher Doman, Dr. Michelle Katz Jesop and Matthew Jesop, Dr. Matthew Clark, Keith Dukavicius, Lynn Stanton, Dontae Latson, Julio Soto and Joe Roos, Sue Miller and John Davis, Richard Baukovic, Natalia Derevyanny Burns, Christina Scott, Nathan Israileff, Jill Ronzio, Scott Perry, Michaelene Tracey, Tina Ellis, and Ricardo Molina.

I am also grateful for the immense support from my fellow clinicians, who put up with me talking about Logan for hours on end: Dr. Gina Frohöich, Dr. Lilia Miramontes, Dr. Jennifer Steel, Marcée Turner, Dr. Nisha Todi, Holly Gartler, Dr. Colin Pickles, Dr. Jami Voss, Clarivel Santos, Maria Grimshaw, Matthew Miescke, Amal Fayad, Dr. Sarah May, Dr. Dereck Byrd, and Dr. Sara Gruzlewski. Thank you for cheering me on when I needed it the most.

I beg forgiveness from all those who have been with me over the course of this journey and whose names I have failed to mention in these pages.

And last, but certainly not least, to Marcus Morales—the love of my life and my partner in crime—thank you for your support and endless patience as I tackled the world of Marvel-topia. Thank you especially for understanding, and even encouraging, my Logan obsession over the past two years. I don't know what I would do without you.

Foreword
by Paul Jenkins

In many respects, the story of Wolverine is the story of us all.

This is the nature of stories: they are supposed to be a mirror held up to their audiences. Stories move us because they remind us of things that we have experienced. Characters reflect us—villains and heroes all—because they succeed and fail in turns, as we do. So why do certain characters appeal to us beyond others?

Well, that's the sixty-four-million-dollar question, isn't it? But maybe that is the point here. It's not that we always find answers in the actions of our heroes; rather, it's that they allow us to ask ourselves the right questions. And we have been asking questions about ourselves since we first crawled out of the mud.

At the beginning of the 21st century I was given the privilege of creating an origin story for Wolverine, which was published by Marvel in 2001. The approach was quite simple, in that we set out to answer two or three simple questions on the minds of the fans: Where and when was Wolverine born, what was his real name, and why did he forget so much of his life? By answering these questions, I firmly believe that we created the opportunity for readers to ask a thousand more questions about their hero: How did he reflect the nurturing personality of his biological father; how did he deal with his biological mother's apparent rejection; what did he learn in his formative years that made him so tenacious; and why does he always—always—stand up to bullies?

These questions and many others are at the core of Suzana Flores's book. Suzie and I spoke in depth about the factors that inspired me to write Logan's origin story and, similarly, what compelled her to psychologically analyze him. We discussed the mythology of the hero archetype,

1

and how the stories behind these characters address our personal experiences of suffering. Ultimately, Suzie and I agreed that the answer to why we both wrote about Logan was *pain*. We have all faced physical or emotional pain on some level, and Logan exemplifies resilience in the face of human suffering.

In these pages you will find a fascinating glimpse into the various factors that have helped shape James Howlett, better known as Logan or Wolverine. Suzie does a wonderful job of peeling back the layers of the character; her book answers a few questions, perhaps, but it will also allow you to ask a few hundred more of your own. This is the story of Wolverine, held under the microscope of insightful psychological analysis.

It is the story of you.

Paul Jenkins has been creating, writing and building franchises in the graphic novel, film and video game industries for more than 25 years. He won an Eisner Award for his work on the Marvel Comics Inhumans *series in 1997, and he has worked on* Spider-Man, Batman, The Incredible Hulk, Teenage Mutant Ninja Turtles *and more.*

Introduction

Have you ever legitimately felt as though you were losing your mind—*truly* questioning what you were seeing and feeling and thinking? Ever been unequivocally pushed to the edge of your psychological precipice? Ever lost every last connection to who you really are, who you know, what you know ... or don't? Ever tried drinking enough to pave over the spiritual anguish that such mental black holes create, or lashed out with a savagery unrecognizable to you or to those around you?

If you answered "yes" to these or other personal mental mysteries, you have something in common with Marvel Comics' most popular character: Wolverine.

Wolverine (a.k.a. James Howlett, and later known simply as "Logan") is a mutant, an antihero, and a human being all in one conflicted carcass. He's the dude with the retractable claws and a dualistic nature—part man and part beast—and driven by the capacity for both ferocity and friendship.

My fascination with the Wolverine character began not during my childhood, as it has for the many fans who collected and traded nearly every issue of the *Uncanny X-Men* and then *Wolverine* comic book series, but, unexpectedly, as an adult.

During a particularly challenging time in my life, I came across a poster from the *X-Men: The Dark Phoenix Saga* series featuring an illustration of Wolverine—alone, aggressively unsettled (if his eyes spoke true) and covered in filth—after he was plunged into the sewers of the Hellfire Club mansion. Sporting a sinister smile, his famous adamantium claws unsheathed, Logan decrees, "Okay suckers—you've taken yer best shot! Now it's MY turn."

It was Wolverine's darkness, his bellicosity—his boldness, if you will—that drew me in.

At once I absorbed the full genius of *Dark Phoenix Saga* writer Chris Claremont and illustrators Dave Cockrum and John Byrne. In this story Wolverine is shown as having been the victim of the rich and powerful, one of many more examples to come of how, as a mutant, he is treated like scum—disparaged by and rejected from all "good" society.

And then ... it happened. Wolverine's breaker tripped! Rising from the sewers, he confronted his enemies and went Mount St. Helens on the Hellfire Club.

On a metaphorical level, I wanted to become familiar with Logan— where he came from, his upbringing (if indeed he had one), who he was, the weapon he was created to be and the wild-card mutant he became. Not to put too fine a point on it, I wanted to *understand* him because, as it turns out, during that tumultuous time in my life, I had more in common with Logan's rage than I cared to confess.

According to an unwritten rule, psychologists are discouraged from disclosing personal experiences because, when assessing a person or a situation (in this case a comic book creation), we are supposed to remain objective in our analysis. It is this detached objectivity that imbues clinicians with the mantle of "expert"—trained professionals who possess a superhuman ability to deflect the emotional effects of traumas that would otherwise trample mere mortals.

This presupposition could not be further from the truth.

We are trained to dissect, interpret, assess, and ultimately understand human behavior. This knowledge base does not make us immune to the emotional hits experienced by others. It just gives us a head start down the road toward figuring out what's broken and where to go to repair the damage.

Such was the case when I was sexually assaulted.

I surmise that here is where I get to say things such as "Clinician, heal thyself" and "This, too, shall pass" and "Yes, the truth shall set you free, but first it will make you miserable."

The fact is that trauma shakes a person to their very core. Depression subdues them, anxiety corners them, and fear circumscribes their every action. Haunting memories of the experience lead to unbearable despair, hopelessness, and terror.

Many victims of assault and trauma choose to isolate themselves from the world. Feeling alone and disconnected, they often suffer in silence as they unsuccessfully try to employ logic where no logic is to be found. Therefore, many victims tend to self-incriminate and torture themselves with unwarranted guilt. In many cases, the psychological anguish is as unrelenting as the traumatic experience itself; it becomes a part of the victim's identity.

My personal experience incorporated all of the aforementioned challenges and more as I struggled to fight my way back to any semblance of my former self. I also endured defamation of character and judgment from a society that likes to blame the victim—a most convenient way to redirect the focus of accountability and culpability from the assailant to the assaulted.

Then, as with Wolverine, one day I had enough. I embraced my own anger at the violation, the subsequent injustice, and the betrayal. I released all the fury I had tried so desperately to mask, causing the depression almost instantly to subside—replaced by an internal auxiliary reservoir of strength that I didn't know I had.

Our current society tries to dictate how the persecuted should feel in the face of prejudice, bigotry, and injustice. We're supposed to turn the other cheek, be the "bigger" person, and pretend that everything is okay when it's clearly not. Wolverine reminded me that, regardless of what was happening around me or how exhausting the battle, I needed to fight back.

Yes, indeed, an altered perspective changes everything. After you allow the fury to pass through your veins, you begin to believe in yourself again, to see yourself as you truly are, and you gain a sense of hope that you can and will win.

Consequently, this book is not just about a short, feisty antihero mutant. It's also about our relationship to the mythos of Wolverine and the X-Men. It's an exploration into the psyche of an unpolished, unhinged, and at first glance "damaged" antihero with the same inner strength to endure the unendurable and move on that can be found in a war veteran, a persecuted LGBTQ individual, a disparaged high school science geek in taped-together horn-rimmed glasses, or a sexual assault victim. This book confirms to the reader that, regardless of circumstance, each of us has an internal fire that will not be extinguished. Just like Wolverine, we can choose to accept our conditions, try to change them or create meaning out of our suffering. And just like him, we can become heroes in our own right. Each of us has the ability to stand up and protect the oppressed and downtrodden.

Courage was at times required to write this book. The chapter on the *Weapon X* series written by Barry Windsor-Smith was especially memorable, as it was distressing. This series—a product of Barry's imagination brought to life by the comprehension of very real atrocities committed against humanity—required me to meet Logan where he was mentally, emotionally, and physically, deep within the dark laboratory where he endured unspeakable acts of torture.

At other times, I found immense inspiration not only in the tales themselves but also through the many interviews I conducted with Wolverine's creators. I was privileged to meet famed writers and illustrators, among them Roy Thomas, John Romita, Sr. and Jr., Joe Rubinstein, Paul Jenkins, and the late Len Wein, who enthusiastically embraced the opportunity to discuss the creative inspirations that went into their creation of this character.

When interviewing these comic book legends, a few commonalities materialized as to why we each chose to focus our attention on the stout and spirited mutant. Paul Jenkins, for example, said that he created Wolverine storylines inspired by his own childhood struggles. Joe Rubinstein told me that he depicts his characters based on people he knows in real life. John Romita, Jr., said Wolverine characterizes the fury he experienced following the 9/11 attacks on the people of New York City; he also mentioned that, like Wolverine, he had to learn how to tame the beast within and replace his immediate desire for malevolent revenge with temperance.

Wolverine's creators bring him to life through their own human experiences and compare this character's strengths and defects with their own. This makes sense, since Wolverine's complex persona could only be captured through human tragedy.

Through an examination of this character, we are able to see layers of ourselves because his dialectic nature reveals something within each of us. Logan's feral nature calls into question whether we are allowed to act upon our anger or continue to submit to the injustices inflicted upon us.

The Wolverine story is our own.

His determination reminds us of our own resilience and our own capacity for angry reprisal. In a prejudiced and unjust world, Logan reflects the potential fights, large and small, that each of us will have to wage one day. And it is in accepting those fights that we discover what we are made of.

I didn't need Wolverine to save me. I was going to save myself. I didn't need him to be "real" either, but there are elements of this character with which I, along with millions of other fans the world over, can relate.

Logan teaches us that it is possible for a person to encompass positive human qualities while also recognizing, and sometimes giving in to, the brute within. He represents this painful life path of ours, but he also represents our healing, resiliency, and growth.

I embraced my inner Wolverine and therefore welcomed my own suffering, with the intent of moving through the experience, regardless of the end result. And just like Logan, through the process of healing I discovered, what I can accept to be, the very best version of myself.

May your journey be as productive as it may be uncomfortable.

ONE

Who Is Wolverine?

I'm the best at what I do, but what I do best isn't very nice.
—Wolverine

Famed comic book writer Paul Jenkins once told me that there are many moments in Wolverine's long lifetime when he "goes insane ... when he's cold, confused, alone, and doesn't know what he's doing." Despite Wolverine's violent temper and surly personality, at his core he is a wounded warrior—tough, unrelenting, and courageous on the outside, yet internally guarded, mistrustful, and fiercely frightened of his own vulnerability.[1]

Wolverine experiences intense berserker rages that he cannot control. He impulsively acts out, and he vehemently and viciously rebels against authority. There are occasions when he "loses time," when he will suddenly awaken in an alien place without any idea of who he is or how he got there or so much as a shred of connection to his past or his current situation.

These factors alone could easily qualify someone as being severely unstable, but would we so hastily categorize our beloved Wolverine as *insane*? And, if so, would we include ourselves in the same indictment? After all, Wolverine's immense popularity stems from *somewhere*. Are we attracted to this character's superhuman strength and unflinching bravery, or are we instead drawn to Wolverine's reckless and anti-establishment "I'm going to do it my way no matter what" attitude?

Logan's densely layered personality is precisely why millions of Marvel fans the world over find him so captivating, and regardless of the level at which he's evaluated, he's fascinating. He exhibits clinical psychological symptoms of PTSD, bipolar disorder, antisocial disorder, dissociative amnesia, even sociopathy, and yet we identify with him, understand his motivations and actions, sympathize with him, and, yes, empathize with him, because Logan mirrors some of the large, ragged chunks of our-selves—sometimes making poor decisions that seem necessary at the time, sometimes hurting himself and those for whom he cares, and sometimes taking irrevocably destructive actions for reasons unknown even to him-self ... just like we mere mortals.

Given Wolverine's violent mood swings and propensity for butchery, mental illness cannot be ruled out as a possible character flaw. Certainly there are apparent markers for mental illness in Wolverine's past: His mother was institutionalized. His grandfather was overbearing, demand-ing, and critical. Logan's interactions with this biological father triggered horrific events. All these factors combined to transform a once joyful young boy into the lethal, razor-armed mutant we think we know today.

But do we reliably know what we think we know? Remember, Wolver-ine witnessing his father's death set the stage for his life of betrayal, manip-ulation, and brutalization at the hands of an uncaring humanity. He experiences a profuse amount of agony and heartache; yet he remains resilient. No matter what he endures, he somehow shines through and fights on another day—and fight he will (brutally if necessary) against any-one or anything that gets in his way.

So, we must ask again: Is Wolverine indeed clinically, irreparably, irre-trievably insane? Or is it just that he is repeatedly thrust into situations over which he has no control save self-preservation or the protection of others dear to him, thus rendering his motivations rational and simply not fully understood by those around him?

The Creative Origins of Wolverine

In fathoming the almost religious reverence in which Wolverine is held by his fans, a short history of the character's conception, develop-ment, and evolution is in order.

In 1974, Marvel Comics editor-in-chief Roy Thomas recognized that Marvel was selling an ever-accelerating number of comics in Canada and suggested the creation of a Canadian superhero. According to Thomas:

> I had only the four requirements that I made to Len Wein: he was to be called Wolverine, he was to be Canadian, he was to be short (because a wolverine is a small animal known to ferociously fight far larger ones), and he was to be fierce. Everything else I left to Len. He was to be introduced as a "villain," in a sense ... but of course, at Marvel, that was often just the preliminary to his being a hero. I'd never have suggested that Marvel's first known Canadian character be a villain, pure and simple. I didn't ask that he be a mutant, or have that in mind ... although

later, when I suggested the international grouping of X-Men that emerged in 1975 after I left the editor-in-chief job, I'm sure I thought he was likely to be one of the new mutant band ... after all, the whole reason for his being created, in my mind, was to appeal to Canadian readers.[2]

In response to these requirements, Len Wein envisioned a character inspired by the wolverine so familiar to Canadians (and, indeed, anyone living in the northern hemisphere). As Wein put it, "I conceptualized a thick sturdy and well-armed character, strong significantly beyond its size, and with a well-deserved reputation for punching well above its weight."[3]

Marvel art director John Romita, Sr., crafted the Wolverine character as a diminutive echo of the animal itself. Romita described the inspiration behind the character:

I went to the encyclopedia and saw that the wolverine is a small, very dangerous creature with cat-like claws. I imagined a 5'3" small nasty guy, half man and half beast, with retractable claws and a capacity for rage and fury. I created a claw image down and explored the cat-like feature. I added the suggestion of whiskers— during the original drawing, it was a mishmash of several ideas which I simplified. I made him dimensional in that I included an illustration of his profile and back view so that it gave him movement. The onlooker could feel what it would be like for Wolverine to be coming towards them in attack.[4]

Thus was born Wolverine the character on the last page of issue #180 of *The Incredible Hulk* (cover dated November 1974).

Wolverine was first drawn for publication by famed illustrator Herb Trimpe; later that role was assumed by legendary artist Frank Miller as writer Chris Claremont wrote Wolverine into the X-Men aggregate in 1982's solo series *Wolverine*.

Equally influential in Wolverine's development was the post–Vietnam War time frame in which the character was first created. It was from the public's perception of Vietnam veterans as tough loners that Wolverine garnered his demeanor, dog tags, leather jacket, love for motorcycles, and volatile antisocial temperament.

As noted by Chicago's "King of Geeks," comic writer and commentator Elliott Serrano, due to its well-tuned psychographics and nonstop action, the *Wolverine* series moved the character from also-ran to star status. As Serrano put it:

Wolverine didn't really take off until Chris Claremont and Frank Miller created the *Wolverine* series. I call this series the "Dark Knight moment." This is when particular characters come into their own. Batman didn't become the real pop-culture bad-ass until Frank Miller wrote *The Dark Knight Returns*. That's when Batman stopped being the Super Friends Batman or the Adam West Batman. Before Claremont and Miller created the *Wolverine* series, Logan wasn't a key figure, but the creation of this series is when Wolverine became Marvel's Batman.[5]

Logan's *"Dark Knight* moment" elevated him to key figure status and offered the opportunity for further character enhancement. From that point forward, enthralled readers were strategically and progressively introduced to Logan's "unwavering code of honor," his protective nature, his mysterious past, and numerous other well-crafted personality nuances.[6] But as the character's popularity increased, the need for further character development and detail emerged.

Thus, with writer Paul Jenkins and artists Andy Kubert and Richard Isanove on board (and despite internal concerns that pulling back the curtain on Wolverine's beginnings might stunt rather than expand his appeal), Marvel launched the tale of Wolverine's genesis in its 2001–2002 limited series *Wolverine: Origin* (discussed in detail in the next chapter). This series told the whole story: where he came from, who he was, what he was, what he is now, and how he came to be such. It revealed how his skeleton and his claws morphed into weapons—it told all. Wolverine was now an open book that made sense, for readers, and mutants, and superheroes, and antiheroes alike.

And so, with that, the die was cast. Logan was able to move from revolutionary solo bad boy to an integral part of the X-Men universe.

Joining the Pack

Now, *finally*, Wolverine had a demonstrable history for readers and fellow superheroes to examine and evaluate. No more mysteries. No more uncertainties. No more bewilderment, or mistrust, or ambivalence, or anxiety. He had a résumé.

Logan had a known lifetime of experiences that others could comprehend, understand, believe, and trust in sufficiently to provide him a seat at a table of exceptional superheroes. He wasn't just a jumble of disturbing uncertainties, however intriguing, to his readers or to the rest of the X-Men. Now he was understandable, worthy of validation. He was a part of the X-Men—to all involved.

With Logan's background on the table, readers could understand the environmental and psychological factors he had endured that turned a young, sickly boy into a strong and powerful, if somber and misunderstood, antihero. Everyone could now see where his stoic antisocial isolationism came from.

If Wolverine isn't exactly "social," it's because his childhood traumas taught him that he was different and to trust no one. He wasn't born a rebellious lone wolf; he was made one. Yet, despite his lifelong preference for solitude, he has come to terms with certain things, among them that even a lone wolf is most efficient in a pack—in his case, one comprising other oppressed mutants trying to find their place in an unjust world. And so he joined superhero groups such as Alpha Flight, Department H, X-Force, the New Avengers, the Fantastic Four, and, of course, the X-Men (more on these crime-fighting teams later).

Wolverine's experience with sidekicks such as Kitty Pryde and Jubilee, and with other superheroes such as Captain America and Spiderman, taught him valuable lessons, as did his friendships with Nightcrawler, Jessica Drew, Havok, Puck, and Agent Zero. His isolative nature notwithstanding, Logan came to understand that team effort is often required for mutual gain and betterment, whether those team members be human, mutants, superheroes, or antiheroes.

Logan is feisty and temperamental, but he is also a loyal friend. Of all the superheroes out there, Logan's your guy. He minds his own business, but he will be the first to step in when you're in trouble. He can be calm and compassionate when not in the throes of his explosive temper, at which times he turns into something else entirely—an uncontrollable beast.

A Deadly Force

Logan simply doesn't fit in a superhero box—or in any box, for that matter. While some of the X-Men team members are analytical or more rational, he is not, and this is precisely what makes Wolverine such an asset and premium addition to the team. At first glance, he doesn't appear to be that big a deal. Logan is short and unassuming; however, his emotional distance and lack of physical stature should not be mistaken for weaknesses.

Wolverine is a visceral, natural-born predator who's battled many adversaries across the globe and off it. He even once fought in hell.[7] His rages and monumental killing sprees can leave readers questioning whose side he's really on, if in fact he has a side, or even if he's psychologically unstable. He himself said it best in the film *X-Men: The Last Stand* (2006): "If you cage the beast, the beast will get angry." When Logan feels caged (that is, when he's pressured to be compliant), he's angry. And when he's angry, he's lethal.

Renowned Marvel Comics illustrator John Romita, Jr., said revenge is a "cut and dried" thing for Wolverine:

When confronted, there's no gray area—it's a matter of kill or not to kill. He's a maniacal revenger.... Inflicting justice on somebody is the part of Wolverine people can relate to, but unfortunately it's your justice and that's wrong. If I were Wolverine, I would struggle with the power to be jury and executioner. But that's who he is, and when he becomes the animal, he's even worse.... He's a complex character because he has these incredible claws, and when angered he will end someone's life.[8]

When provoked, let alone threatened, Wolverine doesn't conduct himself like a typical superhero, who will usually try simply to disarm or disable the opponent in an effort "to cause the least amount of harm." Picking a fight with Wolverine reaps a whole new crop. He attacks with profound ferocity and then, when finished, dispassionately finds a bar, has a beer, lights a cigar, and dismisses the entire matter—just like a one-night stand.

Wolverine's main weapons (although not always needed) are his adamantium claws. He's a boxer with a huge punch. Rogue once asked him, "Wolverine, when will you learn that you can't solve problems with your fists?" His response: "Don't know, Rogue. This far I haven't met a problem I couldn't solve with my fists."[9] He was a samurai in feudal Japan (more on that topic later). He has traveled the world, mastering virtually every known fighting discipline. Logan is a walking weapon. He likes to tell his fellow X-Men, "I'm the best at what I do, but what I do best isn't very nice." Wolverine's most famous catchphrase is a simple one, yet one that perfectly captures the spirit of this character.

Witness the following exchange: After winning a cage fight in the first *X-Men* film, Logan is sitting alone at the bar when the guy who lost the fight approaches him.

> FIGHTER: You owe me some money. No man takes a beating like that without a mark to show for it.... I know what you are.
> LOGAN: You lost your money. You keep this up you'll lose something else.[10]

The fighter draws a knife on Logan, at which point Rogue screams, "Look out!" In a flash, Logan has the fighter disarmed and pinned to the wall, his claws slowly drawing out and positioned at the other man's throat. Game, set, match. Advantage Wolverine.

Now add to his fighting skill his supernatural healing ability. Wolverine has been experimented on, stabbed, shot, burned, choked, even decapitated, but he always recovers. His healing factor even extends his life and his looks. Who knew he's well over 100 years old?

But wait—there's more. He can heal himself not only physically but also mentally. After every traumatic event, he gets a bout of amnesia. As a result, Wolverine will sometimes forget who he is, who his friends are, where he is, or where he's going. Where the injured wolf shrinks off to lick and heal its wounds in isolation, Wolverine shrinks off to lick and heal in amnesia.

Yet, despite his temperament and loner persona, he's not a stone. Wolverine has a romantic layer as well, but while great loves such as Rose O'Hara, Silver Fox, Mariko Yashida, and Dr. Jean Grey have come his way, Wolverine appears cursed when it comes to matters of the heart.[11] Either his prospective partners are unavailable or they get killed off—at times (unintentionally) by him, making his bar brawl assets potential bedroom liabilities while providing additional (if anguished) grist for his emotional growth mill that makes him all the more lethal to his enemies in future conflicts. (Logan's love life will be addressed in more detail in chapter seven.)

Conflicting Natures: Man and Beast

Wolverine encapsulates the age-old conflict between good and evil in that his conflicts are *intra*-personal. Logan once said, "The red rage in me is an animal thing. This is the real reason for anger. It's that curtain of blood in front o' my eyes and the molten lava pumpin' through my veins. It's that roarin' sound in my ears that ain't nothin' but myself howlin'. This is the real reason for anger ... to rev yourself up for killing!"[12] His animalistic nature, physical strength, heightened senses, and nasty temper drive him to attack like a wild creature that cannot be contained or controlled. Yet he longs for a normal and peaceful life. He tries to avoid trouble, but trouble seeks him out.

Thanks to his mutant powers, Wolverine is resilient both physically and psychologically. But, as will be explored in the upcoming chapters, we have to wonder if he ever truly heals from his past traumas. For that matter, does anyone completely heal from their own past hurts? Or do we, like Logan, strive to accept the scars and learn from them?

Who among us hasn't ever felt misunderstood or rejected by someone or something that meant a lot to us? During our most difficult times, many of us may wish that we had Wolverine's healing factor—something that could heal our bodies and protect our minds by helping us forget our most painful experiences. But even if we could forget, traumas have a sneaky way of staying with us. They become a part of who we are.

Throughout his very long life, Logan has experienced a lot of pain, and yet he's able to maintain a sense of humanity. Despite his physical immunity, he's emotionally vulnerable. For example, while his hands heal quickly, every time Wolverine's claws emerge they wound him, and he bleeds. This unique superpower would seem to be metaphorical, as Logan, although seemingly indestructible, still experiences pain every time he fights. In a similar fashion, we mere mortal readers experience a certain level of emotional discomfort every time we face some level of conflict, be it physical or emotional or even existential. These struggles become a part of us too. We accept the scars and move on, ideally learning from them.

Very few superhero characters capture the same scope of human suffering, heartbreak, and redemption that Wolverine does. Tom DeFalco, editor-in-chief of *Marvel Comics* during Wolverine's emergence as a top-tier antihero, put it best when he shared with me, "When you think about Logan you have to think about Chris Claremont's Logan, which was the failed samurai. He is a character who is filled with honor, and yet he is called upon to do dishonorable things for the greater good. Logan also constantly fights himself to maintain control of himself to not get crazy."[13]

Logan's healing factor causes him to forget his past and who he is; yet he regroups and struggles both to gain a sense of purpose and to again define himself. He often has to choose between allowing himself to succumb to his bestial side or doing better and embracing his humanity. Indeed, it is the seemingly endless repetition of his inner conflict between these two opposites that consistently reanneals and reconfirms his humanity. This unknowing endorsement of his benevolence defines who he really is—a kind warrior, lethal in nature and flawed in character certainly, but one with a vulnerable heart.

Perhaps Wolverine's greatest weakness, his tragic flaw—his Achilles' heel, if you will—is his limited control over his emotions. When seriously injured, or when he feels that he cannot take any more punishment, he experiences uncontrollable feelings of rage. This blind rage takes over, reducing his actions to those of pure self-preservation and instinct.[14] The question we need ask ourselves here is: What does this say about Logan? Is he insane, or is he all the more human? And, moreover, what does our answer say to us about ourselves?

Wolverine Is Us

We know Wolverine isn't human in any physical sense. He's only a comic book character, after all—the construct of several prolific imaginations. But his tale reads like a classic hero legend.

Wolverine was born a mutant. As a child, when his superpower literally came out of him, people's eyes didn't open in awe and admiration, as they did when they watched Superman leap into the air. Instead, they were shocked and horrified! People around Wolverine often don't know what to make of him, and razor-sharp claws—whether belonging to a diminutive person or not—tend to strike some serious terror in the audience.

As we shall soon see, his childhood *Origin* story is heartbreaking and wider ranging than most folklore. Mutant powers aside, the tale of Logan, born James Howlett, bears a striking resemblance to violent stories of child abuse and suffering all too frequently seen on the six o'clock news: drunk guy murders his ex-lover and her husband in a fit of rage, children witness the killings, children left traumatized and orphaned.

The *Origin* narrative is gripping and raw, leaving the reader with the impression of young James's story being hauntingly real. An ill-fated child in real life could potentially encounter a horrific sequence of events such as those described in this famous comic series.

James's personality also rings true with endearingly human realism. The adult Logan physically and logically copes with his problems in a very realistic and matter-of-fact manner: "Who won? Musta been me, 'cause I'm still breathing."

Whether Logan's conflicts involve battling a physical opponent or coping with a lost love, his difficulties echo our own. As with Logan, when we are challenged, some of us opt to appear unbreakable and impervious by emphasizing physical strength. Or we may try topping our opponent through the use of sharp intellect. Logan is both physically strong *and* clever—he fights off his opponents through brutal strength and canny wit.

Logan reminds us of who we'd like to be: someone who is smart, fast, and strong, and who stands up to bullies. He's resilient and figures out ways to deal with his problems and adversaries. He also has a great sense of humor and an unwavering sense of kindness. This dualistic nature, a tough exterior combined with a soft heart, is what makes Logan stand out from other Marvel characters.

Within the following pages we're going to look at this character through a psychological lens and answer questions that will unearth the essence of Logan's persona behind his famous pointy coif, his costumes and his outwardly guarded façade. What triggers his amnesia? Why does he drink so much? Why can't this guy keep a girlfriend? Why does this loner fight crime? What makes him so violent? And what horrible things happened to this mutant that caused him to choose a life of solitude?

Most important, what lies within the man with the claws?

Two

Origin

He goes to be with his other self; the piece of him he's kept
hidden.
—Rose O'Hara, *Wolverine: Origin*

From Wolverine's first appearance in the early 1970s until late 2001,
the character's history remained mostly unexplored—vaguely implied over
the years, to be sure, but never detailed. He was a diminutive, rugged,
mutant antihero who fought the bad guys, defended those at risk and, for
reasons unexplored, sometimes experienced amnesia as a side effect of
those conflicts. But that was the end of the available information. At least
until November 2001, when the *Wolverine: Origin* series first began to
crack the code.

Marvel Comics editor-in-chief Joe Quesada initiated an editorial con-
ference wherein Paul Jenkins, former Marvel vice president Bill Jemas,
and thirty-five writers, artists, and editors all gathered in the basement of
Joe's New Jersey home for a brainstorming session that would pursue fresh
themes. Paul and Bill pitched Joe the idea of writing what would become
Marvel's greatest storyline to date: the origin of Wolverine.

Paul Jenkins described the day when the idea to write the *Origin* tale
came to him as follows:

> When Joe Quesada had just become the new Editor in Chief of Marvel Comics he
> asked me to participate in his first conference with all the creative minds of Marvel
> to come up with bold and new ideas. During a break for lunch Bill Jemas and I
> went to speak to Joe and pitched the idea to write about the greatest story Marvel
> never told. Joe asked the group, "Is there any reason why we can't do the origin of
> Wolverine?" Everyone stared back in disbelief. We were about to take on the most
> momentous task in Marvel Comics history.[1]

A few months later Paul and Bill met in New York, along with a few
Marvel editors, to craft various scenarios to explain the well-known

mutant's history. The mandates were that the story had to be character-centric, heartbreaking, cruel, and sufficiently authentic for the reader to empathize with a history capable of producing such prolonged psychological anguish. Paul's talent in writing character-based stories made him the perfect writer to create the story of Wolverine's origin.

Regarding the creative process, Paul recalls:

> We worked the story through and we pitched very hard that we dispense with Weapon X, the adamantium skeleton and even the mutant aspect and concentrate on writing about what makes a person a person. We focused on telling the story of a young boy and how he came to be the type of person driven to protect others. The Achilles' heel was the most important part of the story—Wolverine's memory loss was never explained before. We had to convey a traumatic situation severe enough to cause Logan's mind to act defensively, to protect him from his own memory.[2]

Put colloquially, Logan had to be *"real."* And in response to that requirement, Paul Jenkins ventured profoundly deeper than anyone could have ever fathomed. He elected to write about circumstances not only personal but also visceral. He took the concept of pain, turned it inward and intensified it. He gave Wolverine the literary counterpart of an organ transplant: he gave the character his own background.

On a subconscious level—indeed, on an unconscious level at times—comic book writers and artists project into a character specifics appropriate to that creation that are directly lifted from their own experiences. Every successful fictional character is endowed with some of the personal emotional wounds and conflicts of its creators and therefore gets projected onto every page and/or screen as a representation of how these creative minds think and feel about themselves and about the world. Case in point: Paul's decision to invest Wolverine with the painful particulars of his own life.

In an interview Paul revealed some of the details of his own upbringing and events that profoundly affected him and his older brother, albeit in different ways. Paul grew up with his mother and brother in Kent, England, a diverse southeastern seaboard county. His brother was a loud, rambunctious child who struggled with a hearing impairment. "He could not articulate his feelings well since everyone viewed him as troubled," Paul explained.

Paul found himself in the role of protector and problem solver when the divorce of their parents so adversely affected his brother. At this time, their mother worked for a family of fairly well-to-do farmers, and he and his brother were allowed to play with the children of that privileged household. At the end of the day, however, they had to return home "to the bottom of the hill," as Paul described it. Their father maintained visitation rights but would usually drop the brothers off with their grandmother, whom Paul described as physically and emotionally abusive. Haunting Paul all his life was the memory of how his brother struggled emotionally while (by comparison) Paul thrived. "What developmental factors," Paul asked himself, "shape a child's ability to survive hardship and abuse?"

Any of this sounding vaguely familiar? If not, please read *Wolverine: Origin*, where these and other life-directing personal experiences are so heartrendingly mirrored. Or, more conveniently, just stay here and review the synopsis that follows a few paragraphs further on.

The *Origin* series takes these all-too-human experiences and forges them into modern mythology. It literally makes manifest a comic book character, or (in this case) multiple characters, in that the *Origin* story is primarily (though not exclusively) about the protagonist James, who later becomes known as Logan and the Wolverine, but it is also about his *half-brother* and antagonist Dog, who some writers have hinted is also Wolverine's eternal nemesis and all-around villain Victor Creed (a.k.a. Sabretooth).

Origin goes a long way toward explaining the horrific actions of Thomas Logan—father to Dog and secretly the biological father of James— and how they trigger the never-ending rift between James and Dog. Thomas is the catalyst for unforeseeable anguish inflicted on the entire Howlett family while the physical and emotional abuse that he inflicts on his son transforms Dog into a spiteful villain determined to make James's life a living hell.

The *Origin* series illustrates how early traumatic experiences can transform the psychological structure, and even the physiological structure, of a young adolescent from friendly, trusting, gregarious tweenager into many different malformations, be it a misinterpreted insular time bomb with a propensity for protecting and defending others (in the case of James) or a consummately evil, vengeful, focused sociopath (in the case of Dog). It yields a tale rife with disturbance and ordeal, and one that renders a situation understandably capable of shoving the victim to the edge of insanity.

Through each lurid panel, we see Wolverine's past played out in Stanley Kubrick–grade clarity. *Origin* relates a complex and distressing family dynamic that decrees the fate of two adult half-brothers who begin as friends and end as foes with two very different natures. Page by page, the reader absorbs the realization that this is no ordinary gaggle of family and friends. There are signs of mental illness in this fable and hints at a secret affair that will forever destroy a child's happiness and seal his fate as a tormented mutant.

The Howlett Estate

The *Origin* tale is set in the 1880s in Cold Lake, Alberta, Canada, on a wealthy family estate. The Howlett family consists of Father (John), Mother (Elizabeth), Grandfather (paternal patriarch, unnamed) and one surviving son (James). James's father is loving, respectful, and kind; his mother is brooding, withdrawn, and morose. Grandfather is a cruel, surly, self-made copper mogul, and James is friendly and outgoing despite health issues. The family was deeply wounded by the earlier death of its firstborn son (John Jr.), which institutionalized Elizabeth, who later returned to the estate a somber, sullen shadow of her former self.

Other key players include Rose O'Hara, a young companion to James; Thomas Logan, the estate groundskeeper, who is by any measure a cruel, abusive degenerate; and Thomas's son, Dog, who is a tormented, passive-aggressive whipping boy for his father's problems. Adding a layer of intrigue to this tale, the *Origin* series hints that James is the half-brother of Dog and the illegitimate son of Thomas and Elizabeth, which makes sense since Thomas is depicted as resembling the adult Logan we know today.

The story is set in motion when the young girl Rose comes to this tragedy-ridden, dysfunctional family estate to be a companion to James, whose health issues compromise his daily activities. Rose and James form a close emotional bond over the years and include Dog in their friendship. But just as Paul Jenkins and his brother were aware of their non-privileged status while growing up, Dog is also aware that he was not "manor born" and must return to the bottom of the hill.

Dog often endures physical and psychological abuse at the hands of his father, Thomas, and as Dog matures he is depicted as an "apple that didn't fall far from the tree." He grows up to share his father's inclination for violence and his vehemently negative attitude toward entitlement. In the process he misconstrues James to be the source of all his difficulties rather than seeing his father Thomas as the true catalyst and guilty party.

Years pass, and one day Rose unintentionally stumbles into a room in the manor house and sees Elizabeth with mysterious claw scars on her back. Rose is kicked out of Elizabeth's chambers and then, in the garden, encounters Dog, who makes an unwanted advance. She refuses Dog and pushes him away. James witnesses this encounter and runs to tell his father. Dog attacks James over what he perceives as James's betrayal and, in retaliation, cuts the throat of James's beloved puppy.

The Attack

Thomas and Dog are expelled from the estate. Thomas curses John Howlett and swears revenge. Later he grabs a shotgun and returns to the estate with Dog, where they capture Rose and force her to let them into the manor house. They break into the bedroom chambers and attempt to abduct Elizabeth as well. John hears the commotion and enters the room. James, awakened by the noise, enters Elizabeth's room in time to see John's head disintegrated by Thomas's shotgun blast.

Crying desperately in anguish, James runs to his father's body. Dog grabs the shotgun and moves to kill James, but Rose saves James's life by pushing the gun aside. Overcome with a berserker rage, James screams, "You killed my Papa!" Everyone watches in horror as James makes "an awful, revolting noise—not a scream, but a birth-cry of a new creature that surely had no place on God's earth."[3]

The rising tide cannot be contained. With newfound strength and agility, James strikes out at Dog's face, unknowingly slashing it and temporarily disabling Dog's vision, and then he attacks Thomas, punching him in the stomach. Thomas, looking down, realizes that he is bleeding severely, stabbed and mortally wounded.

The trauma of seeing his father's dead body has triggered James's mutant power—bone claws slowly protrude from his hands. He remains on the ground, shocked, shrieking in pain, and bleeding profusely from the emerged bone claws. Everyone present now realizes that something supernatural is taking place; nature is trumping nurture and has caused some unknown, hideous transfiguration in James.

Oddly, Elizabeth screams, "Not again!" slaps James, calls him a monster and demands that he leave the manor house. James flees the estate, and Rose chases after him. Elizabeth, again acting unexpectedly, cradles Thomas in her arms as he dies, saying to him, "I knew this would happen." Stricken with grief at what she feels she has caused, Elizabeth takes Thomas's shotgun and kills herself.

Later, trembling in fear and hiding in a nearby barn, James remembers nothing of the incident. He asks Rose if he knows her. He tells Rose that he can smell apple dumplings cooking far away and hear people walking by the servants' entrance. James's recent trauma has forced yet another mutant ability to the surface, this time in the form of highly elevated sensory sensitivity. James says that he's having a horrible dream and asks for his mother. Even though Elizabeth neglected James all his life, and attacked him when she should have shielded him from danger, James nevertheless longs for her love and protection.

Rose and James seek refuge at Grandfather's cabin; however, he angrily refuses to listen. Grandfather gives Rose money and tells them to go to the train station, warning them that if they ever return, they will be shot on sight. James is thus rejected and banished by his only remaining living relative.

Complex Childhood Trauma

In the matter of minutes that it takes for the killing scenario at the manor house to unfold, James experiences multiple losses, shock, and trauma. He witnesses his beloved father's head blown apart, absorbs his mother's rejection of him in his most vulnerable moment, is exposed to his friend's betrayal, takes a life for the first time, and is banished from the only home he has ever known. Later, hiding in a nearby shed, he's cold, panicked, and confused. And in the midst of all this he is in blinding pain as he stares in horror at his hands, with blood streaming from the newly emerged bone claws.

In the psychological narrative of James Howlett, it is at this point that the Wolverine persona emerges. From this time forward, his life will never be the same. In this moment he ceases to be a sickly child and transforms into a powerful adult mutant who will experience loss after painful loss and unspeakable trauma throughout his very long lifetime.

Aside from experiencing the mental portion of his self-protective healing factor—a condition termed *dissociative amnesia* by psychologists, in which the normally well-integrated bonds of memory, identity, perception, or consciousness are separated or dissociated (more on this phenomenon later)—James also experiences *hypervigilance*: a heightened state of sensory sensitivity and anxiety. Like dissociative amnesia, hypervigilance is commonly associated with post-traumatic stress disorder. Hypervigilance allows the adult Logan to scan his environment with a keener sensitivity for sights, sounds, life forms, behaviors, smells, or anything else evocative of a threat. This "high alert" state is triggered in Logan throughout his life until he deduces that the dangers he sensed have been averted.

In short, the trauma has triggered a genetically dictated mutational metamorphosis that transfigures Logan's body *and* mind to protect him physically and psychologically—a *physical* self-protection mechanism (a weapon) grew out of his hands, and a *mental* self-protection mechanism grew in his mind to erase all memory associated with his losses, his actions, and, indeed, his past.

Mutation: The Edge of Evolution

"A mutation" according to professor of biology Dr. Eric Snyder, "is a change in a person's genetic code. Mutations can be a minor change called a base pair substitution, or a massive change such as chromosome dupli-cation."[4] Some medically unique mutations include *polymelia*, a birth defect in which causes an individual to have more than the usual number of limbs; *cornu cutaneum*, when humans grow a skin tumor made of wood or coral in the form of a *cutaneous horn*; *ectrodactyly*, more commonly known as "lobster claw hand," where a person has a cleft where the middle finger or toe should be; and a rare genetic mutation, *hypertrichosis*, some-times referred to as "werewolf syndrome," where an individual sprouts thick hair on their faces and bodies.

Examples of more common, yet inconspicuous, mutations include freckles, red hair and even blue eyes. John Travolta and Patrick Stewart have a cleft chin mutation, while Elizabeth Taylor was famous for *distichi-asis*, or thick double eyelashes. David Bowie appeared to don a more dra-matic eye mutation, *incomplete heterochromia*, in which eyes are two different colors. (We hear of this mutation in the major motion picture *X-Men: First Class*, when the young Professor X refers to heterochromia as "a very groovy mutation.")

In the fictional biology of Wolverine, James Howlett experienced what Dr. Eric Snyder refers to as a "massive mutation chromosomal duplica-tion."[5] Just as environmental changes initiate evolutionary alterations toward self-preservation in all living organisms, so, too, in the comic world do a mutant's powers manifest themselves during puberty as a way to help the mutant self-protect, often triggered by psychological trauma.

Part of Wolverine's mutation includes selective memory loss to shield him from the psychological trauma. This "gift" (which the adult Logan later terms a "curse") opens the door to a lifelong quest toward self-discovery. While James's mind stores fragments of information from the past, he has no knowledge regarding the how or the why of his being on the run. Worse, he can only make judgments based upon his incomplete memories of his behavior and his observations of any tangible evidence before him. All he is marginally aware of is that his father died and that he was banished. He knows that "something" is horribly wrong and infers that whatever happened is somehow *his* fault. How did he come to this conclusion?

According to psychologist Robin S. Rosenberg, *self-perception theory* explains how James inferred what happened. This theory, developed by psychologist Daryl Bem, states that people only have limited access to their own beliefs, traits, or psychological states. The theory goes on to say that one must use inference cues from one's environment to find out more about oneself.

James observes his situation and makes inferences about himself and guesses about his past. He *confabulates*—that is, he creates false memories to fill in the blanks. Dr. Rosenberg writes, "Wolverine's autobiographical amnesia puts him on the same playing field as his fans: he (and we) figure out who he is by watching how he acts and reacts, noticing his instincts and habits; we just don't know how he got that way."[6] James's memory loss forces him to make inferences about himself for the rest of his life.

We will address Logan's amnesia more in detail in a bit, but for now suffice it to say that his memory loss, in equal proportion to other ways he appears lost, is a key component of his character. Another prominent character trait is Logan's propensity for solitude. He's a free ranger who avoids getting too close to others, and with good reason. His traumatic past makes it virtually impossible for him to form secure relationship connections in his adulthood.

A Mutant without Attachments

The depictions of Logan's past demonstrate how trauma and neglect affect a child's identity and ability to cope with both immediate and prolonged stress. On a physical level, for the majority of his childhood, James endured a form of corporal confinement, as he was a sickly child required to spend many days bedbound and thus trapped inside the manor house. He was also trapped on an emotional level by two factors: (1) he was unable to escape the intense rebukes of his demanding and authoritarian grandfather, and (2) he had to endure living in a home with his emotionally detached mother as his primary caregiver. Although James's father was very loving, James could not develop his self-identity to its fullest as a function of his overarching belief that he was not "good enough" to merit his grandfather's or his mother's positive attentions.

Origins writer Paul Jenkins described his grandmother as a "horrible human being" who often physically and verbally abused him and his brother. Through his writing, we see Paul's feelings toward his grandmother depicted in the cruel and surly nature of James's grandfather. "It is very likely," this author told Paul during an interview, "your brother's self-doubt, and corresponding emotional and social challenges, were heavily influenced by the negative messages your brother received from your grandmother."

A child's sense of self and his ability to feel secure among others is systematically produced not just by his parents but also by his grandparents and other close guardians. Children who experience abuse or neglect are often left questioning their value and never feel worthy of love or attention. They may act out behaviorally, experience interpersonal conflicts with peers or suffer from a persistent sense of emptiness that lacks joy or other emotions formed through meaningful interactions.

Now one might ask: What happens when a child doesn't feel a strong sense of connection to his parent? Psychoanalyst John Bowlby answers that question through his "attachment theory." Bowlby tells us that there are four main parental attachment patterns: (1) secure attachment, (2) anxious-resistant insecure attachment, (3) anxious-avoidant insecure attachment, and (4) disorganized/disoriented attachment.[7]

According to Bowlby, we come into this world hardwired with an instinct to form attachments with our primary caregivers for survival. Children form attachments with their mothers as a way to explore the world while maintaining a sense of safety and protection. This relationship is critical, as it acts as a model for all future relationships. Any disruption in the attachment can have severe emotional consequences later on and lead to problematic behaviors such as breakdowns in communication, emotional unavailability, a prolonged sense of rejection or emotional abandonment.[8]

Attachment Styles

A *securely* attached child freely explores his world while displaying a strong sense of security, confidence, and an ability to problem solve. James is securely attached to his father, who allows James room to play and explore his world without criticism. However, the emotional neglect from his mother and criticisms from his grandfather profoundly undercut James's ability to form secure emotional attachments.

A child exhibits an *anxious-resistant insecure* attachment to his parents when he tends to be wary of strangers and avoids exploring his surroundings. A child who shows this type of attachment will cry with intense screams when separated from his caretakers.[9] This doesn't sound like James, who is depicted as joyful when playing outside with Dog and Rose, nor does he show signs of preoccupation with returning home.

An *anxious-avoidant insecure* attached child will refuse to explore his world while simultaneously ignoring his primary caretaker. He will show little emotion when his mother departs or returns. This type of attachment is formed when the child's needs are frequently not met. A child with this attachment style believes that his cries and pleas for affection will have no lasting effect on his mother. James would love to interact with his mother more often, but she's emotionally unavailable. Thus, in her absence, James turns to his father for love and support and also seeks him out for protection. Therefore, it's unlikely that James has this form of attachment.

Lastly, children can form a *disorganized/disoriented* attachment when they receive mixed treatment from their caretakers. Children with this form of attachment don't really know how to react. At times they may avoid or resist approaches from their parents, while at other times they may seem confused or frightened, or freeze up when they get too close to their primary caregiver. This pattern of attachment is common in children who have grown up witnessing their parents endure domestic violence or substance abuse. Many such disorganized/disoriented children prove to be the objects of maltreatment or neglect.

James is confused by his mother's distance and he doesn't receive any explanation for her behavior. Throughout his childhood he receives mixed messages: his father shows signs of affection, validating his sense of self-worth, while his mother neglects him. According to Bowlby, these conflicting parenting styles would lead James to display the disorganized/disoriented pattern of attachment.

In his adulthood, one sees in Logan an expansion of this attachment style played out. He is often confused or conflicted about forming close or intimate relationships with others. Early losses and betrayals explain why the future Logan has trust and attachment issues. Thus, he avoids the psychological conflict of a desire to be close to others paired with a reality of past rejection and abandonment. He remains aloof and detached despite his longings to the contrary.

The Consciously Absent Mother

Now that we've looked at the psychology of *why* Wolverine is the way he is, let's look at *how* he got there. Why, or rather how, did his mother Elizabeth do this to him? Why did she distance herself from James in the first place? The answer is a complicated one, as there are several factors that could disrupt a mother's innate instinct to nurture and protect her child.

One study found that most mothers who are detached from their children suffered major losses, severe depression, or other trauma shortly before or after the birth of the infant.[10] Other studies found that unresolved past losses in the mother's own life tended to be associated with disorganized attachment in her child.

We know nothing of Elizabeth's background save that she lost her older son (John Jr.) somehow along the line and that she has Wolverine-style scars on her back. What is traumatic for one person may not be traumatic for another; however, losing a child is often considered the single most traumatizing event that a parent can endure. But while the full details of the absence of the child are beyond us, we easily assume that one strong possibility for Elizabeth's behavior toward James is that losing her first child left her traumatized, unable to conceptualize caring for another child, and perhaps even somehow blaming the loss of her firstborn on the second offspring.

Later we see this distancing coping behavior repeated in Logan's life. Like his mother before him, Logan is insular and avoids getting emotionally attached to others. That Elizabeth is secretive about the claw scars on her back allows the inference that the absence of her firstborn is somehow connected to those scars. In the miniseries *Wolverine: The End*, written by Paul Jenkins and illustrated by Claudio Castellini, we discover that James's older brother, John Jr., shared James's mutation and, as a consequence, was sent away by their grandfather, never to be seen again—thus making for an all the more incapacitating trauma.

Logan's personality is unrefined and volatile. He's guarded and cynical as a coping mechanism to detach himself from others, and he has confabulated explanations in his own mind as compensation for memory loss; yet he can experience profound emotions such as empathy over things that happen to others.

That Logan is able to relate to others at all is due to the strong relationship he had with his father. In many ways John Howlett provided James with his sense of humanity, while the emotional neglect he suffered via his mother instilled in him a strong sense of mistrust of other people and an intense drive toward physical and emotional self-preservation. Losing a parent due to death is the most catastrophic loss a child can endure, but experiencing psychological neglect or abuse from a parent can be even more devastating.

Psychologist Alice Miller, in her groundbreaking book *The Drama of the Gifted Child*, outlines what therapists working with children encounter quite often. Children who are "gifted" or keenly perceptive of their parents' expectations will often do whatever it takes to obtain attention and approval from a distant parent while ignoring their own emotional needs. For example, a child will ignore, or even repress, his need to express anger or sadness in order to soothe his mother's moods. Another child may seek to win his father's approval through excelling athletically, even when the child has no interest in sports. In other words, a child who desperately seeks the love and nurturance from a distant parent will often hide who he truly is in order to become the "ideal" child his parents prefer.

Miller tells us that children become emotionally traumatized when they are not allowed to explore and accept their true nature. Moreover, she expounds on the personality manifestations of childhood trauma, expanding the definition of "abuse" beyond exclusively physical or sexual violence to include a much more sinister variety—psychological abuse performed by one or both parents on their child. Miller believes that psychological abuse and neglect by parents cause the majority of neuroses and psychoses, and she argues that mental illness, addiction, and acts of crime are caused by suppressed rage as a result of subconscious childhood trauma.

Logan clearly displays rage in gargantuan proportions, and Miller's hypothesis pertaining to childhood suppression of feelings can lead us to understand one of the reasons why Logan experiences his berserker rages. As a child, he had to suppress his reactions because his mother often ignored his emotional needs, and his expressions to her of any desire for such needs to be fulfilled were met with rebuke.

That Elizabeth was physically present on the estate but chose to not interact with James makes her rejection of him worse than if she had not been on the estate at all because the message this behavior sends to a child is "I'm here and available to you, but you are not important enough for me to interact with you." Miller would say that this type of message is without question traumatic for James because his mother, being a central figure in his life, is supposed to be a source of nurture, support, and love. A mother is expected to be aware of her child's emotional needs and to soothe and calm when the child is feeling afraid or vulnerable. And while his father John did his best to provide this sort of nurturing environment, the often ill and bedridden (read: vulnerable) James needed his mother's nurturance as well.

Elizabeth's dismissal of her son's emotional needs instills in James a deep-rooted belief that what he feels is unimportant and that he should repress such things, hence explaining his guarded, mocking, and sarcastic nature as an adult. Feeling neglected by his mother imprints negative assumptions about his self-worth, such as "I don't deserve love" or "I will be abandoned." Such negative messages lead to negative *core beliefs*—absolute statements about oneself, others, or the world—treated as if they are absolute facts.

After their escape from the estate, Rose on several occasions attempts to inform James of his real identity and the terrifying events they experienced on that fateful night, but he refuses to listen. While most people would look to obtain such information, James chooses not to believe anything other than the assumption he has formed in his own mind: *he is responsible for his father's death and therefore does not deserve happiness.* This core belief has taken such strong root in his subconscious that he consciously elects to banish suggestions to the contrary.

According to Miller, people repress information about their past when they believe that they are incapable of emotionally tolerating the details surrounding a trauma. She explains, "Without realizing that the past is constantly determining their present actions, they avoid learning anything about their history. They continue to live in their repressed childhood situation, ignoring the fact that it no longer exists, continuing to fear and avoid dangers that, although once real, have not been real for a long time." As such, James chooses to change his identity permanently and embrace his new identity as Logan the hunter.

A child, after enduring repeated emotional rejection from a parent, will stop developing and differentiating his true identity. Such children often feel lonely, empty, and discarded. They never feel "at home" because they've been denied the ability to plant solid emotional roots within their family structures.

Logan never feels "at home" anywhere. He packs his bags, gets on his motorcycle and takes off the minute he feels too comfortable or perceives others getting too comfortable with him. Although he keeps moving from place to place and avoids planting roots, Logan never gives up looking for answers about his past. Miller tells us, "In order to become whole we must try, in a long process, to discover our own personal truth, a truth that may cause pain before giving us a new sphere of freedom."[11] Logan must somehow come to terms with all that he has lost. He spends much of his time removed from civilization and prefers to hunt in the wild. This decision reflects both the profound level of his unvoiced but nonetheless internalized grief and his understanding that he cannot relate or belong anywhere. He has lost too much. He chooses to be unsettled—alone.

The Loss

In her 1969 book *On Death and Dying,* inspired by her pioneering work with the terminally ill, psychologist Elisabeth Kübler-Ross proposed her well-known theory of the five stages of grief. She later expanded her theory to include any catastrophic loss, including the death of loved ones. In those expansions she suggests that the five emotional stages experienced by survivors of an intimate's death are denial, anger, bargaining, depression, and acceptance.

Kübler-Ross later noted that these stages are not a linear and predictable progression.[12] Nor are they immutable. People may skip stages, regress into previous stages or experience an entirely different grieving process altogether.

James experiences amnesia after the trauma, but he later undergoes deep *denial*—the first reaction to grief. In this stage James refuses to listen to Rose speak truth about the past, preferring to cling to a false reality that he himself *confabulated* out of incomplete data. He then experiences *anger*, becoming defensive, frustrated, and distant as he realizes that his denial cannot continue. Certain psychological responses of a person undergoing the anger phase would be asking "Why me?" or "Why would this happen to me?"

Logan doesn't go through *bargaining*—he skips the third stage involving the hope that he can avoid what occurred. During this stage, people typically negotiate for a different reality or the future creation of a reformed lifestyle; however, Logan simply bypasses it, as he has nothing with which to bargain. He has no memory of the actual events; all he has are unsettled emotions with no particulars to evaluate. If anything, as an adult Logan chooses much more unhealthy behaviors and methods of coping with his grief.

He does, however, go through the *depression* stage—he becomes saddened by his reality. After escaping the estate, Rose and James head to the lumber camps in Yukon Territory, where James finds work in a quarry.

Rose gives James the alias of "Logan" while she herself dons the façade of his cousin. The physically demanding work at the quarry amplifies Logan's mutant power of extreme physical strength and stamina. Due to the intensity with which he attacks his work, his coworkers nickname him "Wolverine" after the ferocious little indigenous beast that abounds in the area. Logan grows physically stronger; yet he struggles emotionally. He's stuck in the depths of depression and is obsessed with self-blame and self-loathing.

By all accounts, he is psychologically divided from his past, and therefore detached from his true identity. Logan spends a vast amount of time silent, stubborn, and withdrawn. He isolates himself from the balance of his available human contacts by going into the woods to hunt game, typically among a pack of wolves. Rose delineates her observations of Logan in her journal: "He seems so distant as if he's trying to understand what's happened to him and yet blocked his memories of it at the same time.... I wonder if his brain is trying to heal in the same extraordinary way his body does ... He seems to be retreating even further into his own world."[13]

Traumatized individuals tend to shut down on a psychological level through emotional numbing, which extends to everyday situations. Logan becomes increasingly distant from Rose despite developing feelings for her. He refuses to learn about his past and displays a general sense of emotional detachment.

The *Origin* series also depicts Logan experiencing *acceptance* during a subsequent battle with Dog. Back at the estate, years later, Logan's grandfather begs Dog (who has become physically strong himself) to search for James in order to make peace. Dog agrees, but not with the intention of bringing James back to the estate. Dog's unvoiced resolve is to find James, yes, but to kill him when he does.

Dog locates and confronts Logan; however, Logan does not recognize him. "Who are you?" Logan asks him. In answer, Dog attacks Logan with massive force: "I guess that means you forgot your old pal, Dog. Well I sure as hell remember you!" Dog then sees Rose in the crowd and tells her, "I'll catch up with you soon, girl ... first I gotta see if little James remembers how I was the one who killed his Poppa and you two got the blame."

Dog's attack, along with his words, reawakens the memory and the shock of Logan's childhood trauma—to wit, witnessing his father die horribly. Logan has now *accepted* the truth about his past. Rage pulsing through his body, Logan turns to Dog and says, "You killed my father, you monster ... now I remember you! All these years, I thought it was me."[14]

The realization that Dog murdered his father propels Logan into another berserker rage and into full attack mode. At the *acceptance* stage, people resign themselves to the reality of tragic events. In Logan's case, the truth is now out, and his acceptance of that truth is all important. Logan's father is dead and cannot return, and Dog is the one who killed him. Logan goes from self-loathing and self-blame to focusing his anger on the true villain and exacting vengeance for the deed.

The Rise of Wolverine

Logan beats Dog and pops his claws, closing in for the kill. Rose, rushing in to stop the brawl, accidentally falls on Logan's claws. As she lays dying, she looks at Logan and says, "James I should have told you...." Logan screams, "Rose ... I ... Rose, No ... No." Logan's last chance to know his true past dies with her. In his despair, Logan abandons the fight and allows Dog to live.

The same self-protective metamorphosis that triggered Logan's claws will soon trigger his decision to abandon his life and his humanity. Logan leaves the civilized world and enters both a literal and a mental wilderness. He lives with the wolves in the forest, experiencing another bout of trauma-induced amnesia, and ultimately forgetting the pain of losing Rose. Logan is gone for years to come.

The collage of collaborative artistic effort that created *Wolverine: Origin* confirms the psychology of how parental rearing styles can drastically affect children in different ways. Through Logan and Dog, we see how siblings, even half-brothers unaware of their family ties, can be affected by the abuse inflicted upon them. Both brothers experienced trauma and loss because of one man—Thomas Logan. He is the *true* villain in this tale. Although James and Dog choose different paths along the "good guy" and "bad guy" spectrum constructed by the specific abuse inflicted upon them, without question their lives would have been drastically altered had Thomas never been a part of the picture. The love and hope these boys once experienced as children could not hold a candle to the suffering and rage that Thomas's malicious actions generated in them as adults.

Tragedy has a way of affecting individuals differently. As we shall see in the next chapter, trauma changes us in ways that few other life events can.

THREE

Weapon X

What is the point of this weapon if we can't control him?
—The Professor, *Weapon X*

Since Wolverine's first appearance in 1974, it had been implied that this character was at some level connected to a secret and malevolent government experimental program. In 1991 Barry Windsor-Smith wrote and illustrated the Weapon X story in the *Marvel Comics Presents* anthology in issues #72–84. This series revealed that a project known as Experiment X was responsible for infusing Wolverine with his indestructible adamantium skeleton and claws, with the goal of making him an indestructible weapon of war.

According to the fictional series, Weapon X is a covert government research facility with the mission of procuring, detaining, and (via medically induced torture) reprogramming both willing and unwilling mutants and humans into corporeal weapons of war. Mutants are often experimented upon to enhance their natural superpowers, turning them into flesh-and-blood targetable ordnance. Being the tenth subject of Experiment X, Wolverine became known as "Weapon X" and, as such, was degraded to the level of objectified experiment, stripped of humanity or dignity or the need for compassion.

Windsor-Smith's own perceptive conception of Wolverine's creation is revealed panel by panel through the arrestingly brutal images that chronicle Logan's physical and mental anguish as he struggles to maintain a sense of humanity through his torment. Logan's resilient defiance of his transformation and congruent tenacious grasp on his humanity become apparent in his ability to ultimately harness the mechanically and chemically enhanced capacities of his newly imposed reality.

The *Weapon X* series answered a question long proposed by Wolverine fans: How did Logan get those adamantium claws? The series further presented particulars that more than validated the experiences that had made Logan so cynical, jaded, emotionally distant, and volatile.

Defining Torture

In order to comprehend the true level of agony Logan endured, torture itself must be explored—that is, we must ask what it is, what methods are employed, and how it affects a person on multiple levels both during the actual experience and afterward.

The United Nations Convention against Torture, an international human rights treaty backed by the United Nations that aims to prevent torture and other acts of cruel, inhuman, or degrading treatment or punishment around the world, defines torture as follows:

> Any act by which severe pain or suffering, whether physical or mental, is intentionally inflicted on a person for such purposes as obtaining from him, or a third person, information or a confession, punishing him for an act he or a third person has committed or is suspected of having committed, or intimidating or coercing him or a third person, or for any reason based on discrimination of any kind, when such pain or suffering is inflicted by or at the instigation of or with the consent or acquiescence of a public official or other person acting in an official capacity.

There are multiple motives for engaging in torture. Stated simply, torture can be acknowledged to occur when pain, suffering, and/or intimidation are inflicted upon an unwilling person by an acting authority or entity for the purpose of securing information, asserting racial/ethnic "superiority," repressing political or religious resistance, intimidation, humiliation of the prisoner, inflicting punishment, or coercion to commit or refrain from committing such acts as are beneficial to the acting authority or entity.

Although torture has existed since age-old times, it is now acknowledged as a crime against humanity and is internationally illegal, though 50 percent of the world continues to engage in such practices; worse, 79 percent of the world's G-20 countries do too. Many civilizations have rationalized a perverse justification for torture—namely, conveniently viewing victims as subhuman and deserving nothing more than inhuman treatment. For example, courts in ancient Greece prohibited torture of free citizens but would trust the testimony of a slave only if it had been secured by torture.

In his book, *The History of Torture*, Brian Innes contends that "the official justification [for torture] ... has always been the need to obtain information: from a criminal ... from a prisoner taken in war ... from a heretic ... or from a terrorist.... Sadly, the application of torture in such instances, in itself inexcusable, has been overshadowed by the fact that it is regarded also as a punishment."[1] Some of the most horrific historical torture techniques are still in use today, illuminating the inhumanity and cruelty of this practice.

In 2000, human rights group Amnesty International and African social sciences organization CODESRIA published a manual for overseer groups monitoring prisons where torture is suspected. The handbook offers insight into what qualifies as humiliating, cruel, and inhumane treatment. The guide also discusses the most common forms of torture, including beatings, hanging a person in various positions by their limbs, electric shocks, sexual assault (including rape) and mock executions. In addition to Amnesty International's list, the Boston Center for Refugee Health and Human Rights has cited five other common forms of torture: burning, penetrating injuries, asphyxiation, removal of tissue and appendages, and forced human experimentation. While most of these endured terrors are physical (or black torture), mock executions are psychological (or white torture), and both forms are equally heinous in nature.

The Psychology of Torture

The presenting symptoms of a torture or assault victim should always be understood in the context of their experience since no diagnostic jargon can possibly capture the extent or complete accuracy of the emotional destruction suffered or the deep distrust of others that the victims develop.

Torture has profound and long-lasting physical effects on the victim. Additionally, torture victims often suffer from severe psychological symptoms, including anxiety, depression, difficulty adjusting to unfamiliar situations, post-traumatic stress disorder (or PTSD), nightmares, memory lapses, social withdrawal, insomnia, and somatoform disorders—that is, trauma-induced bodily symptoms, including physical pain without demonstrable physical causes (think fibromyalgia on steroids).

Feelings of guilt and shame about the humiliation experienced during torture are common among victims, as is guilt associated with surviving the torture when others did not. Victims often also experience uncertainty about the future, including the fear of being captured and tortured once more. The stress experienced is amplified by a legitimately acquired deep distrust of others that affects the victim's ability to forge a new or renewed support network.

Victims of torture are often misunderstood and therefore feel alone, frightened, and rejected by society. They will blame themselves for what occurred to them and therefore avoid disclosing their experiences. Then, as social isolation perpetuates, it can lead to even higher levels of emotional distress and perhaps ultimately suicide.

Whether physical, psychological, or both, torture is a deeply personal process between victim and aggressor. Torture involves an attempt to reprogram a victim to submit to an alternative interpretation of the world, one forced upon him by the abuser. Torture is an act of punishing, enduring, and traumatic brainwashing.

As pertinent to Logan, the *Weapon X* series scientists dehumanized Logan by essentially making him a lab rat. He was pushed to his physical limits to measure his "stress levels." Pain became just another metric for the scientists in exploring the depths of their subject and evaluating Logan's complicity with the role of "corporeal weapon" that they forced upon him. The torture inflicted on him explains why Logan has such an intimate relationship with pain, to the point that he almost expects it, or even seeks it out.

WARNING: Agonizing Procedures

Before proceeding, it is important to note that the following section contains graphic descriptions and depictions of horrific violence and, as such, may not be suitable for everyone. Such descriptions are quite real and unfortunately necessary to shed light on the type of physical and psychological agony that Logan is depicted as having suffered within the laboratories of the Weapon X program.

Up to this point, the tone of this work has been that of a professional and clinical discourse in the manner of an objective psychologist reporting the observed events of a mutant's troubled life and the resulting psychological outcomes. However, such pleasantries are hereby suspended for the sake of fully exploring the matter at hand. To fully conceptualize the essence of the horrors inflicted upon Wolverine, one must grasp the essence of the horrors of torture—real, true, revolting torture, overflowing with bottomless anguish, hopeless despair, and searing pain, which, if somehow survived, imposes a life of physical frailty and mental distortion on its victim.

Think back to your first viewings of *Marathon Man*, *Pan's Labyrinth*, *Saw*, or *The Silence of the Lambs*. Envision yourself in Christian Szell's chair being repeatedly asked a question to which you know no answer, or tied to a barn support post as the first hammer strike crushes the right side of your face, or cutting off your own hand to escape the drowning that's about to overtake you.

In reading the subsequent pages, abandon the antiseptic nature of the distant observer. Drop any shred of emotional detachment and move yourself—yes, your SELF—into the primal panic of personal, menacing pain.

Make no mistake: these horrors are real and the daily experience of hundreds of unfortunate people—real people—around the globe. In dark, anonymous dungeons, basements of covert governmental agencies, or nameless bloodstained chambers, with no hope, no way out, and no medical attention, with broken and grotesquely distorted swollen limbs and disgustingly infected sores, abscessed teeth and gouged-out eyes, these confined human beings trudge from egregious minute to egregious minute, with each one feeling like another hour in hell.

Now, envision that person in hell is YOU: feeling your fingers sheared off one joint at a time as they plop into a pool of your own blood, watching your dog disemboweled, your daughter gang raped, and your testicles removed in seconds (without anesthetic) and handed to you with the statement "Here are your balls, asshole."

Canto III of Dante's *Inferno* shows the main character (the Pilgrim) passing into Hell through the main gate with a sign arching above it: "Abandon All Hope, Ye Who Enter Here."

THIS is the real world of torture. This is what you MUST understand. This is what Wolverine has endured!

What follows here are the most prevalent forms of torture endured by victims throughout the world according to science.howstuffworks.com. While the broad descriptions of these torture methods are intentionally clinical and will read as rather sanitized, the actual examples abandon such niceties and are provided for the reader to be able to, in some small, vicarious way, capture the experience.

1. *Beatings*—Regarded the most widely used form of torture, there are some specific methods associated with beatings. For example: (a) the victim's body being beaten and whipped with rods or canes of bamboo or metal or plastic rods, continuing long after the skin ruptures; (b) slashing the victim with cables of varying

diameters and compositions; (c) the soles of the victim's feet being repeatedly beaten as they continue to swell and split, causing lifelong severe nerve pain; (d) the victim's head being repeatedly slammed into walls or bludgeoned with soft, yet heavy, objects such as a bar of soap in a crew sock or telephone books; (e) the victim having his hands and ankles tied together behind him, then blindfolded and forced to kneel on gravel for days at a time while being beaten; (f) the victim being tied to a post from behind and having a bucket of rocks hung about his neck, again for days at a time while being beaten, so that the vertebrae slowly sever and tear into the spinal cord.

2. *Burning*—A victim's extremities or entire body being immersed in boiling or ice water, splashed with corrosive chemicals, or subjected to extreme temperatures for extensive periods of time. These wounds are especially susceptible to infection if not properly treated, and victims frequently carry scars from their torture for the rest of their lives. For example: (a) boiling a victim's entire body in a large metal cauldron; (b) plunging extremely heated or cooled pokers heated into a victim's body parts; (c) cooking a victim's body parts with the flames of gas torches; (d) repeatedly searing a victim's body with cigarettes and cigars.

3. *Penetrating Injuries*—Injuries such as stab wounds and gunshots are particularly traumatic. Although gunshot wounds often occur when a person is initially captured, penetrating injuries are also used methodically to torture victims. For example: (a) nails being driven into a victim's head or into joints or directly through kneecaps and elbows; (b) electric drills boring into the victim's head or into joints or through bones; (c) the plunging of knives into nerve junctions.

4. *Asphyxiation*—Asphyxiation can cause seizures and loss of consciousness, and it always has the potential to kill a victim. Another possible long-term effect is brain damage leading to permanent memory loss or coma. For example: (a) repeatedly covering and uncovering a victim's head with a plastic; (b) waterboarding; (c) overturning a victim's head into a pool of water for minutes at a time.

5. *Forced Human Experimentation (a.k.a. Medical Torture)*—Practitioners of forced experimentation argue that they are pursuing "noble" goals such as curing diseases or advancing scientific

understanding of the human body, but their methods are
beyond repugnant. Think of the names Joseph Mengele, Carl
Vaernet, Carl Clauberg, Herta Oberhauser, or any of the 23
"physicians" tried at Nuremberg for crimes against humanity.
Think of Auschwitz, Bergen-Belsen, or Buchenwald, and you
will be on target. Perhaps the most infamous examples of
human experimentation occurred during World War II and were
carried out by Nazi doctors. Prisoners were forced to sit for
hours in icy water, deliberately infected with diseases and
afflicted with life-threatening wounds. These "doctors of death"
would then "treat" their victims with excruciating and careless
procedures usually ending in death or, at minimum, permanent
disfigurement and lifelong disability and pain. For example:
(a) programmed assembly-line sterilizations of Jews, Gypsies,
homosexuals, and the mentally disabled; (b) the deliberate
infecting of victims with tuberculosis, malaria, and multiple
strains of lethal infectious bacteria; (c) the deliberate insertions
of broken glass, dirt, feces, shrapnel, and various poisons into
deep wounds created by the victim's captors.

6. *Removal of and Deliberate Damage to Tissue and Appendages*—
   Amputation and tissue removal have long been used as forms of
   torture. Torturers commonly remove fingernails, teeth, and dig-
   its from victims, but any body part could be a target. Experimentation on Holocaust victims, for example, involved the
   horrific removal of their arms, legs, and other body parts, followed by either simply observing the victim's unaided recovery
   or transplanting the limbs to other victims, with gruesome
   results. Examples of this torture method include the following:
   (a) crushing, in place, the hands and feet of victims (especially
   artists, musicians, and dancers); (b) nailing hands and feet to
   tables, walls, and floors; (c) the sheering off of fingers, toes, nip-
   ples, and other sexual extremities with hedge sheers and yard
   tools; (d) knives used to cut off ears, noses, eyelids, and other
   soft tissue body parts over prolonged periods of time (see *The
   Death of 1000 Cuts* by historians Timothy Brook and Gregory
   Blue and scientific researcher Jérôme Bourgo); (e) eyeballs
   scooped out with spoons; (f) sticks plunged deeply into ears,
   rupturing all hearing mechanisms; (g) an American Indian torture technique wherein the victim is hung by their wrists from
   above and their torso beaten with clubs until the ribs have been

broken, followed by those broken ribs being pulled out through the skin.

7. *Hanging by Limbs*—History is full of examples of people binding their victims and then using the victims' own weight to execute the torture. For example: (a) the Viet Cong use of a technique called "the ropes" (a.k.a. the Hanoi Hilton Rope Trick), whereby arms or elbows were pulled tight behind the victim's back until they touched or a victim's back was arched with a rope that stretched from the feet to the throat[2]; (b) the victim being hung from the ceiling by another rope attached to the victim's body as in the first example; (c) the victim's hands being tied behind them around a vertical post, then a wire or rope being bound around their neck at a level at which the victim could barely reach the ground even on tiptoe; (d) the Judas Cradle, a tall, stool-shaped torture device with a metal or wooden pyramid on top, onto which a victim would be lowered on ropes (interesting that all languages—French, German, English, Italian—have a word for this same device).

8. *Electric Shocks*—Humans did not discover how to harness electricity until the late nineteenth century. Once established, however, electricity soon came into use as a method of torture. Electrical shocks can be delivered to a victim using cattle prods, stun guns, and electroconvulsive therapy (ECT) devices. One prominent example involves hooking up a set of contacts or wires (e.g., a set of automotive jumper cables) to a victim, grounding the victim with one wire while connecting the other to various body parts, and then turning on the current. Variants of this method include (a) the insertion of metal probes into any of the victim's bodily orifices and then turning on the current; (b) the intermittent rape of the victim during electric torture; and (c) other psychological torture techniques being simultaneously inflicted.

9. *Mock Executions*—Any clear threat of impending death falls into the category of mock executions. For example: (a) a straightforward verbal threat; (b) waterboarding (see the entry on asphyxiation); (c) holding an unloaded gun to a victim's head and pulling the trigger; (d) burying the victim while alive; (e) showing the victim a body being thrown from an airborne helicopter and telling them that they are next; (f) any similar threats to, executions of, or tortures of the victim's family or animals or other objects of affection the victim holds dear.

10. *Sexual Assault/Rape*—Rape of men, women, and children as a form of torture has occurred during conflicts throughout the ages and across the globe. Whether the assaulter uses their body or a device to penetrate the victim's body, the act is rape—pure and simple, and devastating and excruciating. Additionally, while sexual assault is defined specifically, some experts assert that *all* torture is a form of rape because the victim's body is violated.

11. Other forms of torture include sleep deprivation, sensory deprivation, sexual humiliation, extreme thermal exposures, stress positions, and psychological manipulations used in combination with physical beatings and infliction of pain. For example: (a) forcing a victim to choose the instrument with which they or members of their family or pets will be tortured; (b) being forced to observe the torture of those close to them; (c) prolonged isolation/solitary confinement; (d) sensory deprivation; (e) sending a foreign criminal covertly to a country with less rigorous regulations for the humane treatment, to be handed over to practiced torturers, held with no name in a cell without a number, and repeatedly tortured under hopeless conditions.

Although gruesome in nature, the above descriptions slash the curtain of any simple literary description of torture and legitimize Wolverine's experience. They will, or should, much more clearly illuminate why Wolverine is the way he is and why he does what he does.

Put into the form of an analogy, consider how differently one would perceive war, pain, slaughter, death, disfigurement, and dismemberment were they to have experienced such atrocities firsthand. The door to that distinction is the door to understanding Logan and absorbing the reality of his prolonged torment, forced human experimentation, beatings, penetrating injuries, and even rape. Are you now capable of perceiving such things? If so, read on.

The Abduction

As if predicting the suffering he will experience, the *Weapon X* series shows Logan frequenting a bar called "The Prophecy." Alone one evening, he returns to his room, lies down on his bed in a rundown shelter and, to no one in particular, rhetorically asks, "Ever felt like a rat? In a trap? ...

Like you're runnin' for your life ... but you're gettin' nowhere ... 'cept the edge ... of the dark!" Finally falling asleep, he later awakes tense and sweating from another nightmare filled with "pain an' bones an' spikes ... bloodshot with vile stench and horror ... Hell is comin."[3] Wolverine's "hell" will be the long-drawn-out torturous experimentation he is about to endure within the featureless and forbidding laboratories of Weapon X.

On a subsequent night upon leaving The Prophecy, Logan is jumped, sedated, captured, and brought to the laboratory, where he is placed naked in a tank full of red liquid. Unconscious through most of the procedure, Logan awakens to find needles and tubes inserted throughout his body by which a substance called *adamantium* is being infused into his entire skeleton and claws, making them indestructible.

For seemingly months, Logan is experimented upon, tormented, tortured, and brainwashed, all in an effort to make him the ultimate corporeal military weapon. And through it all he is alone. Logan does not know how long he will be kept a prisoner or what is being done to him. Doubtless at points he feels sheer terror at the thought that he might never escape. In brief moments of consciousness, Logan is aware that he is being experimented on, possibly even assessing he is being turned into a monster, and yet he fights on for his freedom in any form that he can secure it.

The three key members of the Project X team are all scientists: Dr. Abraham Cornelius, Carol Hines, and the man ostensibly in control of the project who is referred to only as the Professor. The three monitor the torturous and barbaric Experiment X procedures Logan endures.

The Professor is depicted as a calculating sadist whose sole aim is to transform Logan into the perfect controllable weapon for the government. He considers Logan a mindless brute devoid of humanity and thus not requiring the slightest respect or concern. He convinces the other scientists that Logan was not meant to be human—he was meant to be a killing machine.

Dr. Cornelius is presented as ambitious and yet significantly more cautious than the Professor. At the onset of the experiment, he was unaware of the extent of the torment and mental brainwashing that their unwilling subject would suffer. He protests but ultimately submits to the Professor's demands.

Carol Hines is depicted as the most compassionate of the group. She is meticulous in her work and passive in nature, and she obeys the orders of the Professor almost without question. However, she, too, expresses concern when witnessing Logan's distress.

Objectification and Violation

Logan has brief periods of consciousness when he stares at the wires invading his hands and body, indicating his full understanding that he is being savagely violated. He experiences extreme physical pain, but the Professor is indifferent to Logan's predicament. Logan is *objectified* by the Professor—his opinions or feelings do not matter.

For example, at one point in the procedure, a lab technician expresses concern over Logan's suffering, at which point the Professor instructs him to enter the room to assist Weapon X. By the time Dr. Cornelius and his security staff arrive, the technician is on the floor underneath Logan, seemingly killed. The Professor smiles and is impressed with what he sees.

By definition, to *objectify* someone is to degrade them to the status of a mere object. According to Martha Nussbaum, an American philosopher and a professor of law and ethics at the University of Chicago, there are seven factors involved in the objectification of a person:

1. *Instrumentality*: the treatment of a person as a tool or weapon
2. *Denial of autonomy*: the treatment of a person as lacking in self-determination
3. *Inertness*: the treatment of a person as an unresponsive entity
4. *Fungibility*: the treatment of a person as interchangeable with other objects
5. *Violability*: the treatment of a person as lacking in boundary-integrity
6. *Ownership*: the treatment of a person as something that is bought or sold
7. *Denial of subjectivity*: the treatment of a person as something whose experiences and feelings (if any) need not be taken into account[4]

Nussbaum has also argued that the discussion of *objectification* is as important to a discussion of sexuality as it is to a discussion of capitalism and slavery.

Logan is objectified through instrumentality, denial of autonomy, inertness, ownership, and denial of subjectivity. He is enslaved against his will and treated as property. According to the Professor, Logan is no longer a mutant, but rather government property, and *it* will serve them as an object—a controllable, expendable, and mindless "asset" that can be manipulated to the benefit of the government as it sees fit. And an integral part of that manipulation is stripping Logan of his humanity.

An example of real-life objectification involves assault. Rapists, for example, justify their actions through convenient rationalizations such as "She was drunk," "If she didn't want this to happen to her, why'd she get in the car?" or "I did him a favor." A rapist objectifies his/her victim to remove personal accountability for hurting them. Perceiving a person as worthless, as an object valuable only as being available for domination and control rather than a self-aware being with free will, excuses the rapist's behavior and blames the victim—in their own mind. Similarly, Logan is dominated and treated as an object. During Logan's field testing he is left out in sub-zero temperatures "to toughen him up." In another panel, the Professor is depicted throwing hot coffee on Logan's face as he lies on the floor unconscious.

Although Logan is not raped sexually, his mind and body are certainly violated in the most vicious way conceivable. The Professor forces his agenda on Logan. By the same token, a rapist will often treat his victim savagely. He wants to dominate by asserting power and control over someone who is unconscious, unwilling, or not within their own faculties to consent.

The goal of *angry rapists*, according to psychologist Nicholas Groth, is to humiliate, hurt, and debase their victim. They express hatred of their victim through physical violence. Their aim is to express their anger through defiling and degrading their victim.[5] *Sadistic rape*, by contrast, usually involves extensive, sustained torture, and restraint. These rapists may use some type of instrument or foreign object to penetrate the victim. The torture is often methodical, calculated, premeditated, and inclusive of psychological elements.

Logan's body is purposefully and sadistically desecrated—raped, as it were. He is subjected to horrific misery as the scientists penetrate nearly every area of his body (orifices included) with needles and tubes and then inject a foreign substance into his body.

Dr. Cornelius becomes aware that they are transforming Logan "into a monster ... a mindless murdering animal." He tells the Professor, "I met his eyes for a second filled with hate and fury but I couldn't tell if it was some animal bloodlust or horror at what we have done to him."[6] The Professor neither shows remorse nor cares whether the fury in Logan's eyes is a result of the experiment's success in turning Logan into a creature of controllable bloodlust—an animal—or the experiment's failure in that Logan retains enough humanity to view his current condition with horror.

The Professor justifies the experiment by explaining that Logan was already an "infernal thing" even before the adamantium bonding. "A determinedly violent individual," the Professor calls him, "pummeling his way through a purposeless life." Therefore, they are doing Logan a favor by releasing his primal animalistic nature. Instead of allowing Logan to fight against "the demon," they are essentially helping him to find his true calling.

At this point in the story, comparisons might well be made between the scientists' behaviors within the Weapon X program and the actions of the SS officers and medical professionals under their control within Nazi Germany. In fact, some of the work of Weapon X was based on the experiments detailed in the journals of Nazi scientist Nathan Essex, which were obtained after the end of World War II.

These experiments, along with other sadistic acts, were fueled by Adolf Hitler's theory that the Aryan race was a master race, while Jews, Gypsies, homosexuals, and the disabled were deemed impure subhumans—the Mudbloods of Europe, if you will—all of whom were considered *Lebensunwertes Leben,* or "life unworthy of life," due to their perceived inferiority. The Third Reich perceived these individuals not as people but as mindless objects without value who must be extorted for their physical labor and disposed of when no longer useful.

Torturers often convince themselves and their victims of their invincible power. "Sometimes they present themselves as supermen who have other men at their mercy, and sometimes as men, strong and severe, who have been entrusted with the most obscene, ferocious, and cowardly of animals, the human animal."[7] Within concentration camps, prisoners were referred to and recognized exclusively as an assigned number, which was typically tattooed on their skin. Similarly, the Professor insists that the scientists refer to Logan solely as "Weapon X" in order to extinguish any belief that he is human or deserving of sympathy.

"Just Following Orders"

Given the magnitude of torture Wolverine endured, surely one would think that one or more of the research practitioners would feel enough compassion toward their test subject to cease the experiments, but they make no such effort. At several points in the series Dr. Cornelius questions the Professor's inhumane tactics; however, he still follows the Professor's orders. Why would someone obediently follow orders to harm another despite such directives directly conflicting with one's own personal values or sense of morality?

One of the most famous studies of obedience in psychology was carried out by Dr. Stanley Milgram, a psychologist at Yale University. Dr. Milgram's experiment focused on the conflict between obedience to authority and personal conscience. The aim of this study was researching how far people would go in obeying an instruction if it involved harming another person.

Milgram's study began in 1961, a year after the trial of Nazi Adolf Eichmann, who famously argued that he was "just following orders" when he sent Jews to their deaths. Milgram's study was inspired by the justifications presented during this trial for acts of genocide. He devised an experiment to answer the question: "Could it be that Eichmann and his million accomplices in the Holocaust were just following orders? Could we call them all accomplices?"[8]

Dr. Milgram told his participants that a man was being trained to learn word pairs in an adjacent room. An experimenter wearing a grey lab coat (appearing as the authority figure) ordered the test participants to press a button delivering an electric shock of escalating strength to the learner when he made an error; when they did so, they heard his cries of pain. In reality, the learner was an actor, and no shock was ever delivered. Milgram's aim was to see how far people would go when they were ordered to step up the voltage from 15 volts (mild shock) to 450 volts (dangerous/severe shock). The learner provided mainly incorrect answers (on purpose), and for each of these errors the teacher/test subject was to give him an electric shock. The drawing below, obtained from simplypsychology.org, illustrates the layout of this experiment.[9]

The learner would give the impression that he was screaming in pain from the electric shocks. When the teacher/test subject refused to administer another shock, the experimenter (in the grey lab coat) gave the teacher/test subject a series of orders pressuring them to continue with the experiment. There were four verbal prods the experimenter stated aloud to the teacher/test subject:

Prod 1: Please continue.
Prod 2: The experiment requires you to continue.
Prod 3: It is absolutely essential that you continue.
Prod 4: You have no other choice but to continue.

Routinely, an alarming two-thirds (65 percent) of the teacher/test subject participants continued to step up shocks to the highest level of 450 volts even after the learner was no longer responding and supposedly rendered unconscious. All of the teacher/test subject participants continued to shock the learners up to 300 volts.

Milgram explained the behavior of the teacher/test subjects by suggesting that people have two states of behavior in social situations: (1) the *autonomous state,* in which people direct their own actions and take responsibility for the results of those actions, and (2) the *agentic state,* in which people allow others to direct their actions and therefore pass off responsibility for the consequences to the person giving the orders.[10]

Milgram's agency theory suggests that people will obey an order when they believe the authority figure will take responsibility for the consequences of their actions. For example, when the teacher/test subjects were reminded that they bore responsibility for their own actions (shocking the learner), almost none of them were prepared to obey. In contrast, the teacher/test

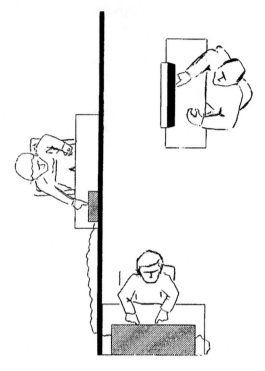

The Milgram experiment (1963) was conducted by Yale University psychologist Stanley Milgram with the goal of examining justifications of genocide through the conflict between obedience to authority and personal conscience. Male participants were instructed to administer shocks, gradually increasing in intensity, to "learners." The results were disturbing, with the majority of men fully obeying orders.

subject participants who at times refused to continue to shock the learner did so if the scientist in the lab coat said that he would take responsibility.

Modern takes on this study produced similar versions of Milgram's work. Patrick Haggard, a cognitive neuroscientist at University College London, led such a study, the results of which were published in 2016 in *Current Biology.*[11] The new findings appear to suggest that the "only obeying orders" excuse reveals a hidden truth about how one feels when acting under the command of an authority figure.

The new study was designed so that volunteers (all female this time) sat across from each other so they faced one another. They knowingly inflicted real pain on each other and were completely aware of the experiment's aims.

In a separate experiment, volunteers followed similar procedures while electrodes placed on their heads recorded their neural activity through electroencephalography (EEG). When they were ordered to press a key, their EEG recordings were quieter, implying that they were not processing the outcome of their action. Some participants reported feeling reduced responsibility for their actions. The test produced a similar outcome: giving the order to press the key caused the volunteer's sense of responsibility to be reduced whenever she was ordered to shock.

Another study examining the psychology of imprisonment was conducted at Stanford University in 1971 by a team of psychologists led by Dr. Philip Zimbardo. The college student participants adapted well to their roles as either prisoner or prison guard. The guards became authoritative, even cruel, ultimately subjecting some prisoners to psychological torture, while several prisoners passively accepted the abuse. Even the researcher, Dr. Zimbardo, became affected when, in his role as superintendent, he allowed the abuse to continue.

Additionally, an abuser may at first experience reluctance to participate in a sadistic act; however, with time he will become desensitized. The social pressures within one's environment will cause abusers to experience a lessening of moral inhibitions and behave in ways not coinciding with their moral convictions.

And, most pernicious of all, once torture becomes a social norm, its use increases in frequency over time. For some abusers, torture becomes enjoyable. Within a sadistic environment, torture invokes a person's inherent cruel nature, not otherwise displayed in any other setting. After a while, a torturer will experiment on his victims, if for nothing else than out of pure curiosity and experimentation.

Crimes against humanity are not ordinary crimes, but rather *crimes of obedience*—crimes that take place not in resistance to a governing body but under explicit instructions from an authority figure to engage in cruel and gruesome acts. Torture provides a clear example of a crime of obedience: as mentioned previously, torture is illegal and considered immoral by the international community; yet the authorities of these very states often encourage, tolerate, or order systematic or sporadic acts of brutality.

These above studies explain the conformity—indeed, the obedient tendencies—of Drs. Cornelius and Hines. Throughout the *Weapon X* series panels, we see Dr. Cornelius's internal conflict regarding the adamantium bonding and brainwashing procedures. However, when the Professor reassures Dr. Cornelius that the experiment will benefit Logan in the long run and that the Professor is taking sole responsibility for the procedures, Dr. Cornelius willingly chooses to continue to inflict immense suffering on Logan. Similarly, in the Milgram experiment, although volunteers were informed that they had the right to withdraw from the experiment at any time, only 35 percent of participants chose to withdraw.

The *Weapon X* series exemplifies how authority figures can hold both hierarchical power and psychological control over their subordinates. This abuser-to-abused phenomenon also explains why so many people, even in a seemingly "informed and enlightened" society, are willing to blindly follow the orders of an authority figure with a domineering personality, even when those orders are cruel or inhumane—or don't make any sense. Concurrently, the studies additionally confirm how it is that, when following commands, people feel less responsibility for their own actions—whether they are told to do something evil or benign.

In short, the chilling reality is that under the right circumstances, we are all capable of horrendous acts toward others.

"The Shadow" Knows Revenge

During the adamantium bonding process, Logan's brutish impulses are as greatly enhanced as his capacities to act upon them. As more experiments take place, Logan awakens, sits up, and grabs Hines by the throat. Images generated by Logan's subconscious appear on a screen, revealing that he is in piercing pain and confused as to why he is being hurt by the scientists.

The Professor directs Logan to release Hines, which he does, only to then grab the Professor instead. Security blasts open the doors and sedates Logan. As Logan sleeps, his subconscious continues to project images onto the screen, detailing the bloodbath Logan would dearly love to inflict upon the scientists as part of his revenge.

According to psychoanalyst Carl Gustav Jung, the *collective unconscious*, an inborn layer of the psyche, assists us in receiving and creating themes that match nonconcrete and innate mental patterns known as *archetypes*. Being unconscious in nature, the existence of archetypes can only be presumed indirectly by examining behavior, myths, images, or dreams (more detail on the various archetypes will be provided later).

Although the number of archetypes is boundless, there are a few particularly notable types, including the *hero*, the *trickster*, and the *shadow*.

The *shadow* represents our dark side—the part we prefer to keep hidden from the world—and refers to (1) an unconscious aspect of the personality encompassing largely negative, and therefore less desirable, aspects of one's personality, or (2) the entirety of the unconscious, which may include positive aspects of our personality outside of our consciousness. The less conscious we are of our shadow, the "blacker or denser" it is.[12] The shadow may also be a powerful link to our more primitive animal instincts.[13]

Jung says that the shadow is largely instinctive and mostly hidden but can be prone to psychological *projection*—when a perceived personal inferiority is experienced as a perceived moral deficiency in another person. For example, if you are a person prone to bouts of anger, you may perceive another person as the one with the anger problem.

Within the walls of the Weapon X laboratory, Logan's "inferiority," if we wish to call it that, is that he is trapped in a tube, unconscious, and vulnerable. However, Logan is not one to be trapped or restrained. Even subconsciously he fights against his glass-wall prison in the only way he can, a fact to which the on-screen projections of his subconscious rioting attest.

Logan was already prone to furious fits of rage before the experiment even started. Add to this the scientists' medical enhancement of not only these primal animal instincts but also Logan's matching (and now invincible) physical capacity for limitless carnage, and you have a detonation of seismic dimensions just waiting to happen. Logan's darkness—that is, his *shadow*—is played out on the monitors, full screen, to express his desires for the scientists: he wants to savagely tear them apart.

The Test of Extinguished Humanity: Phase 1

All as a part of Logan's medically induced enhancements and psychological reprogramming, his mind has been implanted with false mental sequences wherein he kills several wranglers, who, armed to the teeth with sedatives and weaponry, are set to recapture him. The implantation of these sequences serves the dual purpose of not only testing Logan's capacities relative to his reprogramming in general but also assessing Logan's responses to an outside handler's direction of his possible future actions.

In mentally running through these implanted test sequences, Logan shatters the laboratory doors and severs the Professor's hand. Logan then butchers all of the security guards as he follows the Professor, Dr. Cornelius, and Carol Hines to the adamantium reactor, where he kills Dr. Cornelius by thrusting his adamantium claws into Cornelius's stomach.

Fleeing Logan, the Professor and Hines continue their run for the reactor, wherein the Professor uses Hines as bait to lure Logan inside. Logan appears at the reactor and enters its pit, there encountering Hines, causing her to scream in terror. She begs for mercy, and Logan hesitates. He tells her, "You don't matter to me," seeking to convince himself.[14]

Again, while this is a series of implanted psychological scenarios and response tests for Logan, note that Logan still exhibits the last remnants of his humanity. As Weapon X, he has every reason to kill Hines. His violent instincts and enhanced abilities, in his subconscious dealings with the implanted test scenarios, have created a bloodbath of everyone in his path, and now Hines, one of his main oppressors, kneels before him begging for the mercy she never showed him.

But he can't kill her.

He stands before her and experiences a very human emotion—compassion. Through all the anguish, medical torture, and psychological trauma of being used against his will, the Weapon X experiment has not wholly extinguished Logan's humanity. It has failed to transform him into a mindless killing machine. Although primal and lethal, he remains Logan. He is a living being who shows mercy to an undeserving, yet unarmed, living being.

As the subconscious mental "trials" continue in Logan's mind, the Professor opens the fission gate (the "purge") of the reactor, and Hines warns Logan to run. But it's too late! The Professor turns the reactor on, searing Logan's body. Thinking he's accomplished his goal, he foolishly pauses to gloat that he has indeed killed the Canadian government's experiment. But he's foiled in his attempt by the monitoring of the very same government he's just ridiculed, which takes control of what it perceives on the grid to be the reactors' and the fission gates' purge, closing the gate before the purge can be completed.

The Professor now turns around and sees Logan's charred flesh coming toward him.

> LOGAN: Am I dead? Is that what you done to me? Walking dead man?
> THE PROFESSOR: You are ... an animal!!!
> LOGAN: I AM LOGAN! LOGAN! I AM A MAN! And you—are the animal![15]

Logan now slices off the Professor's other hand and plunges his claws straight into the Professor's skull. Logan has made his final strike: he has killed the Professor.

Logan's perpetual fight for his humanity caused the Professor's goal for Weapon X to backfire. One could say that Logan accentuated his human essence through rebelling against the animal that the scientists aimed to create and simultaneously against the animals that the scientists have become.

The Test of Extinguished Humanity: Phase 2 and Escape

In this continued subconscious dreamscape and experiment testing Logan's acceptance of all his torture, trauma, reprogramming, and response to control, he "awakes" to the sound of voices belonging to the scientists. He sees blood and bodies everywhere. In that instant Logan recalls another dream or memory—he's unsure which.

But amid all the chaos in Logan's mind and the monitoring and controlling intrusions of the Professor, Dr. Cornelius, and Carol Hines, a subtle intrusion is about to take place that will unexpectedly redirect the course of the entire experiment. The scientists may be in "control" and monitoring Logan now, but the Canadian government is about to step into the play in a most unanticipated and unpredictable way.

But back to the experiment.

Logan's recollections are fragmented and uncertain. He recognizes one of the bodies lying on the floor and wonders if he is responsible. He recalls some of the particulars of what he's currently internalizing as the "reality" of the experiment's previously installed scenario. He is confused, believing that perhaps he is dead, or should be dead, following the reactor/pit encounter he's mentally endured. He recalls struggling and fighting for freedom:

> I'm running ... running in a dream! ... And something's behind me, moving with me—like a livin' shadow—it's at my heels ... and if I slow down it'll get me—I'll suffocate in it—in its darkness ... And I won't be able to scream ... or yell ... or fight it off 'cos it'll be inside me ... under my skin—in my guts—inside my bones.[16]

The terror Logan experiences is his subconscious becoming an induced "reality." But his mental healing factor will not allow him to gain full access to his memory, induced though it may be. The "reality" of the induced events and his rage-driven responses to them within Weapon X are too shocking and dreadful for his conscious awareness to retain.

According to famed psychoanalyst Sigmund Freud, a defense mechanism known as *repression* occurs when our minds unconsciously block unwanted, unpleasant, or traumatic memories, feelings, or impulses from our consciousness. Some examples of repression may include losing the memory of a car accident or of some abuse suffered during childhood.

Repression is helpful to us when we need to block intense negative emotions associated with painful memories. But while our innate self-protective mechanisms repress the negative emotions associated with painful memories, the memories remain with us. Symptoms of repression manifest themselves via other indicators, such as anxiety, panic, or depression, which will in turn affect our behavior.

So it is with Logan.

Logan exits his current real location and immediately enters the building housing the scientists. The series does not reveal what takes place while Logan is inside the facility; however, it is *implied* that he causes some damage. Logan is finally free from the facility and once again heads for the snowy wilderness of isolation and rebirth.

Logan's identity as James Howlett collapsed with his mutation and subsequent dissociation from his childhood experiences. In the same way, his identity as Logan was forever changed when he was forced into the tank, violated, and transformed into Weapon X. Despite his escape, a part of Logan died in that laboratory, and he was resurrected as part man and part unrelenting weapon.

Logan is a mutant who has now been thrice stripped of his identity, not to mention his dignity and his body. And now, following his escape from the compound, he carries with him evidence of the torture—he is infused with an adamantium skeleton and claws and experiences flashbacks involving the desecration and violation of his body. As we shall see in the next chapter, Logan's experience in the Weapon X program exacerbated the trauma he experienced as a child. The combination of both developmental and torture-induced trauma has forever morphed him into the Wolverine we know today.

FOUR

What Does Trauma Have to Do with It?

> What they ... what they did to me, what I am, that can't be undone.
>
> —Wolverine

The *Wolverine Origin* miniseries, discussed in chapter two, elucidates the terror and shock that the young Logan (a.k.a. James Howlett) experienced when he witnessed the death of his beloved father. The horror and pain of this event caused James's mutant powers to appear: heightened animalistic senses, berserker rages, super strength, and the physical manifestation of a weapon—bone claws protruding through the backs of his hands, which he used to kill Thomas Logan. James also obtained a healing factor that heals his body from most injuries and protects his mind from maddening memories.

In the previous chapter, we discovered that these healing powers served Logan well when he endured months or years of agonizing mental and physical torture within the laboratories of the Weapon X program. Logan was treated like a prisoner and a lab rat—trapped in a test tube, his mind and body were repeatedly violated in the most gruesome manner. Suggestions of violence were implanted in his mind, and he was forced to kill—first from brainwashing, and then out of survival.

Both of these events explain why Logan is the way he is. As a child, he lost everything: the love, support, and compassion of his father and a missed opportunity to win the affection of his mother. In a matter of seconds Logan went from privileged child to a murderer on the run. He lost his family, his home, his identity, and his childhood innocence. If Logan's childhood experiences were bad enough to form some symptoms of trauma, such as social isolation, depression, memory problems, and fits of rage, his emotional wounds and berserker rages worsened and became solidified at the hands of his torturers in the Weapon X laboratory. What does this level of suffering do to a person?

Psychological Trauma

Psychological trauma occurs when a person experiences an event or enduring situation in which (1) his ability to process the painful experience is overwhelmed, or (2) the experience (real or perceived) threatens his life, bodily integrity, or sanity. Trauma psychologist Van der Kolk tells us, "Traumatization occurs when both internal and external resources are inadequate to cope with [an] external threat." Thus, an event becomes traumatic when a person either experiences or witnesses a terrifying event that overwhelms them emotionally, mentally, and physically. Emotions following a traumatic experience are often fear, panic, horror, emotional numbing, or helplessness. Trauma can be so severe that it can even leave a person fearing death, eradication, disfigurement, or psychosis.[1]

The definition of what constitutes trauma is fairly broad. A trauma may involve emotional reactions to intense and sudden events such as crimes, natural disasters, serious accidents, and other violent events. Trauma may also include situations in which an individual endures prolonged and repeated stress, such as an abusive relationship, child abuse or neglect, combat, community violence, physical pain, and psychological manipulation.

A tragedy does not necessarily cause trauma. The loss of a parent can cause immense grief and a sense of loss (depending on the closeness of the relationship); however, based on a parent's expected life span and the understanding one has of their parent's mortality, the death may or may not cause trauma. Conversely, a traumatic event is one in which a person experiences a *sudden* threat (or perceived threat) of death or serious injury to either themselves or others. Additionally, unexpected events, which blindside a person, can be traumatic. These types of situations often involve a betrayal of trust or abuse of power followed by a sense of pain, confusion, loss, and helplessness.

Determining whether a situation is traumatic is ultimately up to the victim. The more someone believes they are endangered, threatened, or blindsided by circumstances beyond their control and then experiences subsequent prodigious emotional responses, the more likely it is that they will develop symptoms associated with post-traumatic stress disorder.

Post-Traumatic Stress Disorder (PTSD)

Many psychologists who are also knowledgeable about the Wolverine character believe that he has PTSD. He trusts no one, has trouble sleeping, experiences problems with memory, and has frequent flashbacks and nightmares. Logan is also impulsive and isolative. He has trouble connecting emotionally or committing to relationships. And, let's face it, he also has some serious anger-management problems. These are common symptoms associated with PTSD; however, we cannot be quick to diagnose Logan without carefully examining each criterion of the diagnosis. After all, a person can present with some of these symptoms and still not meet criteria for PTSD.

What we do know about Logan so far is that, as a child, he endured prolonged emotional neglect from his mother and then was traumatized by witnessing the murder of his father. As an adult, he has experienced even more losses and was repeatedly tortured, attacked, and threatened. As we will soon learn, Logan is also no stranger to combat or war. The more a trauma is repeated, and the longer a person suffers, the heavier the emotional impact ... and the more likely that he will develop PTSD.

Someone can experience severe stress or shock without developing the full disorder. Post-traumatic stress disorder refers to the type of anxiety severe enough that it causes a person to experience problems functioning in, and adapting to, most areas of his life. According to the *Diagnostic and Statistical Manual of Mental Disorders* (5th ed.), the characteristics of PTSD include the following symptoms[2]:

Criterion A: Exposure to actual or threatened death, serious injury or sexual violence.

Yes. Logan has been directly exposed to trauma and endured multiple injuries, violations, and physical pain throughout his life. He has also witnessed loved ones die, including his father. Additionally, Logan experienced violent violations during the Weapon X program without his consent.

Criterion B: Presence of one (or more) of the following intrusion symptoms associated with the traumatic event(s) beginning after the trauma occurred:
[1] Recurrent, uncontrolled, and disturbing memories of the trauma.
[2] Recurrent distressing dreams related to the trauma.
[3] Flashbacks in which one feels or acts as if the trauma was recurring.
[4] Intense or prolonged psychological distress at reminders of the trauma.
[5] Bodily reactions to cues that resemble the trauma.

Yes. Logan has flashbacks (or fragmented visual recollections) of his experience with Weapon X. The *X-Men* films, particularly the motion picture *X-Men Origins: Wolverine*, portray Logan suffering from frequent nightmares, from which he often wakes up screaming, with his claw blades protruded ready to fight. In most new situations, Logan presents as guarded because he feels that at any moment he may be attacked, or captured, all over again. Logan's anxiety spikes when he experiences events that remind him of his trauma, and if he acts on his instinct to fight—look out.

Criterion C: Persistent avoidance of stimuli associated with the trauma, beginning after the trauma occurred, as evidenced by one or both of the following:
    [1] Avoidance of painful memories, thoughts, or feelings of the trauma.
    [2] Avoidance of people, places, thoughts, or feelings related to the trauma.
    Not really. Logan is constantly digging for answers associated with his past. In the motion picture *X2*, Logan is confronted by William Stryker, who begins to tell him about Weapon X. Logan does not shy away from Stryker. In fact, when Ice Man creates a thick ice barrier between Logan and Stryker in an effort to protect Logan, Logan places his hand on the ice wall, demonstrating a desire to connect, in some way, to his past. One could argue that Logan avoids violent situations by maintaining a life of solitude; however, when a threatening situation arises, he won't shy away from it either.

Criterion D: Negative changes in thought and mood beginning or worsening after the trauma, as evidenced by two (or more) of the following:
    [1] Inability to remember an important aspect of the trauma.
    [2] Exaggerated negative beliefs about oneself, others, or the world.
    [3] Inaccurate thoughts on the cause of the trauma, leading to self-blame or blame of others.
    [4] Prolonged negative emotions (e.g., fear, horror, anger, guilt, or shame).
    [5] Decreased interest or participation in meaningful activities.
    [6] Feelings of detachment or estrangement from others.
    [7] Persistent inability to experience positive emotions.
    Yes. We cannot assess whether Logan has lost interest in activities he enjoyed prior to the trauma because he was a young adolescent during his first traumatic experience. However, in the *Origin* series we see the first signs of memory loss following the trauma. Logan blames himself for his father's death. He feels horror and shame for his (self-perceived) actions and therefore isolates himself from Rose. He also experiences prolonged sadness. For the most part, Logan chooses to remain solitary and detached because he doesn't trust himself not to hurt the people he cares about. Although Logan certainly displays positive emotions during the brief periods of time when he allows himself to join a group, fall in love, or mentor a fellow mutant (more on this topic later), a hallmark character trait is his sarcastic and at times desolate nature.

Criterion E: Marked changes in reactivity beginning (or worsening) after the trauma, as evidenced by two (or more) of the following:
    [1] Irritability and angry outbursts (with little or no provocation).
    [2] Reckless or self-destructive behavior.
    [3] Hypervigilance.
    [4] Exaggerated startle response.
    [5] Problems with concentration.
    [6] Sleep disturbance.
    Yes. Logan is a mutant with a volatile temperament and is at his most lethal when he feels even mildly threatened or when his friends are getting bullied. Logan can also be self-destructive. Despite his incredible healing ability, he loves to take risks that could potentially cause harm to himself or others. He drives his motorcy-

cles super-fast, often finds himself in "shady" situations, and drinks excessively. Logan approaches most situations and challenges with reckless abandon. He also shows signs of *hypervigilance*—an intensified awareness of the environment—many times in an effort to predict trouble (more on this phenomenon in a bit).

Criterion F: Duration of the disturbance (Criteria B, C, D, and E) is more than 1 month.

Yes. Definitely. Logan began showing signs of trauma in his adolescence, and they have continued ever since.

Criterion G: The disturbance causes clinically significant distress or impairment in social, occupational or other important areas of functioning.

Yes. Logan doesn't allow himself to stay long enough in any situation to form meaningful and lasting relationships. Logan is a skilled hunter, warrior, and samurai; he is more than capable in his occupation as a superhero, but early in his crime-fighting career, he sometimes allows his impulsive and explosive nature to cloud his judgment.

Criterion H: The disturbance is not attributable to the physiological effects of a substance or medical condition.

Yes. Logan loves to drink, but beer doesn't cause his symptoms.

The magnitude of a person's harrowing experience, prior traumatic distress and level of social support during (and after) a traumatic experience appear to be the three most significant predictors for developing chronic PTSD. During the Weapon X program, Logan was completely alone as he endured months of torturous confinement. This torture, compounded by losing many friends on and off the battlefield, makes Logan a prime candidate for PTSD.

Our intricate human brains distinguish our intelligence, memory, and processing abilities from those of other mammals, and yet our intelligence and memory capabilities make us susceptible to negative long-term effects of trauma, such as the fight, flight, or freeze response, learned helplessness, severe mood swings, favored over thought, feeling on edge, dissociative amnesia, emotional numbing, and traumatic reenactment.

Evolution's Safety Net

Before we jump into the topic of how trauma affected Logan, we need to look first into the role that evolution played in bringing us the emotion of anxiety.

At its core, anxiety is nothing more than a warning to be mindful of our surroundings; it keeps us safe. Without anxiety, we would walk around without a care in the world. Although this prospect certainly sounds appealing, having no warning system also leaves us vulnerable.

Abetting our survival, anxiety was formed as an evolutionary response to danger.

One way evolution has influenced our responses to a threat is teaching us to gather in packs in order to increase our chances of survival. In chapter two we learned the importance of children forming secure attachments. Psychoanalyst John Bowlby believed that the tendency of primate infants to develop attachments to familiar caregivers was the result of evolutionary pressures, since attachment behavior would facilitate an infant's survival in the face of dangers such as predators or exposure to the elements.[3] Another way we cope has to do with our physical impulses and actions.

Fight, Flight or Freeze

The fight, flight, or freeze physical impulse is evolution's response to coping with fear. When we feel overwhelmed, the shock of what we are experiencing, along with corresponding intense emotions, can wreak havoc on our ability to think clearly. Our cognitive ability to process information carefully is temporarily "turned off" during an attack. Therefore, we tend to implement the fight, flight, or freeze response to protect ourselves. These responses kick in during a dangerous situation due to the perceived unpredictability of the outcome, a sense of immediate helplessness and a confrontation with our own mortality. In prehistoric times, this would mean that we would attack the cave lion, run away from it, or freeze up. In today's world, we cope with stress through less drastic means. For example, we could blame someone else for our problems (fight), run away from them (flight), or experience writer's block when faced with a deadline (freeze).

Wolverine's isolative nature, berserker rages, and superhuman strength highlight the legacy of our primitive past as featured in the fight, flight, or freeze response. He enacts all three reactions and uses them at different times in different situations.

Logan engages in the *flight* response whenever he isolates or brushes off a problem. When the world becomes too much to bear, or when he feels a little too emotionally connected to someone, he will leave town or isolate himself emotionally (we'll discuss this tendency more in detail in a bit).

Logan experiences the *freeze* response when genuinely shocked or during episodes of disorientation and dissociation. When thrown into a violent exchange, he sometimes experiences a gap in memory. Put more tangibly, Wolverine finds himself in a forced freeze response when he encounters Magneto in the first *X-Men* film. Magneto's initial impression of Logan is both inquisitive and commentary. He criticizes Logan's inability to fight a mutant of Magneto's caliber. "You must be Wolverine," Magneto tells Logan, a sinister smile forming on the edge of his lips. "That remarkable metal doesn't run through your entire body, does it?" Magneto then holds Logan in the helpless space of the freeze response as he manipulates the adamantium, forcing him to remain suspended in midair.

We all know which response Logan enacts the most. He primarily embodies the *fight* response rooted in anger at the level of rage. We can almost hear the sound of his claws coming out of his hands: "*Snikt!*" Just like a predatory animal, Logan's animalistic instincts kick in whenever he senses that he will need to bury his claws—into someone else.

Learned Helplessness

When a trauma victim is repeatedly subjected to an aversive situation (such as prolonged torture) that he cannot escape, eventually he will stop trying and behave as if he is utterly helpless to change the situation. Similarly, trauma can cause someone to undergo a form of mental "block" whereby he does not realize that escape is an option.[4]

Logan doesn't display learned helplessness at all, save for one time in his life—in the *Origin* series. After escaping the Howlett estate, the emotional disturbance that young James feels after losing his father causes him to believe that he is powerless to escape future problems. He becomes brooding and depressed and accepts his "fate" as an outcast.

The theory of learned helplessness was developed by American psychologist Martin Seligman at the University of Pennsylvania in 1967.[5] Using dogs to test his theory, Seligman discovered that those dogs which had received unavoidable electric shocks failed to take action to escape the shocks (even when escape was clearly possible). Comparatively, dogs that had not received the unavoidable shocks took immediate action.

When the experiment was later repeated on humans, with the substitution of loud noises for electric shocks, it yielded similar results. Seligman coined the term *learned helplessness* to describe the expectation that a negative outcome is completely out of a person's control.

Shameful experimentation on dogs during the 1960s aside, learned helplessness has become a valuable principle of behavioral theory, because it reveals that prior and repeated exposure to an extreme trauma can cause humans to remain passive in long-term hostile or negative situations. For example, a victim of long-term physical, emotional, or sexual abuse may remain with the perpetrator because they have been psychologically brainwashed, in a sense, to accept their miserable reality as unescapable.

Learned helplessness has also been applied to conditions such as depression, domestic violence, poverty, drug abuse and alcoholism. Seligman argued that this sort of negative assumption (that the misery will continue no matter what) can be caused by other factors, including physical illness, profound sadness, a dire financial situation, lack of social support, and low self-esteem.[6]

After James and Rose escape from the Howlett estate, James is withdrawn and acts in a helpless manner. He is unable to think analytically, to the point that he becomes vulnerable to his coworkers' taunts and insults. James cannot protect himself or avoid danger.[7] He continues to rely on Rose for guidance until he slowly grows physically stronger and discovers his ability to stand up for himself. Shortly thereafter, we see another trauma-induced trait—an inability to regulate his emotions, especially anger.

Berserker Rages

Severely traumatized individuals can appear ill tempered or impatient; at times their tempers are set off without cause. They can go from zero to sixty in a few seconds. In fact, intense mood swings can lead some people with post-traumatic stress disorder to be erroneously diagnosed with bipolar disorder. One minute they are calm and collected; the next, they're cycling through extreme mood shifts.

Research has shown that many traumatized people, including assault victims, do not respond to stress the way other people do. Under pressure, they may feel (or act as if they were) traumatized all over again.[8] According to trauma therapist Ed Ottesen, "Common feelings associated with assault include, but are not limited to, self-loathing, shame, confusion, and insatiable fury. Self-loathing occurs with the confusion of experiencing oneself as a victim. Confusion then triggers personal detachment to the belief that such an atrocity could happen. In the mind of the survivor, fury is experienced as a call to justice."[9]

Of all the superheroes out there, Wolverine is most notorious for his berserker rages. One second he's calm, perhaps even friendly; the next second he "sees red" and is in full attack mode. But most of the time Logan is on edge, irritable, and hyper aware of his environment.

Many war veterans and first responders, who have experienced extreme levels of threats and violence, report experiencing similar mood shifts. These shifts in emotion can be extremely challenging not only to themselves but also to those around them. Such mood swings, along with other post-traumatic symptoms such as extreme levels of anxiety and aggression, can become debilitating for those whose professions may require them to return to a threatening environment.

Retired clinician and Navy veteran Larry Yarbrough says this about trauma-induced mood swings: "The violent/kind demeanor of vets who witnessed war is paradoxical. Logan has an extremely reactive temper, but he's also a kind person. He copes with pain any way he can: he smokes, drinks, loves the adrenaline rush, and he can be violent, but he's a good guy. The violent mood swings are a symptom of trauma, not a reflection of his character."[10]

Logan's berserker rages persist throughout his life and reflect his dualistic nature.

Action Over Thought

When we find ourselves in dangerous situations, physiologically, our survival instincts kick in and we tend to act on impulse. A threatening situation pushes us into action, and the choices we make are often direct and inflexible, such as pulling the trigger on a gun in order to save our own life.[11] In situations such as these, reacting without thinking can cause some people to make critical mistakes, such as running into a closed alley, forgetting to call for help or (as depicted in bad horror films) running UP the stairs, away from any possible exit. Others, however, find that in situations of acute danger it is best to respond immediately without wasting time on contemplating the options.

Gerald Newport, retired U.S. DEA agent, describes what instinctual behavior means to military personnel and first responders: "Action over thought is a part of your training and will save your life because when you find yourself in acute danger seconds count, and if you wait too long to make a decision, you are compromising your life and the lives of those around you."[12]

Firefighter and EMT Joseph de la Rosa shares how first responders respond to hazardous conditions: "When firefighters face enough danger, we gain experience in mitigating certain situations. At times, we only have seconds to act before a condition goes sideways. Other times, we have to take into consideration risk management or risk versus reward. Firefighters are taught to study building construction and the behavior of smoke and fire. Whenever possible, we must first assess the setting, the position and direction of a fire, accessibility, and other factors, and then make a decision based on what we see."[13]

A traumatized person can also acquire a drive for survival that overtakes everything else. For example, a war veteran returning to a civilian lifestyle may not be aware of reacting to a stressful situation in an extreme manner because he continues to operate on his ingrained training principle to act first and think later. He has learned to trust this instinct because it kept him alive and may continue to function as though he could experience a possible threat at any given moment.

Wolverine's physical strength and endurance afford him the ability to act first and think later. He's a bad ass. He knows that he can't be permanently wounded; if he is injured, his healing factor will protect him from lasting damage. This mindset alone drastically changes his outlook on safety compared to the average person. When faced with an intimidating person, most of us try (to the best of our ability) to consider whether it's worthwhile to act or walk away (unlike Wolverine, who rarely, if ever, walks away).

Wolverine also behaves impulsively because of trauma. We don't know exactly what kinds of tests the Weapon X scientists performed on Logan; however, based on the adamantium bonding to his entire skeleton and the monitoring of his vital signs and biochemical levels, we can surmise that his central nervous system (CNS) was affected. According to Lawrence Kolb, excessive stimulation of the CNS at the time of trauma may result in permanent neuronal changes that have a negative effect on learning, habituation, and stimulus discrimination.[14] In other words, the experiments Logan endured may have affected his ability to distinguish between threatening and nonthreatening stimuli.

Just like other trauma victims, Logan can overreact and erroneously assess a person or situation as more threatening than they really are. Many times, Logan's impulsiveness serves him by enabling him to accurately evaluate the dangerousness of his opponent. At other times, however, his judgment is off. It takes a long time for him to trust Charles Xavier from the X-Men, although Charles ultimately proves to be one of his greatest allies and mentors. Wolverine seems to go by the old saying, "Trust is earned." He's forever on guard because of what he remembers, and also because of what he doesn't remember.

Feeling on Edge

Hypervigilance refers to the experience of being constantly edgy or "on guard." A person with PTSD will maintain an increased awareness of their immediate surroundings, sometimes frequently scanning their environment to identify potential sources of threat. If you have PTSD, you are likely to scan an unfamiliar area for exit signs, or you may notice the harsh conditions of a strange neighborhood faster than anyone else can. Your senses are also likely sharper than others'.

Most people presenting with hypervigilance wish to maintain their state of hyper-alertness because it keeps them safe. They tend to believe that if their hypervigilance is eliminated, they will become vulnerable. In certain settings, this belief is repeatedly reinforced. Gerald Newport told me, "Hypervigilance to law enforcement and military personnel is a skill acquired through training. You learn to sharpen your senses and notice every detail in one's immediate environment."[15] Retired Special Forces veteran Joe Garcia further highlights the importance of hypervigilance for military personnel:

> When you first go on a mission, you don't move or speak. You sit there; you listen to the sounds around you. You wait for your eyes to adjust to the light. You become a werewolf in that you are acutely aware of your environment. Then, when it is time to get moving, if anything or anyone approaches, you are going to hear it. Hypervigilance in the military is good because you are doing exactly what the enemy is doing. You are both noticing details like "Is that the smell of an American cigarette or a foreign cigarette?" You're trying to outwit your enemy in his own backyard by noticing even the slightest changes around you.[16]

Logan's animalistic senses are trauma induced but serve him throughout his entire lifetime. In the comic book world, this ability translates to psychological hypervigilance. Logan's trauma causes his mutation to emerge. He can see, smell, and hear with wolf-like precision.

Dissociative Amnesia

Wolverine's greatest natural-born mutant gift is his ability to heal quickly from most attacks and injuries. He can slow the aging process, regrow damaged tissue, absorb bullet wounds, fight off infection, and ward off poisons. Aside from healing his body, his enhanced X gene allows Wolverine to protect himself mentally. After enduring a horrendous ordeal, Logan's healing factor triggers a kind of amnesic effect—his memories surrounding the trauma are soon eradicated.

Mild dissociation (sans healing factor) is a coping mechanism used by those seeking to minimize or tolerate stressors, including those associated with conflict. Most of us have experienced mild dissociation, such as daydreaming or zoning out while driving or getting lost in the moment while working on a project—this is normal. However, *dissociative amnesia* (also known as *psychogenic amnesia* or *functional amnesia*) transpires when a person has gaps in memory for long periods of time related to a trauma.

In Freudian psychology, dissociative amnesia is an act of self-preservation. Your memories are blocked subconsciously in order to protect you from experiencing severe psychological symptoms. The alternative might be overwhelming anxiety or depression severe enough to trigger thoughts of suicide. Another way of thinking about dissociative amnesia is that, while conscious, a person experiences a kind of subconscious censorship. If they had access to all of the traumatic information, they might not be able to cope with the intense emotions—at least not around the time that the trauma occurred.

In the movie *X2* (2003), Logan's claws slowly retract back into his hands when he hears the voice of William Stryker speaking to him. Stryker's voice is something Logan remembers, but he just can't place it. We can see Logan struggling to remember and focusing completely on the distinct nuances of Stryker's voice. When a thick ice wall is raised between them to protect Logan (thanks to the help of Ice Man), Stryker places his hand on the wall in a gesture signifying "I miss my creation." Logan then places his hand next to the shadow of Stryker's hand in a manner that suggests "You are the only link to my past." Later in the film, Logan confronts Stryker:

> Logan: "You stole my life!"
> Stryker: "You make it sound as if I stole something from you."
> [Logan pauses, a hint of detection on his face.]
> Logan: "Who am I?"
> Stryker: "You are just a failed experiment. If you only knew about your past, what kind of person you were.... People don't change, Wolverine. You were an animal then, and you're an animal now. I just gave you claws."

Cognitively, Logan has no idea what Stryker is talking about, but we witness a hint of recognition on his face.

Logan experiences dissociative amnesia quite often, and with good reason, but this state is also counterproductive. After forgetting his trauma, Logan has the major advantage of not being prevented from moving forward following a violent exchange. However, being denied the ability to reflect on his suffering denies him the opportunity to emotionally process how a traumatic event has affected him. If his memory continues to get blocked or repressed, Logan will never be able to fully heal from his traumas.

Emotional Numbing

Another way we dissociate from trauma is by splitting off the actual experience from our *feelings* about the experience. Most of us practice this form of detachment on some level. When someone we care about suddenly leaves us, we convince ourselves that we didn't really care about this person as much as we formerly thought. An extreme form of splitting off our feelings is called *emotional numbing.*

During a traumatic experience, some individuals show emotions that do not seem to match the situation. For example, if someone's house catches on fire and they escape unharmed, they may tell their friends that they're happy it happened because now they're free to purchase another house. Some people perceive this behavior as a type of positive coping skill. Psychologists refer to such a positive shift in cognitive perception as *reframing.* However, when someone's emotional response is extremely counter what it typically should be, that could be a sign that this person is protecting himself through disconnecting from his emotions. As a consequence, the person's ability to interact with others on an emotional level is compromised.

In chapter two, we addressed how the young James emotionally cut himself off from Rose shortly after their escape from the Howlett estate. Based on his faulty assumption that he had killed his own father, Logan convinces himself that he does not feel—*anything.* If he allowed himself to grieve over his father's death, the suffering would overwhelm him, and the subsequent emotions of guilt and shame could be too much to bear.

Traumatic Reenactment

One way traumatized individuals heal themselves subconsciously is through reenacting a trauma. In Logan's case, he repeatedly attacks people with his claws. Now, most of his adversaries have it coming, but other times Logan's attacks are either unavoidable or accidental. Nonetheless, the act of violence is an integral part of Logan's life journey because, without the ability to learn from his memories, Logan is destined to reenact what he cannot remember. Freud said of this process, which he named the *repetition compulsion*, "He [the traumatized individual] reproduces it [trauma] not as a memory but as an action; he repeats it, without of course, knowing that he is repeating.... He cannot escape from this compulsion to repeat; and in the end we understand that this is his way of remembering."[17]

Logan searches the world over for ways to control his berserker rages and to stimulate his memory. In the *X-Men* and *X2* films, we witness Logan join the X-Men on the condition that Professor X provide him with some answers about his past. Until he finds the answers he is searching for, Logan subconsciously reenacts acts of violence as a form of healing.

All of us reenact our stories in some way. You can say that, in various settings, we subconsciously "hint" at each other to play certain roles from our past in the hope that we will be provided a different script—this time containing a positive outcome. For example, if someone grows up with an emotionally abusive mother, he may subconsciously select a verbally abusive partner in the hope that his partner will validate him. However, in order to truly heal, one must return to the *source* of the problem. Unfortunately for Logan, returning to the Howlett mansion and confronting Thomas is not an option. Furthermore, he has lost all memory of his father's death; therefore, he continues to search for bad guys to confront. Logan will maintain a pattern of violence throughout his life until he can emotionally heal.

Another reason why people reenact trauma is due to a developed addiction to endorphin elevation. Endorphins help us in our everyday functioning by regulating our moods, but they especially help us during times of stress. In Logan's case, they provide him with enough pain relief during an altercation that he can continue to fight. We all know that he heals quickly, but he can still experience pain.

Every time Logan fights, he is exposed to repeated stress; therefore, he's also hit with repeated doses of endorphins. When a person gets addicted to endorphins and only feels "calm" after experiencing stress, fear, or anger, he becomes addicted to trauma.[18] Endorphin and trauma addiction help explain why certain people are labeled "adrenaline junkies" or "someone with a death wish." Logan certainly falls into this category.

The Search for Meaning

Plato once wrote, "Madness, provided it comes as the gift of heaven, is the channel by which we receive the greatest blessings." Meaning that trauma, unlike any other experience, can shake us to our very core; however, we can make meaning out of our suffering and therefore redefine who we are and who we will become after the trauma experience.

Psychiatrist Viktor Frankl wrote *Man's Search for Meaning* in 1946, chronicling his experiences as an inmate at the Auschwitz concentration camp during World War II. When Frankl, along with his family and many other doctors, was sent to the Nazi concentration camps, he carried with him the manuscript for his first book, which was taken from him and destroyed at Auschwitz. His desire to reconstruct that volume on psychotherapy helped him endure three harrowing years of imprisonment. *Man's Search for Meaning* is a personal account of the most appalling event in modern history and describes Frankl's psychotherapeutic method of *logotherapy*, or existential analysis, as a means of discovering the purpose of despair.

Clinician Roumen Bezergianov tells us, "In spite of the extreme conditions, Frankl had positive comments about human possibilities. Although most inmates yielded to general apathy or learned helplessness, some inmates displayed compassion, giving away their last piece of food and offering comfort toward other inmates."[19] Frankl suggests that the kind of prisoner one becomes depends on some *inner decision*, not solely on environmental conditions. He notes that there is a last human freedom available in even the most horrible conditions: the freedom to *choose* one's attitude toward one's suffering.

How does Logan find meaning in his tragedy? Does he succumb to desolation, or does he decide to find his purpose?

Some superheroes become superheroes simply because they want to make the world a better place, while others become superheroes because they have a sense of purpose inspired by trauma. When a burglar killed Peter Parker's Uncle Ben, he vowed to use his abilities to protect his fellow humans by becoming Spider-Man. He was driven by his uncle's words: "With great power comes great responsibility."

Logan avenged his father's death; however, he has no memory of doing so. Therefore, his motivation to fight crime appears to be driven by his protective nature and his search for answers.

Logan defends those who cannot defend themselves. This is his nature—his calling in life. His trauma, his suffering, strengthened him physically and transformed him into Wolverine. Although he lacks an understanding of his own history, he embraces his power and generally uses it for good. Sometimes he uses his power to get even—Logan never said that he was a role-model superhero. Logan's main purpose in life, it appears, is his ongoing search for answers. Fragmented memories, flashbacks, and nightmares haunt him. He believes that if he can discover his origins, the nightmares will stop.

In the miniseries *Wolverine: The End*, a mature Logan continues to seek purpose through his past. He cannot obtain a sense of closure until he makes sense of where he grew up, who his parents were and how he came to be known as the Wolverine. He tells his companion George, "That's all I ever wanted … to connect the pieces together again. To connect with the person I was."[20] Logan does not give in to disillusionment. He never fully obtains the answers that he seeks, but his life purpose is to reconnect with his humanity. Logan knows that there is more to him than the animal.

Frankl states, "It is one of the basic tenets of logotherapy that man's main concern is not to gain pleasure or to avoid pain but rather to see a meaning in his life."[21] Logan eventually gets his memories back, albeit temporarily. In the 2005 *House of M* miniseries, the Scarlet Witch uses her power to create a world in which mutants rule. At this time, Logan recalls his past: "I hate the memories. For so long, I wanted 'em back. An' it's like the saying goes: 'be careful what you wish for.'"[22] In a flash Logan gets re-exposed to his past, and it's not pretty.

Answering questions may bring a trauma victim relief, or it may cause the searcher even more anxiety and possibly exacerbate their PTSD symptoms. Logan does not find solace in getting answers, but rather in retaliating against those who have wronged him.

Traumatic symptoms may remain with a person long term, if not throughout most of their lifetime. Learned helplessness, emotional numbing, traumatic reenactment, and dissociation will produce more PTSD symptoms. However, individuals report less depression after they allow themselves to feel the unpleasant emotions that accompany recalling the details surrounding their trauma. Flashbacks and anxiety can transform into introspection and purposeful contemplation. In this manner, trauma victims may be able to find purpose and value in their pain.

Logan chooses to search for meaning and therefore has made the quest for answers his life purpose. Psychologist Lisa Gaudet emphasized this point by stating, "Despite Logan's inability to remember his past or past traumas, he has total freedom to choose his path through his decision to seek meaning. He is on the precipice of dictating who he is and who he will become."[23]

Chaos forces you to learn about yourself and those around you. Pain has a way of stirring up the soul. The process of loss forces a kind of death on your psyche, but eventually, when you learn to embrace the loss, you are resurrected. The trauma healing process is a complicated one and unique to each individual, but it can change and shape you in a positive way. You learn a thing or two about your resiliency, and just when you think that you cannot overcome the pain, you realize that you are stronger than you formerly thought.

FIVE

When the Claws Come Out

They're just gonna keep comin'. Anywhere I go ...
Guys like you, not caring who gets in the way, who gets hurt,
who dies.
                                                            —Wolverine

Villain: (noun';vi-lən) A cruelly malicious person who is
involved in or devoted to wickedness or crime; A scoundrel;
or a character in a play, novel, or the like, who constitutes an
important evil agency in the plot.
                        —Random House Unabridged Dictionary

As a directional arrow for intellectual focus, the thrust of this chapter is the illumination of several of Wolverine's more salient foes and a potential psychological identification of those rogues' operative personality dysfunctions and antisocial behaviors. In this chapter we will concurrently examine but a few of the primary villains with whom Wolverine endlessly engages and the relevant psychological disabilities and malformations with which these villains are burdened, afflictions that drive their contra-social actions (and those to which Wolverine takes such exception).

When one has an explosive anger-management problem and has lived as long as Wolverine, one is bound to make enemies. Logan's surly nature has gotten him into trouble with a century's worth of opponents, including Sabretooth, Silver Samurai, Ogun, Omega Red, Lady Deathstrike, Viper, Romulus, The Hand, and Hellfire Club, to mention just the salient members of the "Loathe Wolverine" fraternity. Logan has taken on several X-Men foes and even his own family members—family members can certainly cause even the best of us to "snap" and lash out—but his most memorable adversaries are the villains who hit close to him emotionally (in addition to being sliced and diced by him).

There are several theories as to *why* people commit terrifying acts of violence, but very little guidance is available when it comes to predicting *who* these people will be. Some serial killers grow up knowing nothing but physical and emotional abuse, while others have upbringings filled with love and comfort only to go over to the dark side.

If a person's malicious nature can't entirely be blamed on his or her upbringing, then are flawed genetics perhaps equally to blame? Or, if we buy into Magneto's philosophical bent, is evil the true future of the human condition, and gentility and compassion the real evolutionary flaw? Can someone actually be *born* evil?

Psychologists have long debated this issue, calling to question whether nature or nurture primarily drives social development and whether genetics or environment plays the larger role in a child's future sadistic acts (or the lack thereof). Certainly, genetics influence a person's demeanor, but the penchant for aggressive acts can also be heavily influenced by environmental exposures along with negative learned behaviors.

If such is indeed the case (and it likely is), then "evil" is applicable as both an adjective and a noun. And again, assuming that such is the case, if we are to assign someone the label of *evil*, we would be abdicating our intellectual responsibility if we failed to consider the cause(s) of their actions just as strongly as the tangible realities of their actions. In order to gain insight into what propels a person to deviate from moral society, we must first examine what psychologically drives a person to commit aberrant behavior.

Drives Toward Destruction

In sociology, *deviance* describes a thought or action that violates social norms, rules, laws, and socially approved behaviors.[1] Someone is considered *deviant* when they lack the ability or willingness to conform to social benchmark standards or rules.

Social norms differ from culture to culture. For example, within one society an act may be committed that is considered deviant and breaks a social norm there, while that same act may be normal and acceptable within another society. For the sake of discussion here, we will be dealing with generally recognized civilized standards of societal gentility, peace, and counter-carnage.

Often considered deviant behaviors, acts of aggression and violence may just as readily be reactive, defensive, impulsive, or predatory in nature, possibly stemming from childhood abuse or neglect, traumatic experiences, or threatening circumstances. Additionally, stress, personal issues, societal or peer group status, and social factors and political climates may all play key roles. Aggression can also be perceived as a narcissistic compensatory behavior—the best defense being a strong offense, if you will. For example, in order to mask one's own insecurities, a person may avoid the focus of negative attention on themselves by acting violently toward others.

Aggression manifests itself in two major groups: (1) aggression with no intent to harm, and (2) aggression with the intent to harm, be that harm physical or psychological. Differentiated psychologically, the main types of aggression we experience include emotional hostility, direct physical aggression, indirect aggression (or using our words to transmit hurtful messages) and instrumental aggression, which is behavior aimed at hurting someone to accomplish some other goal.

Within these two broad headings, aggression is found in four major subtypes: *accidental or non-intentional aggression* (when we accidentally run into someone while trying to catch a cab), *expressive aggression* (intentional aggression without the intent to cause serious harm, such as yelling at the television screen during a football game), *hostile aggression* (reactive hostility or bullying with the intention of causing physical or psychological suffering) and *instrumental aggression* (when we fight another person over territory, rights, property, or partners that we believe to be ours).[2]

Psychoanalyst Sigmund Freud proposed that aggressive acts serve a purpose in and of themselves. His interpretation of human drives originally included a *life instinct*, or self-serving drive to ensure our reproduction and survival. However, after witnessing the devastation of World War I, he soon postulated the existence of a *death instinct*—a drive to end one's own life. In so hypothesizing, however, Freud noted that the death instinct clearly conflicted with the life instinct, and so he suggested that we tend to redirect our self-destructive aggression away from ourselves and onto *other* people, such that, under profoundly stressful and threatening circumstances, the death of others could be an extensional and marginally satisfying surrogate for our own death.

Taken from another angle, a death instinct may have evolved through natural selection, given that aggression can provide an edge toward survival.[3] Animals that choose to fight to survive tend to live longer as compared to their counterparts who make a run for it only to be caught and consumed by a speedier or more aggressive predator.

Evolutionists argued that Freud's death instinct theory conflicted with Darwin's theory of evolution.[4] This makes sense given that we know all too well that we are not Wolverine and do not possess claws, an indestructible skeleton or an innate ability to quickly heal. We know without question that if we readily jump into to-the-death battles, we risk our own lives. But what of individuals who seem to act with hostility for no apparent reason?

Personality disorders are a group of mental illnesses that involve enduring patterns of unhealthy and inflexible thoughts and behaviors, which can lead to aggression, thus causing serious social and interpersonal problems. Individuals diagnosed with these disorders often experience difficulty coping with everyday stresses and problems. The exact cause of these disorders remains unknown; however, genes and traumatic developmental experiences have been known to play a role.

The symptoms of each personality disorder are different and can range in intensity from mild to severe. As we shall soon discover, personality disorders are some of the most difficult conditions to treat, as those afflicted often lack insight into the role played by their disorders in their turbulent relationships. To the victims, they are the "normal" ones while everyone else has the problems.

But enough preamble. Wolverine always fights—always—and, to the unbridled enjoyment of Marvel fans, so do his enemies! In the mutant world, as in our own, individuals are inclined to place the blame for their problems on sources outside themselves, and to identify specific individual entities as focuses for their anger and hostility. Some commit crimes of passion, while others become lifetime criminals, seeking money, power, or admiration.[5] Other notable motivations for violent acts include, but are certainly not limited to, pure detestation, dishonor, pride, greed, lust, or jealousy, the last of these motivations being central to Logan's distaste for his most unlikely adversary—Cyclops.

Cyclops

Created by Stan Lee and artist Jack Kirby, Scott Summers (also known as Cyclops) first appeared in the 1963 *The X-Men* #1 issue. A founding member of the X-Men, Cyclops can release powerful rays of energy from his eyes; however, he cannot control the beams without the use of special eyewear, which he must wear at all times.

Often portrayed as the straight-laced, prototypical hero of the X-Men themselves, and the polar opposite to Wolverine, Cyclops is one of Logan's most controversial villains in that he isn't a true enemy. Rather, Cyclops is the sole person Logan could not defeat on an alternate field of "battle"—that is, the fight for the heart of Jean Gray.[6]

Logan's struggle with Cyclops is that he has always believed himself to be the better man for Jean, especially since the attraction was mutual. But while their chemistry was undeniable, Jean remained forever faithful to Scott.

After a few skirmishes between Scott and Wolverine, things would cool down a bit, but never completely. Until much further into their association, Logan never fully acknowledged Cyclops's hegemony within the X-Men cabal. Not to put too fine a point on it, Logan rarely respects *anyone's* authority. But because Cyclops enjoyed the devotion of the woman many believe to have been Logan's true love (more on this subject later), Logan detests him. Applying an exponential "10" to that loathing, and exacerbating Logan's internal struggles, is Scott's personification of precisely what Logan wishes he could be: deliberate, sensible, calm under pressure, urbane, and adroit—qualities Logan envies and strives to internalize.

In a stunning reversal of fortunes, years after their rivalry begins, the two foes switch roles: Wolverine the leader of the Jean Grey School and Cyclops the fugitive. After the complications created by the Phoenix Force, Logan and Cyclops replicate a rapport similar to that of Professor X and Magneto (more on these adversaries later): two former allies driven to opposite sides of a conflict due to incompatible ideologies on how to realize a shared dream.

Cyclops does not possess a personality disorder, or any mental disorder for that matter. In fact, when he's not blasting people with his laser beams, Cyclops can be perceived as the Dudley Do-Right of the group. He is habitually squared away, rational, calming, and managerial in nature. In many ways, he is the barometer of normalcy (and psychological progress) among the X-Men, and the one against whom the others are measured. Still, Logan and Cyclops fight primarily out of jealousy. Studies show that men act aggressively toward each other to defend their status in a peer group.[7] In our evolutionary past, loss of status could be harmful for survival and reproduction. Even though status is largely irrelevant for survival nowadays, aggression triggered through sexual jealousy is an evolved behavior that is passed on genetically (more on genetics and aggression in a bit).

The Banner / Hulk Character—
Dualistic Personalities

Created by Stan Lee, penciled and co-created by Jack Kirby and inked by Paul Reinman, Hulk first appeared in the debut issue of *The Incredible*

Hulk in May 1962. The Hulk is yet another unlikely Wolverine foe, given that these two not only have fought on the same side but also have more in common than any other Marvel characters.

Both tender and terrible, Hulk was intellectualized as an inspired synthesis of Dr. Jekyll and Mr. Hyde and Frankenstein's monster. Stan Lee also directly compared Hulk to the Golem of Jewish mythology.[8]

Hulk was conceived as a metaphor for the potential lingering effects of atomic weapons use in World War II and the nuclear pall that hung over the world in the post–World War II and erstwhile U.S./Russian Cold War era—an expansion on other fictional characters during this period made popular by worldwide perceptions that exposure to nuclear radiation had the potential to transform living creatures of all varieties into monsters.

In the 1960s, famed comic book artist Herb Trimpe first penciled the Hulk, with the character's robust reception becoming Trimpe's signature achievement to date. Trimpe also became the first artist to draw for publication the character Wolverine as an antagonist for the Hulk in issues *#180–181.*

Created by an accidental exposure to gamma radiation during the detonation of an experimental nuclear bomb, the character is a dualistic composite of two distinct personalities: Dr. Bruce Banner, an isolative, emotionally reserved, physically weak physicist,[9] and his alter ego the Hulk, a massive, green-skinned raging savage of insurmountable physical strength. Both personalities resent each other. Whenever Dr. Banner is subjected to extensive stress, he transforms into the Hulk, who can destroy practically anything (or anyone) in his path as he bellows out his most famous catchphrase: "HULK SMASH!"

In the comic book world, Hulk personifies the destructive nature of our humanity: Hulk's displays of physical strength and rampaging anger depend heavily on Dr. Banner's level of stress prior to morphing. In this manner, Hulk and Wolverine are almost perfect rivals. Both are possessed of a berserker fury and an incredible will to survive. Both are nearly impervious to death or permanent damage, and neither has ever backed down from a fight, even with each other.

While never especially "friendly," Wolverine and Hulk haven't always battled each other. At times these two brawlers have joined forces, fighting side by side with the Avengers and the Fantastic Four. An interview with Patricia Trimpe, wife of the late illustrator Herb Trimpe, reveals how the legendary artist theorized the Hulk/Wolverine interactions:

Herb drew the Hulk for eight years. The Hulk was his baby. He absolutely loved this character and so developed him into a simple, yet complex, character—much like Wolverine. Both characters have their own life ideology. Wolverine and Hulk are courageous characters, and they are also gentle. They have two sides to their personality, just like we do. My husband drew his characters to represent who we are inside. Drawing them was his life. He truly had an amazing career.[10]

In addition to brawling, another personality trait shared by Wolverine and Hulk is what one would reasonably think of as the mutually exclusive capacities for aggression and gentleness, and therein lies the disorder in need of review for the Hulk character. The Hulk embodies two distinct personalities reflective of a psychological condition called *dissociative identity disorder.*

Dissociative Identity Disorder

As the *Diagnostic and Statistical Manual of Psychiatric Disorders,* 5th edition (*DSM-5*), notes, a dissociative identity disorder (DID) is characterized by symptoms including the presence of two or more distinct personality states accompanied by the failure to recall personal information beyond normal forgetfulness. One of the more controversial diagnoses of the *DSM-5*, some clinicians believe that DID is actually a derivative of other psychiatric conditions, such as borderline personality disorder, or the result of an incapacitating inability to cope with the stress associated with emotionally trusting others.

All of us dissociate from time to time, such as when we get mentally "lost" while working on a project. However, DID is a *severe* form of dissociation—a mental process that causes a lack of connection among or between an individual's thought process, emotions, memories, behaviors, and sense of identity. People with this disorder commonly have two or more distinct personality states.

A clinical presentation of DID can vary in intensity and severity. The majority of patients presenting with this disorder experience distress when confronted with the consequences of their actions while they were a different persona and may not be able to recall specific information from the dissociative episodes. The multiple identities may be aware of each other and therefore can make efforts to suppress one another, resulting in the patient experiencing chaos in their personal life and relationships. The disorder can stem from childhood trauma, with the dissociation itself being understood as a coping mechanism.

The primary identity of a patient—often a person's given birth name and personality—tends to be withdrawn, depressed, or passive, as seen in

Dr. Bruce Banner, while the other personalities (or "alters") embrace more "lively" and erratic natures, as seen in Hulk or in Jean Grey's alter, The Phoenix. *Switching* occurs when each "alter" asserts itself and controls a patient's thoughts, behaviors, and overt being.

Unlike Hulk, who switches between personalities, the majority of Logan's enemies reflect traits more associated with what psychologists refer to as *personality disorders*, as expanded upon earlier in the introductory portion of this chapter.

Sabretooth—Sadism Personified

Created by Chris Claremont and artist/co-writer John Byrne, Sabretooth first appeared in the 1977 issue of *Iron Fist* #14. Originally depicted as a serial killer without any special powers, he was later repositioned as a mutant with powers similar to Wolverine's. Cloaked in mystery, his background is later partially revealed to include voluntary participation in the Weapon X program, which, as with Logan, altered and erased his memory.

Of all Wolverine's aggressive enemies, Sabretooth (also known as Victor Creed and, by some accounts, Dog, Logan's earliest foe) is without a doubt Wolverine's most enduring archenemy. A trained killer shaped by the same Weapon X program that gave Logan his adamantium skeleton, Sabretooth is Logan's physical duplicate as well as his humanistic antithesis. He possesses all of Logan's abilities but none of Logan's integrity. These two have a long, if mostly forgotten, history together.

Sabretooth continually attacks Logan on both physical and psychological levels, particularly reveling in exploiting Logan's gaps in memory. At one point, Sabretooth even manages to make Logan believe that he is Logan's father. Sabretooth will occasionally fight on the side of right, but he inevitably returns to his gratuitously violent antisocial ways. And no matter how many times Sabretooth "dies," he (as with many of Wolverine's foes) doesn't ever seem to "die" for keeps. It would seem Logan put it best when he said, "Folks don't die like they used to ... these days, nobody remembers how to stay in their plots." As long as Sabretooth lives, Logan will never be safe.

The *Wolverine*, Vol. 2, #10, series explores their long rivalry in greater depth. Here, readers learn that Sabretooth was responsible for murdering Logan's lover, Silver Fox. Sabretooth quickly followed up that act of butchery with a prolonged beating that taught Logan to fear suffering and death for the first time since childhood. Worse still, Sabretooth made these beatdowns an annual tradition. Wolverine dreads his birthday since it includes the inevitable renewal of attacks.

The Backstory of Two Half-Brothers

Claremont had originally conceptualized Sabretooth as Wolverine's father, though several writers have contradicted this relationship. For example, in *Wolverine*, Vol. 2, #42, the counterterrorism agency S.H.I.E.L.D. performed genetic tests confirming that Sabretooth is not the father of Logan. Regardless, Sabretooth appears to share some of Logan's blood, and not just on the battlefield: by multiple accounts, Victor Creed is also Dog Logan, introduced to fans in the *Wolverine: Origin* miniseries (see chapter two).

Dog is consistently depicted as an "apple that didn't fall far from the tree" (meaning his father, Thomas Logan). He grows up to share his father's violence and his vehemently entitled attitude. And, in the process, Dog misconstrues James Howlett/Logan to be the source of all his difficulties rather than seeing Thomas as the true catalyst and culpable party. Dog's upbringing endorses the "nurture" side of the "nature-versus-nurture" argument: Do we behave the way we do because of genetic or environmental factors?

The feature film *X-Men Origins: Wolverine* is a prequel/spin-off of *The X-Men* focusing on Wolverine's violent past and his relationship with his half-brother, Victor "Dog" Creed. Loosely based on the *Origin* comic, the plot suggests a close bond between the half-brothers. In the movie, after James's mutation manifests itself and James kills Thomas Logan, the two half-brothers flee the estate together. Their consanguinity too obvious to dispute, they grow to display similar traits: they are both impulsive, possess bad tempers, and love fighting in wars. The primary difference between Logan and Victor, however, lies in how they attempt to channel their anger.

Their mutant genetics being what they are, the two brothers spend the next century as soldiers fighting in the American Civil War, both world wars and Vietnam. Then, while in military custody during the Vietnam era, the brothers are recruited by Major William Stryker to join Team X, a group of mutants including Agent Zero, Wade Wilson, John Wraith, Fred Dukes, and Chris Bradley. James eventually quits the team, finding himself incapable of accepting the team's abject contempt for life. In response, Victor feels abandoned and refuses to accept James's departure: "I just can't let you walk away." Victor decides to act out—violently.[11]

Merciless and sadistic, Sabretooth will never stop killing. He thrives on it; his bloodlust is insatiable. But digging deeper into the presentation, what is being depicted is a textbook case of *antisocial personality disorder* (APD). Certainly not all APD sufferers are sadistic serial killers, but the disorder does manifest itself in varying levels of severity, and it is thus characterized by varying levels of aggressive, sadistic, manipulative, and demeaning behavior. Individuals with this disorder tend toward abusive and violent reactions in their relationships because they lack empathy and gain pleasure from humiliating or harming others.

Antisocial Personality Disorder

Someone is termed *antisocial* when they are averse to, and resist acting within, generally accepted societal norms or rules and are indifferent to the results of these dismissals. In the eyes of these people, such rubrics apply to them only when convenient.

Individuals with this disorder can initially be charming, but they soon turn dictatorial and cold. No matter how much pain they inflict, they show no remorse for their actions. They can be impulsive and reckless, and they fail to consider the consequences of their actions. They lack moral sense or conscience and tend to compile a dossier of crime, legal problems, and impulsive/aggressive behaviors. They may be habitual criminals or may manipulate and hurt others in noncriminal ways widely regarded as immoral, irresponsible, or unethical. At times, their unruliness may jeopardize the safety of others, or even their own safety.

Given this description, it could be argued that all of Marvel's villains (and several antiheroes) have some antisocial traits. However, Victor Creed raises the bar on the severity of the particulars of this condition. He takes the notion of being antisocial to another level: he IS antisocial personality disorder incarnate.

Initially identified and defined in the 1830s, APD was then referred to as "moral insanity." By the 1900s the terminology had changed to "psychopathic personality," with some clinicians supplanting the term "antisocial" with *psychopathy* or *sociopathy* being used synonymously.

Antisocial personality disorder is defined by a pervasive and persistent disregard for, and violation of, the rights of others. In other circumstances, a *sociopath* or a *sadist* is differentiated from a *psychopath* in that sociopathy is rooted in environmental causes, while psychopathy is genetically based. Whichever term one chooses to use to describe people who are manipulative, sadistic, or violent, the overarching opinion of their behavior is this: these people are bad news and need be avoided at all costs!

One of the main characteristics of APD is an inability to attach emotionally to others. Whatever relationships those with APD do sustain are maintained primarily for purposes of exploitation and manipulation. They will keep their prey around as long as they are needed, but once that need is fulfilled, the victim will be kicked to the curb. In the film *X-Men Origins: Wolverine*, however odd it might seem, Victor's attachment to Logan appears to be fueled by some distorted sense of loyalty absent any real emotional connection.

Another example of an APD mutant is Daken, the mutant son of Wolverine and the deceased Itsu, who possesses powers nearly identical to those of his father but has none of Logan's integrity. Depicted as a highly intelligent, bisexual sadistic killer who manipulates everyone he meets to suit his own ends, Daken loves to psychologically torture Logan. His trump card with Logan is that he's "family" and therefore knows full well that Logan doesn't want to kill him. They share many battles until the 2012 *Uncanny X-Force—Final Execution* story, written by Rick Remender, in which Wolverine is eventually compelled to drown Daken with his bare hands.

So where, it might be asked, does this sadistic nature come from?

The Nature versus Nurture Debate

Psychologist Vijay Jain suggests that "while nature and nurture both play a role in inducing deviant behavior, several studies suggest nature has by far less influence on aggressive and criminal behavior than nurture. Clinicians tend to focus more on nurture because they have at their ready the tools and techniques to address the environmental psychological causes for aggression. That having been said, it takes time to explore in several prior generations any genetic pattern of aggression in a client's family."[12]

There are, however, some substantively valid and reliable studies to which one might look for direction. For example, a genetic analysis of almost 900 offenders in Finland has revealed two genes associated with violent crime: (1) the MAOA gene, dubbed the "warrior gene" because of its link to aggressive behavior, which plays an important role in controlling the amount of dopamine and serotonin in the brain, and (2) a variant of cadherin 13 (CDH13), which had been previously associated with substance abuse and attention-deficit hyperactivity disorder (AHDH). The Finnish study, published in the journal *Molecular Psychiatry*, noted that at least 5–10 percent of all violent crime in Finland could be attributed to individuals with these genotypes.[13]

Other "nature" authorities have found that violent criminals tend to have higher levels of testosterone than the average person. Additional research has provided corroborative testimony in the form of children with head injuries, especially to areas such as the limbic system that could amplify violent and aggressive signals in the brain. Also supportive is the fact that traumatic events have been shown, in some cases, to affect a child or adolescent's development of the central nervous system, hormones such as testosterone, and neurotransmitters such as serotonin (5HT), which, in turn, can influence levels of aggression, impulsivity, and unhappiness.[14]

On the "nurture" side of the argument, a child's social experiences, along with family dynamics and social values, can determine sociopathy later in life.[15] Psychologists have found that most people who bully others have been bullied themselves as children or adolescents. Later in life, they are motivated to assert power due to their own deeply rooted sense of helplessness.

Other paths to sociopathy are also available given that a child can be raised in a healthy and happy home and still grow up to be a bully. The reason for this outcome is that group dynamics and peer pressure also play a role in determining future behavior. After a certain age, a child will want to "hang out" with certain peers and groups, which are then in a significant position to exert a far more powerful (read: negative) influence on behavior than any positive guidance provided by caregivers.

Dr. Jon McCaine, psychologist and expert on high-risk youth, reveals that a child's moral maturity is determined by the functional role that the family plays in the child's formative years. Basic factors such as a child's physical health, safety, and cognitive growth influence his ability to develop a sense of moral maturity. Dr. McCaine explains, "Emotional security is contingent on an ongoing presence of feeling safe from external threat and harm. This occurs in the consistent and familiar presence of a caring adult. This familiar and consistent reassuring presence is a prerequisite for the development of interpersonal trust."[16]

Dog Logan experiences the complete absence of these positive familial influences. He has never known the kind of consistently safe and healthy environment that might have fostered cognitive or moral growth. His father, Thomas, was abusive, and Dog had every reason to fear his father rather than respect him. "There is a recipe for making a violent person," Dr. McCaine expounds, "and it involves five factors." Namely, that the parent will: (a) undermine confidence and ensure persisting doubt, (b) compromise a child's capacity to relate at an emotional level, (c) create feelings of endangerment or personal threat, (d) become a role model for the use of violence and intimidation, and (e) provide a child with a personal experience of being emotionally and/or physically dominated.[17]

As the *Origin* series emphasizes, the differences in James's and Dog's parental upbringing and their social status, along with their roles in the tragic events at the Howlett estate, caused them to develop two different personalities and outlooks on life. From birth, Dog was taught to resent James, which he ultimately does. He becomes angry and hostile in his adolescence and shows signs of *conduct disorder*—a range of antisocial behavior displayed in childhood or adolescence.

According to *DSM-5* criteria, *conduct disorder* is a psychological malady diagnosed in childhood or adolescence that presents itself through a repetitive and persistent pattern of behavior in which the basic rights of others or age-appropriate norms are violated. There are four categories that could be present in a child's behavior in order to meet criteria for this diagnosis: (1) aggression to people and animals, (2) destruction of property, (3) deceitfulness or theft, and (4) serious violation of rules. These behaviors are often referred to as "antisocial behaviors" and are seen as precursors to antisocial personality disorder, which is not clinically diagnosed until an individual is 18 years old.[18]

Whether violence is motivated by nature or nurture, we cannot ignore the fact that violence and evil exist. But although any of us are capable of carrying out awful acts under the right circumstances, some are more likely to do so than others, and those who do typically show early symptoms in their childhood.

So, we have come to the point where we must ask, "Is there hope for Sabretooth?" And here we must answer, "Not very likely." Antisocial personality disorder of this caliber is one of the most difficult personality disorders to treat. The prognosis for positive remediation and resolution of this disorder is poor because people with this condition usually attend therapy only when pressured or forced, such as when they are court-ordered. Medications are also of very little help. Physicians tend to prescribe medications for people with APD only when they have a *comorbid condition* (a coinciding mental disorder) such as anxiety or schizophrenia.

Behavioral treatments, such as *cognitive behavioral therapy* (which focuses on changing the way a person thinks in order to alter the decisions they ultimately make) or *behavior modification* (which rewards appropriate behavior and provides negative consequences for inappropriate behavior), may work in some cases. Additionally, *trauma therapy* (which provides insight into the painful childhood roots of aggressive behavior) can be beneficial when a client is willing to collaborate with a clinician. However, in many cases, people with APD lack insight as to the problematic nature of their behavior. In fact, they frequently view *other* people as the problem. Therefore, it is challenging for them to trust clinicians or be genuinely interested in changing their ways.

Hellfire Club—Social Status in the Criminal World

In an effort to add a whiff of historic intrigue (think *Da Vinci Code* or *League of Extraordinary Gentlemen*) to its mythological world of fiction, the creative experts at Marvel developed the Hellfire Club. Established in the late 1700s, the Hellfire Club began as a meeting place for the societal elite of London, where, within a private and privileged mansion, they secretly indulged in pleasures forbidden by the morality of the time.

In the 1770s, two of the club's leading members immigrated to New York City, where they formed the American branch of the Hellfire Club. In the modern age, members include celebrities, politicians, CEOs, and socialites. However, an agenda-specific secret faction of the club known as the Inner Circle formed, its members high-society mutants intent on gaining both political and economic power through illegal means, though under the altruistic guise of helping all mutant kind.

In *The Uncanny X-Men: The Dark Phoenix Saga*, written by Chris Claremont and penciled by John Byrne, Logan took on these aristocrats after they kidnapped the X-Men and held them hostage. During a battle, Logan is literally dropped into the sewers, leading to an incredibly iconic call-to-action scene. In this sequence (also found in the final panels of the #132 issue), Wolverine emerges from the sewers at the lowest point of an extravagant New York City mansion, alive, well, and infuriated, having survived the Hellfire Club's "best shot" and sufficiently enraged to return the courtesy. Logan then proceeds to bring down the highest members of society, revealing their filthy underbelly, despite the club's seemingly unassailable status and position.

Coincidentally, this story falls in the middle of *The Dark Phoenix Saga*, known as one of the most defining and controversial *X-Men* story arcs of all time. In it Logan vows to protect the woman he loves (Jean Grey, despite the fact that she is in love with Cyclops) from becoming possessed by the Dark Phoenix, even if he has to kill her at the height of the Dark Phoenix's corruption in order to save the universe.

Members of the Hellfire Club are arrogant, self-serving, exploitative, and manipulative. One club member in particular, Jason Wyngarde (better known as Mastermind), hypnotizes Jean Grey, making her believe that she is her ancestor, a woman hailed as the Black Queen of that era's Hellfire Club. Mastermind haughtily brags to Sebastian Shaw of how he controls Jean completely, ignoring any emotional and physical consequences that his exploitations cause her to experience. In one panel, Shaw congratulates Mastermind, though he privately thinks him arrogant; then "Wyngarde and the Black Queen embrace like long-lost lovers. When they finally part, Jean's eyes are lit with a cruel wanton passion she's never known before."[19] Through his psychic ability, Mastermind forces Jean Grey to envision him as handsome. He needs her to revere him unconditionally.

Narcissistic Personality Disorder

Narcissus was a handsome man in Greek mythology who inspired love in anyone who saw him and often toyed with their affections. Ultimately, Narcissus became a victim of his own attractiveness when he caught sight of his own reflection in a pool of water. He sat and gazed at his reflection in complete adoration and died from lack of food or water. Upon his death, the Greek gods turned him into the flower named *narcissus*, which stands with its head bent as though gazing at its reflection.

People often refer to those showing vanity as *narcissistic*, but those with narcissistic personality disorder (NPD) suffer from a serious psychological defect characterized by a deep-rooted need for admiration, a lack of empathy or compassion for others, and a magnified sense of their own importance. Behind a mask of self-importance, sufferers of NPD hide a fragile ego that is vulnerable to the slightest perceived criticism and causes numerous problems in their relationships.

DSM-5 criteria include the existence of any 5 of the following 9 standards: (1) a grandiose logic of self-importance; (2) a fixation on fantasies of infinite success, control, brilliance, beauty, or idyllic love; (3) a belief that he or she is extraordinary and exceptional and can only be understood by, or should connect with, other extraordinary people or institutions;

(4) a desire for unwarranted admiration; (5) a sense of entitlement; (6) interpersonally oppressive behavior; (7) no form of empathy; (8) resentment of others or a conviction that others are resentful of him or her; and (9) a display of egotistical and conceited behaviors or attitudes.[20]

Although some features of NPD would seem to allow for an easy identification of those with the condition, NPD breaches the threshold of healthy confidence and crosses well over into pathological or paranoid thinking. In the throes of NPD, individuals so heavily self-aggrandize that they enshrine themselves on an undeservedly elevated pedestal and simultaneously work to demean others, all in an effort to maintain their own egotistical self-importance.

Viper—The Seductress

Logan has a well-documented weakness for the ladies, and the terrorist Viper is no exception. The woman who ultimately became the Viper, sometimes known as Madame Hydra (real name Ophelia Sarkissian), was born in the 1920s. She became an orphan at a young age after her parents died in an Eastern European political revolution. During her escape from her war-ravaged homeland, an accident scarred the right side of her face, a disfigurement she subsequently wore her hair long to hide. Through her teen years and into adulthood, Viper wandered Europe, where she survived on her wits and criminal cunning, leaving a trail of encounters with all manner of superheroes and villains; in the recounting of such tales, she became one of the comic world's most well-known (not to mention treacherous) terrorists.

Viper's anarchistic nature surpasses even that of the most aggressive Marvel villains, a nearly guaranteed turn-off for almost everyone she encounters despite her supremely intoxicating allure. Yet her attraction can prove irresistible under certain circumstances. At one point even Red Skull fell prey to her charm and seduction. However, that relationship ran aground when Red Skull discovered that Viper had covertly squandered his ample resources in financing her massacres.[21]

One of Viper's most diabolical schemes involved blackmailing Wolverine into marrying her as a means of securing her criminal empire in Madripoor. Although this was a marriage of convenience, she insisted on consummating the agreement. Sometime later, the spirit of Ogun briefly inhabited Viper's body, and Wolverine gravely wounded her as a means of driving the spirit from her dying body. In return for saving her life,

Wolverine demanded and received an uncontested divorce, simply citing irreconcilable differences as the mutually agreed-upon reason for granting the decree.[22]

Histrionic Personality Disorder

It appears that Viper most likely suffers from histrionic personality disorder (HPD), a disorder characterized by a pattern of excessive attention-seeking emotional displays, a powerful need for the notice of others, and the display of inappropriately seductive or flirtatious behavior, all typically beginning in adolescence or early adulthood. People with this disorder can be described as theatrical, behaving in an exceedingly dramatic, lively, and charming manner. However, they are also easily influenced by how they observe others as perceiving them and are prone to self-indulgence and engaging in manipulative behaviors to achieve their own needs.

Persons with HPD often imagine relationships as running deeper and being more intimate in nature than they actually are. Where the narcissistic person expects (or even demands) attention, the HPD sufferer fears not getting attention and will attempt to dispel that fear by acting in an over-the-top manner to secure that notice. They are known to display flirtatious or seductive behavior, including dressing provocatively; to exhibit theatricality, at times displaying an exaggerated degree of emotional expression; and to share vague statements lacking in detail, giving them the appearance of being intelligent while being disingenuous and insincere. This artificially exaggerated behavioral style often precludes the development of seriously intimate relationships and contributes to continuing discomfort with being alone.

Physically, Viper is tall and beautiful, with hydra-green hair. In her direct interactions with Logan, she manipulates his mind and seduces his body. This constant undercurrent of sexual tension (a dynamic not often found with his other foes) adds a level of complexity to their hostility; their fights are chess matches of ego and affections and are lavished or withheld more than the usual Marvel Comics all-out clashes that most readers have come to expect.

Another example of a histrionically afflicted villain is Marvel's Arcade. In his 1978 debut in *Marvel Team-Up*, Vol. 1, #65, Arcade wasn't the most unnerving of bad guys. This changed dramatically, however, with his appearance in *Avengers Arena*, an episode in which Arcade abducted 16 superhero children. In a style analogous to the Hunger Games, Arcade forced the children to fight to the death at Murderworld—a perverse execution camp masked as an amusement park designed to sadistically murder its captive inhabitants via carnival-like robotics and traps.

Arcade is wealthy and obnoxious, and he uses his wealth to create elaborate settings for his perverse love of twisting death into an extended spectator sport. In most ways, he's also dramaturgical—that is, he cares intensely about his physical appearance, with his behaviors and mannerisms being greatly embellished and exaggerated in an effort to generate attention from others and self-stimulation bordering on auto-erotica.

Lady Deathstrike

Created by writer Dennis O'Neal and artist Larry Hama, Lady Deathstrike is a highly trained warrior, mercenary, and assassin. Writers Chris Claremont and Bill Mantlo protracted her cyborg abilities, while artist Barry Windsor-Smith enhanced her physical cyborg appearance in general (and countenance in particular).

Lady Deathstrike (original name Yuriko Oyama) is a profoundly efficient killing machine obsessed with the adamantium bonding process. She believes that she invented the formula based on notes from her deceased father, Lord Dark Wind.[23] She blames Logan for the "theft" of this scientific breakthrough; therefore, killing Logan and removing the adamantium from his skeleton has become her sole focus.

In *Alpha Flight* #33, Lady Deathstrike battles Logan with her cyber-genetic enhancements and the razor-sharp talons that extend from her fingertips. She is defeated, but her resolve to steal back the adamantium remains unbroken. While Deathstrike's preference is to operate alone, she infrequently finds herself in the company of the Reavers, a group of cyborgs with a grudge against Wolverine and the X-Men. Truth be told, Deathstrike's bottomless bloodlust and penchant for retribution make Logan look docile by comparison.

Obsessive Compulsive Disorder (OCD) vs. Obsessive Personality Disorder (OPD)

An *obsession* is a thought or belief that persistently preoccupies and haunts a person's mind. Obsessions can cause a person significant distress and anxiety, since that person finds it difficult (if not impossible) to "turn off" their obsessive images or impulses. A *compulsion* is distinguished from an obsession in that a compulsion grows out of, or is considered to be, a consequence of an obsession, specifically repetitively and persistently performing an act and feeling thwarted when unable to follow through with the performance of these activities.

Obsessive compulsive disorder (OCD) is the carrying forward of the deeply held desire into the deeply desired act—the amalgam of both the idea and the idea made manifest. While most people try to ignore or suppress their obsessions or consequential compulsions, almost every criminal and villain in Marvel's comic universe embraces their nefarious and murderous impulses. Wolverine's nemeses seem quite comfortable with obsessing over his death and their compulsion to make the attempt.

Obsessive personality disorder (OPD), however, ups the ante substantially from, dare we say, "garden-variety" OCD. OPD is hallmarked by an unswerving pattern of orderliness and perfectionism, as well as a pervasive need for mental and, at times, interpersonal control. A pattern of inflexibility and rigidity is characteristic of OPD, leading to organizational manifestations congruent with the most efficient completion of the obsessions and compulsions. Think lists of various particulars to acquire, in what order, time elements required to secure and assemble such elements, the manner in which to accomplish such acquisitions without attracting attention or leaving a trail, and so on, and you have OPD.

These types of obsessions can be so pronounced that people who experience them may notice a corresponding inflexibility in ethics and morality, especially when influenced by religious or cultural practices.[24] The accomplishment of the task is paramount, yes, but in OPD the methodically efficient and organized accomplishment of the task is paramount on steroids.

Most of us have experienced minor obsessions, even compulsions, at some point in our lives. We may become anxious over whether we locked the front door or obsessed by the thought of a former lover. When these thoughts and behaviors begin to cause significant distress, we try our best to overcome them.

Some people with OCD may well have insight into the irrationality of their obsessions, while others do not. In the case of Lady Deathstrike, though she is conscious of being consumed with thoughts of obtaining Logan's adamantium because, in her view, it "belongs" to her, she presents zero insight into that assumption's lack of logic.

What we sometimes fail to realize is that a villain is just a victim whose story hasn't been told. Deathstrike "needs" the adamantium to credibly establish or validate her self-worth. Given her history, though, even if she one day obtains Logan's adamantium, it is very likely that she will find some other victim or idea over which to obsess.

Logan Himself

In Logan's mind, he is his own greatest enemy. The moment he escaped the Weapon X laboratories and resurrected as a living weapon, he has struggled with maintaining his humanity. Fearful of losing control and hurting those he loves, Logan detests his feral nature. Aside from fearing emotional vulnerability (as discussed in chapter two), he keeps others at a distance out of fear of turning on them.

While Logan views his uncontrollable berserker self as his greatest failing, his internal battle between good and perceived evil could never be fully realized until the appearance of Victor Creed. Creed provides Logan with his greatest challenge: the opportunity to simultaneously engage a detested physical equal and channel his tyrannical rage in a battle "mano a mano."

We have covered Victor's propensity for aggression and his corresponding diagnosis of antisocial personality disorder. And given that these two characters share so much in common, at this point one might be tempted to ask whether Logan himself has APD in addition to his given diagnosis of PTSD (covered in detail in the previous chapter). The answer is as complex as his character.

Logan has depth of feeling and a strong sense of compassion and empathy, but there is no question of his deviant nature in that he, without the slightest compunction, would slice the throat of anyone who threatens him or someone he loves.

Comic writer Jeph Loeb's assessed Logan's behavior in comparison to Sabretooth's sociopathic tendencies in the 2013 issue *Wolverine: Sabretooth Reborn*. As stated by Loeb, "Sabretooth is that road not taken by Wolverine—he kills without mercy and actually enjoys it. Logan is by far the better, and in some ways, more evolved character. But make no mistake they are metaphorical brothers who are dealing with their own demons."[25] Victor embraces his antisocial nature, while Logan eventually strives to rid himself of his chaotic and violent past.

In many ways, when Wolverine battles Sabretooth, he is fighting himself, since Creed is everything Logan could have been had he not joined the X-Men and learned to develop his sense of empathy. And just when Logan believes that he is controlling his rage and becoming more humane,

Creed will appear out of nowhere to remind him of where he came from and who Logan fears he will eventually become. What Logan believes about himself torments him more than any enemy or any attack.

As much as Logan longs for peace of mind, he also believes in pursuing justice, sometimes at any cost. Another Marvel antihero, Frank Castle (also known as the Punisher), once said, "In certain extreme situations, the law is inadequate. In order to shame its inadequacy, it is necessary to act outside the law. To pursue ... natural justice. This is not vengeance. Revenge is not a valid motive; it's an emotional response. No, not vengeance. Punishment." Logan appears to agree with this philosophy— that is, until he meets Charles Xavier.

As we shall see in the next chapter, Charles Xavier, or Professor X (as he's affectionately known among his X-Men pupils), the leader of the X-Men, exudes a sense of calm and control that Logan has never known. It is in this position of metered, balanced, and considered leadership that Xavier helps Logan soften to the point that he is able to refer to some X-Men members as friends.

SIX

The X-Men

Oppression and the M-Word

> Mankind has always feared what it does not understand.
> —Magneto

A young Jewish boy walks in a crowd of prisoners heading toward the Auschwitz death camp. Suddenly his mother and father are pulled away from him as SS officers separate children from their parents. His mother screams out his name: "Erik!" He yells back, "Mama! No! Mama!" Tears streaming down his face, he stares at the disappearing figures of his parents. Overwhelmed by rage and terror, he stretches his hands toward the iron gates. With staggering force, his mutation surfaces: manipulating the magnetic fields around him, Erik bends the gates open—until an officer strikes him unconscious.

The haunting origin story depicted above belongs to the boy mutant Max Eisenhardt, later known under the multiple cover identities of Magnus, Erik Lehnsherr, and then ultimately "Magneto"—nemesis of Professor X, enemy of the X-Men, and leader of the Brotherhood of Evil Mutants.

According to his comic book biography, Magneto's life became a living hell in Germany's 1930s as the Nazis began to institutionalize their xenophobic ideology, spewing an odorous brand of propaganda that blamed the Jews for Germany's defeat in the First World War, its subsequent decline and subjugation to its European foes, and its economic collapse then being experienced. Specifically identified as "undesirables" by the Civil Service Law and the Enabling Act of 1933, and later the Nuremberg Laws of 1935, Jews, along with the disabled, individuals of Romani ("Gypsy") and African decent, homosexuals, and children of mixed African-German heritage, were forced out of Germany's economy. As permitted under these statutes, they were harassed, beaten, unwillingly sterilized and barred from interacting with the balance of German citizenry.[1] Then, via a last wave of legislation immediately preceding Germany's plunge into World War II, the Nazis escalated their tyrannical practices to include unspeakable acts of torture and murder (for more details on this topic, see chapter three).

At this point a reader might legitimately ask, "What does Nazi ideology, group oppression, and racism have to do with the fictional stories of Wolverine or the X-Men?"

As it turns out, quite a lot.

Author Clark Zlotchew explains, "Fiction has been maligned for centuries as being 'false,' 'untrue,' yet good fiction provides more truth about the world, about life, and even about the reader, than can be found in nonfiction." In other words, when it comes to the notion of conveying any global theory or concept in a story—be it one of marginalized group oppression, as expressed through the X-Men fables, or any other—there must be some grounding level of truth underpinning that fiction for it to be received as plausible by the reader.

Comic book writers and illustrators channel real-life experiences in their work so their readers may more easily abandon "reality" and plunge headlong into the mythology and allegories of their crime-fighting characters. As famed comic book artist Joe Rubinstein once said, "I always conceive of a real person when I ink or draw anything. In my mind, I make the characters someone real, such as a film star or somebody in my life, so that instead of just being a character or a bunch of features they are the more heroic version of a real person."[2]

The X-Men comics tell the stories of costumed mutants searching for acceptance and equality in a world that hates and fears them. In addition to defending themselves against bigoted humans who wish to capture, control, or experiment on them, they must combat societal prejudice, intolerance, and oppression. Given these entrenched obstacles, no matter how many battles they fight or how powerful they become, achieving what would seem to be equitable and realistic goals eludes them. As such, the X-Men are an allegory for marginalized groups and the oppression they experience at the hands of the privileged and powerful.

As legendary *X-Men* writer Chris Claremont explains in his book, *X-Men: God Loves, Man Kills*, "Mutants in the Marvel Universe have always stood as a metaphor for the underclass, the outsiders, they represent the ultimate minority."[3] Although certainly not a watertight comparison, mutants serve to represent all oppressed groups because they suffer harassment, persecution, systemized oppression, and hate analogous to what is inflicted on real-life minorities on the grounds of baseless fears about their race, religion, or sexual orientation. Additionally, within the fictional universe, such repeated oppression has caused many mutant characters to feel ashamed of their own mutations.

Since rejection from their parents is often concurrent with their mutations emerging, mutants are driven to build communities with other mutants for physical survival, emotional support, and defense against a government either indifferent to their struggles or aggressively disposed to exterminate them altogether. Laconically capturing the essence of that struggle in the movie *X-Men: The Last Stand* is Magneto, who warns young mutants against the humans in saying, "No one ever talks about [extermination]; they just do it. And you go on with your lives, ignoring the signs all around you. And then one day when the air is still and the night has fallen—they come for you."[4]

Parallels between the seemingly fanciful X-Men storylines and the real-life confrontations experienced by marginalized groups such as African Americans, Latin Americans, LGBTQ populations, and various religious (or non-religious) groups are conspicuous. More to the point, such connections provide readers with opportunities for introspection and conversations on subjects such as bigotry, racism, homophobia, misogyny, xenophobia, misandry, and political oppression.

Mutants Are Minorities

First published in 1963 by writer Stan Lee and artist Jack Kirby, *The X-Men* introduced the original five team members: Cyclops, Marvel Girl (later known as Phoenix), Angel, Iceman, and Beast, as well as their leader, Professor Charles Xavier (a.k.a. Professor X). Their main über-antagonist was also revealed to be Magneto, leader of the Brotherhood of Evil Mutants.

Several years later, *Giant-Size X-Men* #1, written by Len Wein and illustrated by David Cockrum, introduced a new and more diverse international team of powerful mutants, sparking regenerated interest in the series. Then, in 1975, when Chris Claremont began writing for the X-Men series, the comic began its rapid advance toward becoming Marvel's most popular franchise. That series, later renamed *Uncanny X-Men*, received worldwide popularity thanks to Claremont and eventually generated numerous X-Men spin-offs, such as *New Mutants*, *X-Factor*, *X-Force*, *Excalibur*, *Generation X*, and the simply titled *X-Men*.

"The success [of the X-Men], I think, is for two reasons," comic book writer Mark Millar said. "The first is that, creatively, the book was close to perfect ... but the other reason is that it was a book about being different in a culture where, for the first time in the West, being different wasn't just accepted, but was also fashionable. I don't think it's a coincidence that gay rights, black rights, the empowerment of women, and political correctness all happened over those twenty years and a book about outsiders trying to be accepted was almost the poster-boy for this era in American culture."[5]

A prominent (if rather underplayed) feature of the mutants as an aggregate is their diversity in terms of their ethnicities, nationalities, genders, religions, and sexual orientations. The characters originate from homelands as far flung as Canada (Wolverine), Africa (Storm), Germany (Nightcrawler), Russia (Colossus), and Mexico (Velocidad). As illustrated by the introductory paragraph of this chapter, Magneto is Jewish, while Nightcrawler is a devout Catholic, Dust and M are Muslim, and Thunderbird is Hindu.

While not a primary focus of friction in the Marvel universe, religion is one of many confrontational topics addressed by the X-Men series, which portrays religion as both a cohesive and an adversarial element of dispute among humans and mutants alike. Some stories represent combative religious fundamentalism, such as when William Stryker (a human), believing mutants to be "children of Satan," forms an anti-mutant group whose aim is mutant experimentation. Conversely, religion is also depicted as a source of hope and solace, such as when Nightcrawler speaks of forgiveness and is often depicted praying his rosary. Whereas most mutants fear or hate humans, Nightcrawler feels only pity for them, branding the bulk of humanity as simply cognitively circumscribed in noting to Storm, "Most people will never know anything beyond what they see with their own two eyes."[6]

More recently, and in keeping with the recognition that sexual identification and orientation is on the radar of those who would oppress anyone other than those who identify as heterosexual, several mutants have been identified as members of the LGBTQ community. Among the most notable of these characters are Rictor, who found comfort in the arms of Shatterstar (their kiss being one of the first mainstream comic representations of same-sex love); Karma, whose affection for Kitty Pryde was not reciprocated, though the encounter gave her the strength to come out to her teammates; Mystique, who defies categorization when it comes to her sexuality and preferences; and even Daken, the deadly son of Logan, who has welcomed both genders into his bedroom.

This expansion of such diversity among the X-Men characters was neither happenstance nor an obeisance to political correctness. Rather, it was a conscious tactic selected by Marvel's X-Men creators to reinforce the need for expanded equality and inclusion in today's world in general (and in today's America in particular). Particularly relevant to such modern-day existential realities and social climates (as we'll address in a bit), X-Men tales illustrating societal stigmatization and segregation continue to serve as metaphors for the daily realities of beleaguered minorities of every stripe.

Oppression by Any Other Name

Systemic (a.k.a. institutionalized) oppression occurs when a society's laws, customs, or practices mistreat individuals of a particular group based solely on their affiliation with or membership in said group. Past examples of such oppression in the United States include slavery, denying women the right to vote, denying equal rights to people with disabilities, and refusing LGBTQ populations equal protection under the law in their legal right to marry the person of their choice.

Examples of recent laws and practices that oppress marginalized groups include profiling individuals from Middle Eastern countries at airports, prejudicially (and without probable cause) anticipating that Mexicans who cross the U.S./Mexico border are "rapists, murderers, and drug dealers," restricting transgendered individuals to the use of restrooms congruent with their biological birth genders, and the excessive use of force by police against African Americans without reason, provocation, or probable cause—a practice is so common it is often referred to as "walking while black."

Oppression is often so pervasively woven into the fabric of a society that members of minority populations frequently experience what is referred to in psychology as *internalized oppression* or *internalized racism*—that is, when a member of said group begins to *believe* the negative messages proliferated about one's race, gender, religion, or sexual orientation to be fact. Again, in psychological parlance, long-term endurance of these or other such oppressions can cause victims to alter their worldview and question (if not outright reject) their self-worth, with the end result being the achievement of precisely the aim of the oppressors.

Examples of internalized oppression may include someone with an accent or speech impediment believing that no one would choose to speak with them, an immigrant parent disciplining children in an overly harsh manner so the children will "fit in" better with their peers, an LGBTQ individual preferring to remain closeted due to religious shame or guilt, and women or African Americans not voicing valid opinions for fear of being perceived as "uppity," "demanding," "bossy" or "bitchy."

In Marvel-topia, society sees mutants as repulsive, if not outright dangerous, freaks of nature who must necessarily be kept contained, quarantined, and (ideally) eradicated. They are not celebrated or revered as role models or exemplary characters because, unlike those superheroes who obtain their powers through exposure to some accident, external elements or noble service (think the Fantastic Four or Captain America), mutants are *damaged goods*, born afflicted and dangerous. Yet, while their genetic mutations are in most cases simply physical peculiarities that in rare cases render them *Homo superior*, it is precisely that distinctiveness that makes them a target for jealousy, suspicion, prejudice, and societal persecution, and their superiority a focus for fear and hatred.

In this vein, one of the most iconic X-Men storylines is the 1981 *Days of Future Past*, in which Chris Claremont and artist John Byrne provide readers with a glimpse into just such a genocidal dystopian universe. The plot unfurls within two parallel storylines: the then present (1981) and the future (2013).

Following human acts of carnage against the X-Men, the last remaining mutants find themselves in concentration camps fearfully hiding from the Sentinels—human-produced robots programmed to eradicate mutants. Here the Sentinels have all but taken over, with the world teetering on the edge of the use of nuclear weapons.

Fearing annihilation, the mutants (led by one-time adversary Magneto) send Kitty Pryde, a young mutant recruit, back in time to avert the sequence of events that will lead to this future's bleak reality—the keystone of which is an assassination attempt made by the Brotherhood of Evil Mutants (this was Magneto's anti-assimilation horde, remember?), which raises human loathing of mutants to a boiling point. The dark future seen in this story became the basis for the similarly titled 2014 feature film *X-Men: Days of Future Past*, wherein it is Wolverine who is sent back in time instead of Kitty Pryde to pacify a government that the mutants rightly believe is moving to exterminate them.

These illustrations of mass violence in X-Men storylines mirror the abuse and debasement that minorities worldwide have and continue to face. For example, in *Uncanny X-Men* #235 the controversial issue of the island of Genosha is addressed, a prison colony in which mutants are incarcerated, isolated, enchained, and numbered via an imprint on their foreheads. This storyline is generally accepted to be an allusion to the enslavement of Africans, but it is more directly connected to the concentration camps of 1940s Nazi Germany, in which the arms of Jewish prisoners received such incarceration ID tattoos.

Some storylines incorporate themes of hate groups that tyrannize mutants at every turn, such as the disingenuously named Church of Humanity, the Purifiers, and Humanity Now! In equating such fictional organizations with real-life hate groups, readers almost universally first think of the KKK; beyond that, they might be able to innumerate perhaps another two or three examples at most. There are, however, literally hundreds of U.S.-based organizations legitimately classified by the Southern Poverty Law Center (SPLC) as hate groups, with that number growing to 917 by 2017—up from 784 as little as one year earlier.

The *New York Times* editorial board has laconically noted, "Hate crimes don't happen in a vacuum. They occur where bigotry is allowed to fester, where minorities are vilified and where people are scapegoated for political gain. Tragically this is the state of American politics, driven too often by [certain] politicians who see prejudice as something to exploit, not extinguish."[7] And just as one-off, lone-wolf hate crimes are perpetrated upon singular minority individuals unlucky enough to come under the watchful eye of individual minority haters, so, too, are minority aggregates preyed upon by organized minority hate groups, albeit with more systematized savagery and multiple victims.

Since 1981, the SPLC's Intelligence Project has published a quarterly *Intelligence Report* that monitors what the SPLC considers hate groups in the United States. The SPLC also publishes a weekly newsletter documenting racism and extremism, as well as the *Hatewatch* blog, the subtitle of which happens to be "Keeping an Eye on the Radical Right." As one might expect, the SPLC's hate group listings have been criticized by some political observers and prominent Republicans.[8]

According to the SPLC, hate groups are defined as those that "have beliefs or practices that attack or malign an entire class of people, typically for their immutable characteristics."[9] Hate group activities can include quasi-legal or ostensibly benign actions such as marches, rallies, publishing, speeches, meetings, or borderline criminal acts, but the actual goal of such activities is a purely a deliberate and willful intent to denigrate or inflict emotional and/or physical harm on, or incite racial, ethnic, religious, or political tensions among, other groups holding views, practices, or memberships antithetical to those of the hate group (e.g., seeking publicity for their particular grievance and sporting burning torches and wearing uniforms or swastika arm bands reminiscent of those worn by the Nazis while carrying a large swastika flag). A 30-member Wisconsin chapter of the KKK in 1977 petitioned to stage a now infamous march through the northern Chicago suburb of Skokie, Illinois, a city of some 70,000 people, 40,000 of whom were Jewish (and 5,000 of them Holocaust survivors).

Power Concedes Nothing without Demand

Recently, Marvel's depictions of the struggles of various minority groups have expanded to include those of the LGBTQ community. The topic of being transgendered could be considered equitably represented in the characters of mutant shape-shifter Raven/Mystique, who can morph into either human physical gender at will; Bobby Drake (a.k.a. Iceman); and Angel.

Mystique has struggled with her identity since childhood, an issue that resonates deeply with individuals who identify as LGBTQ. Witness the following exchange between Mystique and Nightcrawler in *X2: X-Men United*:

> NIGHTCRAWLER: Why not stay in disguise all the time? You know, look like everyone else.
> MYSTIQUE: Because we shouldn't have to.

The aspects of visibility and acceptance are just as much a part of "rights" to an LGBTQ community member as they are to the fictional X-Men and Marvel's mutant community at large. Witness another exchange, this time between X-Men members and the parents of Bobby Drake/Iceman when Bobby "comes out" as a mutant in the film *X2*:

> MOM: When did you first know you were a mutant? ... We still love you, Bobby—it's just that this mutant problem is a little...
> LOGAN: What mutant problem?
> MOM: ...complicated.
> [She redirects her attention toward Bobby]
> Have you tried ... *not* being a mutant?

This interchange is unambiguously analogous to the coming-out process that many in the LGBTQ community experience with their own family members. Some mutants, after "coming out" to their families, eventually free themselves from the pressure they feel to assimilate.

As James F. Barnes, university ombudsman and professor of government and justice studies at Appalachian State University, might say, this metaphor allows for "the injection of the dimension" of why and how minorities tend to collectivize, live, work, and socialize with their own, to prefer insular environments—or, as members of the accepted general mainstream would pejoratively cast it, to isolate themselves in ghettos and refuse to assimilate. So let us ask: Why would they so choose?

The answer is simple: It's a choice of avoidance. Ask yourself why someone would choose to seek out *more* rejection or remain in an environment in which it came to them daily and without provocation. Bluntly, they wouldn't. Quite the contrary, in fact—in the face of widespread societal exclusion and rejection, the rejected would seek *more* acceptance, *increased* affiliation, *enlarged* opportunities for camaraderie, and, when all else is said and done, *expanded* protections from a world seemingly bent on meting out affliction and repression.

And where might social outcasts receive such positive attentions? By asking their oppressors for it? Oh, PLEASE! Clearly, they would seek acceptance and support from their peers, from themselves, from "their own who know the pain." Hence the genesis of the NAACP, SCLC, SPLC, Black Panthers and the Black Lives Matter movement. Here is where LULAC found its roots. ILGA, GATE, and GRIN were likewise born out of rejection and persecution. It's the fountainhead of labor unions and atheist societies, just as it is the reason for political parties, the Irish Republican Army, FARC, and very likely the beginnings of today's multiple terrorist groups (even as they have ultimately spun out of control, to the detriment of all involved).

The old saying is right: power does corrupt, and absolute power does corrupt absolutely. And in that escalating "quid-pro-quo" gyre of perceived necessity, responded to by resistance, countered by insistence, and followed by outright opposition, what was once a legitimate and reasoned response to a societal issue left unnegotiated becomes a corrosive bigotry that begets a downward and unresolvable spiral of hatred on all sides.

But enough of the whys and wherefores of real life. It is Marvel Comics' use of its fictional mutant franchise to depict (and hopefully make headway against) societal bigotry and prejudice that is being discussed here. Art does indeed reflect life, and so let us return to the topic of Marvel's mutants and their metaphors for civil injustice.

At this point one might ask, "Aren't mutants powerful? Why would they need to fear humans?" Again, we arrive at a simple answer: While there are the rare few mutants who are profoundly powerful, preternaturally gifted and even combat trained, the vast majority of mutants are not.

As the Seized See It

Yes, the X-Men team members all have superhuman powers of one kind or another: Cyclops can project powerful laser beams from his eyes, Storm is capable of manipulating the weather, Wolverine is capable of bludgeoning an adversary to death and slicing the remains beyond all recognition—and as formidable as all these abilities are, they pale in comparison to the psychic capacities of Phoenix. But these are the exceptions, the rarities, the Hope Diamonds of the mutant order.

As examples of mutant normalcy, let us look at several of the more "commonplace" mutants, such as Skin and Long Neck (named for their exaggerated bodily manifestations), whose membership in mutant-dom consists of rather purposeless and downright off-putting physical aspects. And while some precious few mutants are indeed extraordinarily powerful individually, so is the government (to say nothing of its ability to marshal forces both profoundly formidable and infinitely more numerous than those of the mutants).

While their atypical abilities grant some mutants advantages over their human counterparts, they also set the mutants apart from literally all other communities. After all, as impressive and potent as melting a truck with one's eyes or disemboweling an adversary with indestructible claws radiating from one's hands can be, being able to do so is not likely to secure an invitation to join the local yacht club.

Psychologist Jon McCaine tells us, "For people identified as a member of a minority, exceptionalism has as many liabilities as cost. Becoming conspicuously accomplished provides the mainstream [with] evidence of the absence of racism and prejudice while simultaneously posing a threat to the status quo. For example, the Secret Service reported unprecedented increases in death threats leading up to the inauguration of President Obama."[10]

Mutant powers do not confer privilege or legitimacy in a powerful society that detests them. Case in point: Professor X's telepathic powers are viewed as damning evidence when he is denied equal rights under the law. For example, in the first *X-Men* movie, the government pushes a Mutant Registration Bill aimed at registering and tracking mutants. A different proposed law known as Proposition X, floated by Simon Trask and his anti-mutant rights group, would subject all mutants to enforced birth control procedures and deny them marriage rights in an effort to regulate (read: eradicate) all mutant reproduction.

What's more, in the film *X-Men: The Last Stand* a pharmaceutical company develops an antibody to "cure" the mutant "disease." Rogue is the only team member who wants the mutant cure, but Storm angrily affirms, "They can't cure us. You want to know why? Because there's nothing to cure! There's nothing wrong with you, or any of us for that matter"—a concept no doubt painfully familiarly to the LGBTQ community.

In *Avenger's A.I # 2*, with advanced technology, overwhelming force and xenophobic fervor, the government hunts down mutants. Humans build laser guns, inhibitor collars, and other high-tech gadgets designed to keep mutants "in line." Millions of dollars are spent building the Hadron-Class Kilgore Sentinel—a robot designed to attack mutant nations "just in case" mutants decide to build any countries.[11] There's a name for the notion of seeking to eradicate entire populations: *genocide.*

In response to this persecution, many mutants conceal their true identities and go underground, while others choose to face the oppression head on, ready to confront any human who dares attempt to contain, control, or exploit their powers. Thus, underpinned by two utterly divergent philosophical bulwarks, two radically variant political subgroups of mutants emerge, both based on the similar goal of achieving respect, but with very different ideologies: inclusion versus exclusion.

The disparities between the pursuits of inclusion or exclusion are never more clearly on display than when comparing the two former friends who now serve as the leaders of each respective camp: Professor X and Magneto. Magneto adopts the "by any means necessary" aggressive resistance philosophy that some have associated with Malcolm X, fighting the government with the aim of overpowering humanity. Professor X, however, adopts a "passive resistance" posture analogous to Gandhi or Dr. Martin Luther King, Jr., with whom he shares a "dream" of inclusion—ideally a respectful and mutually beneficial collaboration between humans and mutants.

The Pacifistic Professor

An expert in genetics, biophysics, anthropology, psychology, and psychiatry (whew ... you GO, boy!), Charles Francis Xavier, the founder of the X-Men, possesses one of the world's most formidable telepathic mutant minds. Putting his combined talents to good use, he serves humanity as a leading authority on genetics and mutations. In this capacity, Xavier is best known for creating a device called *Cerebro*—advanced technology that expands his telepathic powers so that he can detect and monitor mutants found across the globe.

As the owner and operator of an ultra-high-end private school in Westchester County, New York, exclusively dedicated to the shelter, guidance, and education of mutants, Xavier is portrayed as both father figure and mentor to his charges. Through his teachings, he strives to help his students "become the better man" and serve the greater good in a world filled with clutching avarice, hatred, and bigotry.

An illustration of Xavier's sensei-like position occurs in the film *X-Men: First Class* when Charles reads Erik's mind and sees his memories filled with joy and anguish. Charles tells Erik, "There's so much more to you than you know—not just pain and anger. There's good too; I felt it. When you can access all that, you'll possess a power no one can match—not even me."[12]

Another example of Xavier's telepathically nuanced tutelage can be seen in his interventions with Wolverine. Being so powerfully clairvoyant as to be able to read in the subconscious of others what is buried beyond even their own reach, Xavier knows the details of Logan's past but will not reveal them to anyone, not even Logan himself.

Xavier believes Logan must take his own journey toward meaning and self-discovery. He believes that in doing so Logan will encounter the opportunity to fully embrace his humanity, a goal that Xavier deftly applies his psychological skills in guiding Logan toward when he advises him, "The mind is not a box that can be simply unlocked and opened.... Sometimes, the mind needs to discover things for itself."

Xavier devotes his life to shepherding all his disciples while protecting humanity from the equally gifted followers of Magneto, who wish to rid the world of humankind. And in so doing, Xavier demonstrates his firm belief in the abilities of humans and mutants alike to peacefully coexist.

As is true for most leaders, mutant or otherwise, Xavier is often forced to send his X-Men into harm's way. From a social and political standpoint, however, Xavier deeply resents the violent methods so antithetical to his aspirations for peaceful coexistence that are employed by his former close friend and current nemesis, Magneto.

Xavier often acts as a mediator between humans and mutants—a most challenging task given that humans despise, persecute, and segregate mutants. Yet, in his pursuit of equality and mutual benefit, his chosen methods remain passive and nonviolent in nature: witness his counsel that mutants should be sensitive to the biases of humanity. For instance, in *X-Men: First Class*, Xavier encourages Raven/Mystique to shield her mutation so that she appears more human (read: nonintimidating). To be sure, in this respect Xavier acts less the civil rights activist and more the accommodator, but he remains well within his overarching inclinations toward inclusion.

By contrast, Erik (later Magneto) *encourages* Raven to embrace her mutation. "I prefer the REAL Raven," he tells her. When she switches back to her innate mutant appearance inclusive of her scaled blue skin and nuclear-chartreuse eyes, he stares at her achingly and before kissing her proclaims, "Perfection."

A Magnetic Personality

In stark opposition to Xavier is Magneto, who arrives at his philosophy of aggression as a result of negative nurture rather than Xavier's enlightened nature. An examination of Magneto's history reveals a once innocent child turned tyrannical "monster" via anguish and loss and the brutality of his childhood captors, a man whose ultimate aim is the domination of those who once dominated him.

In *X-Men: First Class*, Sebastian Shaw (depicted as a Nazi SS officer) forces a young Erik into an inhuman psychological dilemma. "I'm going to count to three," Shaw threatens Erik, "and you're going to move the coin. You don't move the coin, I will pull the trigger." Shaw then points a gun at Erik's mother.

Try as he might, Erik cannot move the coin with his mind. And so, on the count of "three," Shaw kills Erik's mother with a shot to the head. Filled with unbearable wrath, Erik converts Shaw's laboratory into a crime scene by trashing every piece of metal there. He then proceeds to crush the skulls of two nearby German stormtroopers with their own steel helmets.

Thus is forged the character of "Magneto," a powerful mutant overflowing with fury against humanity for the horrors inflicted upon him and his family in the concentration camps and imbued with intractable resentment toward governmental authority for the oppression that it imposes on him and his fellow mutants. Determined to prevent another Holocaust, Erik embraces the use of deadly force.

Experience has taught Erik that the privileged and powerful will never accept mutants as equals; therefore, he repudiates any thought of assimilation. Instead, Erik wants mutants to join him in his rejection of inclusion. To hell with the humans! Who needs them? Ultimately, Magneto wants mutants to be "Mutant and Proud"—to acknowledge life as a zero-sum pursuit: either we win or they do!

Magneto would thus seem to be channeling Frederick Douglass, who once said in a speech, "Power concedes nothing without a demand. It never did and it never will."

Whether consciously or subconsciously, Erik embraces some of the same ideologies as his captors. In line with Nietzschean philosophy as bastardized by the Nazis, Magneto believes mutants to be the Übermensch and that the inferior humanity should be annihilated. But despite adopting that perverted Nietzschean bent, Erik never bonds emotionally with the Nazis. Witness Erik enact his revenge against Sebastian Shaw in *X-Men: First Class*:

> SHAW: I don't want to hurt you, Erik. I never did. This is our time. Our age. We are the future of the human race—you and me, son. This world could be ours.
>
> ERIK: Everything you did made me stronger—made me the weapon I am today. It's the truth. I've known it all along. You are my creator. I'd like you to know that I agree with every word you said. We are the future. But unfortunately, you killed my mother.... This is what we're going to do. I'm going to count to three, and I'm going to move the coin.

Erik then slowly moves the coin in the air toward Shaw's forehead. Completely defenseless and terrorized, Shaw has no choice but to witness his instrument of psychological torture become his own demise as, on the count of three, Erik drives the coin straight through Shaw's skull. In Erik's eyes, classic revenge, as with Vichyssoise, is a dish best served cold.

Nietzsche is known to have said, "Whoever fights monsters should see to it that in the process he does not become one." In the moment that Erik enacts his revenge against Shaw, he goes from oppressed to oppressor and embraces his new identity as the magnetic master of the new master race.

With most of the Nazis either dead or incarcerated after World War II, Magneto refocuses his anger upon rebellious mutants such as Logan who have not accepted his teachings. A famous battle between Magneto and Logan occurs in the major X-Men crossover *Fatal Attractions* (written by Fabian Nicieza and Scott Lobdell and illustrated by Andy Kubert, Adam Kubert, Greg Capullo, Joe Quesada, Ken Lashley, and John Romita, Jr.). In this series Wolverine ferociously injures Magneto, who retaliates by ripping the adamantium from Logan's bones, forcing the metal through

Logan's open wounds and pores. Observing Wolverine screaming in horrific agony, Magneto sardonically informs him, "We are all but bit players in a tragedy far larger than any of us ... a tragedy called life, Logan."[13]

Freedom Fighter or Terrorist?

As is to be anticipated in any compelling "good versus evil" saga, the X-Men chronicles provide the reader with a stellar pair of iconic combatants. In his rejection of any possibility for peaceful coexistence between humans and mutants, and in the lethal methods he employs in the pursuit of human eradication, Magneto is unswervingly identified as the premier antagonist to Xavier's objective of calm cohabitation and mutually beneficial cooperation. Thus, by extension, Magneto's furious rejection of Xavier's world vision is positioned as "evil" while Xavier's placatory ideology is alleged to be socially desirable and thus "good."

In these confrontations, the suggestion that mutants should somehow be required to "turn the other cheek" has been challenged by X-Men devotees as inaccurate and even offensive in that this approach reinforces the assumption that oppressed groups tacitly accept offensive and racist rhetoric—or at least *should* accept such steerage-class treatment. The notion that Magneto is somehow immoral or criminal for rejecting the supposed dominance of the numerically superior also directly contributes to the victimization of marginalized groups.

Sadly, the inclination to blame oppressed groups for their own victimization is neither a comic book mythology nor an idea relegated to the pages of history books. This mindset persists to this day, such as when one suggests that gay men "choose" to be outcasts or that African American men provoke the lethal *response* of police officers in circumstances absent criminal activity or signs of lethal threat.

Regardless of how far we've come in terms of societal tolerance and inclusion, oppression remains. One need look no further for a tangible example of such contemporary oppression than the events that occurred following the election of Barack Obama to the office of president of the United States. Once elected, Obama was thought to be the most powerful man on earth, and yet, being the first black president, he was obstructed from day one (and at every turn) by the traditional, white male power structure he was "uppity" enough to challenge. Privileged groups even went so far as trying to disprove his U.S. citizenship in an effort to de-legitimize his eligibility to hold the highest office in the land, with *traditional* congressional leadership announcing the day after his election that their primary job was to deny him the slightest victory and certainly to deny him any opportunity for a second presidential term.

Many X-Men devotees and dilettantes alike empathize with Magneto and acknowledge the validity of his position. Such support has led to the mass marketing of T-shirts, hats, bumper stickers, campaign buttons, and other miscellaneous trinkets inscribed with the tagline "Magneto was Right," indicating the possessors' affiliation with the minority's opposition to an institutionally imposed reduced station in life, and with the notion that minorities have a uniform birthright to justice, fairness, and equality under the law.

Identity Through Community

Should mutants seek accommodation with the regular human population in the spirit of inclusion and compromise, or should they show resistance and enmity, effectively exiling themselves from a society that fears and hates them? As with gangs in a prison or on the mean streets of any urban environment, a mutant's answer to this question will likely be driven by the most basic of existential requirements: physiological needs for shelter and sustenance, personal safety, security (however limited), and protection, leading to an affiliation with one of the two main mutant camps.

The mutant gene, aside from giving mutants unique physical characteristics and abilities, also reveals what it means to be a unique entity in a "normal" throng—that is to say, being average or "normal" in society is safe, whereas being unusual (let alone extraordinary) will invite persecution. And when one is persecuted, be it on a physical or a psychological level, one is driven to seek the safety of numbers.

According to clinician Max Stoltenberg, "Being part of a community or group is not just about learning skills and about your abilities and empowerment but also about learning who you are. The expression of being one's own person is problematic in light of how our interactions with others define who we are via how we influence and are influenced as well as being reminded of our commonalities and dissimilarities."[14] In other words, we learn about ourselves (and others) through our social interactions, and it is through such interactions that we become aware of how well we "fit in" or are willing to conform to a community's acceptable norms—or not!

Question: Why does Logan, the ultimate loner/rebel, join the X-Men (and many other crime-fighting teams) in the first place? Doesn't assimilation or affiliation go against the very core of who he is?

Answer: Wolverine chooses to associate not with crime-fighting teams per se, but rather with a "fraternity" of mutants who happen to wind up combating what they see as evil or injustice. He associates with them out of a need to surround himself with those who have the best chance of understanding and receiving him. He seeks community and acceptance—or, more correctly, he seeks avoiding rejection. The crime fighting is happenstance, a seemingly necessary corollary of the affinity.

Aside from enjoying the exhilaration of the fight in general, and fighting alongside his comrades-in-arms in particular, Wolverine's association with the X-Men has led to the most important friendships of his life. For example, in *Amazing X-Men* #4, Logan is slowly freezing to death while walking in the barren tundra of purgatory. In his last moments, he recalls the words of his friend Kurt: "No one wants to die alone."

Being one of Logan's closest companions, Kurt would never leave Logan in his time of need. Freezing alone in the snow, Logan suddenly hears Kurt's voice:

> KURT: I hope you weren't planning on dying out here, *mein freund*. Not when we've whiskey to be drunk...
> [Logan reaches over to Kurt and embraces him tightly.]
> LOGAN: Is there really whiskey?
> KURT: No, sorry. Just wanted to make sure you had a reason to live.
> LOGAN: You're real. You're really here. You're not dead anymore.[15]

Hugh Jackman, well known for playing Wolverine on screen in the *X-Men* movies, once said, "I don't want to be too earnest about it, but I've always felt that *X-Men* has something thematically that is beyond just escapism, beyond superheroes saving the day.... It's about alienation and discrimination. And, of course, there's that great wish fulfilment of the person being alienated having claws or can fly or being able to read minds, and having the ability to overcome those powers."[16] Jackman would seem to be implying here that it's a relief for the oppressed to encounter the fact that they are not alone in their persecution, and liberating to "see" a creature like themselves with the capacity to destroy their provocateur should they choose to dispense with restraint.

The difference marker between the two available camps of mutants is that Professor X grants Logan and the other mutants an opportunity to become "more"—to grow within themselves, and to control/manage/channel/restrain their powers. Magneto, by contrast, simply wants to unleash mutant fury, regardless of the havoc such unrestrained bedlam creates.

Danny Fingeroth, author of *Superman on the Couch*, wrote about why we are drawn to mutants: "The most popular culture franchises are those that make the viewer/reader feel special and unique, while simultaneously making him or her feel he or she is part of a mass of people experiencing and enjoying the same phenomenon. The plight of the mutants is universally compelling. Many people feel a need for a surrogate family, one composed of those the world has abused and persecuted in the same way they have been their whole life. This is especially true in adolescents, which may in part explain some of the draw of mutants."[17]

Most minorities, at one point or another, have felt like outcasts. Marvel's mutants are metaphors for these minorities, those who feel themselves to be society's broken pieces, its huddled masses yearning to be free (or at least not persecuted). Mutants are united as an unconventional species living an alternative lifestyle, uniting into teams, bound together in their desire for acceptance and their struggle for equality. In that alliance mutants protect and defend one another. They embrace and honor their differences, all in the pursuit of being seen as equals establishing their place in society—and all mirroring the journey of the marginalized.

The Need to Belong

In the Marvel comic universe, mutants have *always* been attacked and exploited by outside forces. Whether this entails the government turning them into super killing machines, humans exploiting mutant powers to further their own ends, or simply being convenient targets for prejudice and abuse, it makes sense that mutants would be averse to trust. Despite this, many of them (Logan in particular) repeatedly join teams through their very long (or reincarnated) lifetimes. Their decision to affiliate can best be explained through Maslow's Hierarchy of Needs.

In 1943, psychologist Abraham Maslow unveiled his now widely employed theory of human motivation, a five-tier model of human needs, motivation, and fulfillment, frequently illustrated as hierarchical levels of a pyramid (as illustrated in the diagram).[18]

The original hierarchy of needs five-stage model includes the following tiers: (1) *biological and physiological needs*—air, food, drink, shelter, warmth, sex, sleep; (2) *safety needs*—protection from elements, security, order, law, stability, freedom from fear; (3) *love and belongingness needs*—

friendship, intimacy, trust, and acceptance, receiving and giving affection and love, affiliating, being part of a group (family, friends, work); (4) *esteem needs*—achievement, mastery, independence, status, dominance, prestige, self-respect, respect from others; and (5) *self-actualization needs*—realizing personal potential, self-fulfillment, seeking personal growth and peak experiences. The five-step model is further divided into *deficiency* needs (the first four levels) and *growth or being* needs (the top level).[19]

According to Maslow's theory, certain needs take priority over others—thus the proposed hierarchical pyramid. For example, deficiency needs become more insistent the longer the needs of that level go unsatisfied (e.g., the more we are deprived of water, the thirstier we become). Once basic survival needs are met, one moves to address the needs of the next higher level, and so on all the way to the self-actualization level.

It is important to note that the totality of each hierarchical level need not be 100 percent fulfilled before the individual begins seeking satisfaction

Self-Actualization

morality, creativity,
spontaneity, acceptance,
experience, purpose,
meaning and inner potential

Self-Esteem
confidence, achievement, respect of others,
the need to be a unique individual

Love & Belonging
friendship, family, intimacy, sense of connection

Safety & Security
health, employment, property, family and social stability

Physiological Needs
breathing, food, water, shelter, clothing, sleep

Maslow's hierarchy of needs, first proposed by Abraham Maslow in "A Theory of Human Motivation (1943), is a five-tier pyramid displaying humans' most fundamental needs at the bottom and the need for self-actualization at the top. Abraham Lincoln and Albert Einstein were among the "self-actualized" subjects studied.

of the demands of the next (or still higher) level(s) of need. It is sufficient that the bulk (usually nearing 80 percent) of the needs in any given level are met before moving on to satisfy the needs of subsequently higher levels.

Maslow tells us that one of humanity's strongest needs is to feel a sense of belonging and acceptance among our peers. Just as with humans, mutants need to love and be loved by others. Mutants are especially susceptible to depression, loneliness, anxiety, and fear when facing the world alone. This is why they group with other mutants, why minorities spend time interacting with other oppressed groups, and why Logan—who doesn't get along well with most people and who attains his safety needs through his solitude—will abandon his loner lifestyle in favor of feeling the camaraderie of a crime-fighting group. Just like anyone else, Logan wants to belong to something greater than himself.

The film *X-Men: Days of Future Past* is loosely based on *The Uncanny X-Men* #141 and #142, in which Charles Xavier receives a serum that "cures" both his mutation and his paralysis. In the film Xavier is seen grappling with the choices that the serum provides—either taking the serum and satisfying the needs inherent in the four lower "deficiency" levels while surrendering his mutant capacities or relinquishing the serum and regaining his mutant abilities at the cost of satisfying his "deficiency" level desires (inclusive of ever walking again).

For the most part, physiological and safety needs take precedence with any living organism, mutant or otherwise. Whether they experience war with humans or other mutants, physical violence or systemic institutionalized oppression as a result of anti-mutant discrimination, mutants (as a comic book stand-in for minorities) struggle to find respite from physical harm, psychological neglect, and resultant economic insecurity—that is, until they enter the well-appointed sanctuary of Charles Xavier.

As Xavier Promised

Kitty Pryde and Wolverine, a limited six-issue comic book series written by Chris Claremont and illustrated by Al Milgrom, introduces readers to a new aspect of Logan—namely, that of mentor. A spin-off of *Uncanny X-Men*, this series chronicles the Japanese adventure of two unlikely friends: Kitty Pryde, a young, innocent, appealing, and insecure "kid sister" type, and the much older, tainted, off-putting and aggressively recalcitrant Wolverine.[20]

Regardless of her diminished capacities at the beginning of the story, the plucky Kitty runs off to Japan to assist her father with the trouble he has encountered there. She is captured by mob bosses Shigematsu and Ogun, who brainwash Kitty into becoming a deadly ninja assassin (yes, a lot of brainwashing takes place in the Marvel-topia).

After a brainwashed Kitty overpowers a group of ninjas (think of it as the Marvel counterpart of the "hypnosis" or "miracle drug" fantasy transformation themes of LGBTQ pulp fiction), she is ordered to kill Logan, which she attempts and nearly accomplishes before she is knocked unconscious by Logan's friend Yukio. Having come to her senses, and mortified by her actions, Kitty tries to flee, but Logan's sense of loyalty forces him to impel Kitty to draw on the inner strength that Logan knows she possesses in combating and finally overcoming her conditioning.

Through his mentoring of Kitty, and later another mutant named Jubilee, Logan realizes that he has the capacity to impart his wealth of valuable (if hard-won) experience. In this respect, he reaches Maslow's highest level in the hierarchy of needs—that of self-actualization. Whether counseling young mutants or actually mentoring protégés, Logan finds meaning, purpose, a sense of morality, and (most important) a sense of belonging to something greater than himself.

So Is Magneto Right?

As we have discussed, Marvel's mutants can well be read as a collective metaphor for the minority "other." In reality, bias takes many forms and pervades virtually every country in the world. Everywhere there is humanity there are minorities resisting intolerance and subjugation, fighting for religious, ethnic, political, social, civil, and economic parity. And if one erroneously believes minority oppression to be ancient history in this enlightened modern world or in the ever-so-egalitarian United States of America, think again. Remember, it wasn't until 1967 that the Supreme Court declared statutes against mixed-race unions unconstitutional.

Nor is such oppression exclusively an American issue. Since the 1990s, United Nations human rights mechanisms have repeatedly expressed concerns and condemnations of human rights violations around the globe, with equal rights activists and diversity proponents struggling against great odds to make the world a better, safer, and more egalitarian place for all its inhabitants.

As with Joseph Conrad in *Heart of Darkness*, and as with Frederick Douglass, Dorothy L. Sayers, Loraine Hansberry, Bertrand Russell, Frank Byrne, Howard Zinn, Langston Hughes, Eric Berne, August Wilson, James Baldwin and myriad other intellectual luminaries, it would appear that Professor X has a point when he tells us, "It is a historical fact: sharing the world has never been humanity's defining attribute."[21] And in this respect, Magneto *is* right.

Audre Lorde put it best when she wrote, "For the master's tools will never dismantle the master's house. They may allow us to temporarily beat him at his own game, but they will never enable us to bring about genuine change. Racism and homophobia are real conditions of all our lives in this place and time. I urge each one of us here to reach down into that deep place of knowledge inside herself and touch that terror and loathing of any difference that lives here. See whose face it wears. Then the personal as the political can begin to illuminate all our choices."[22]

Indeed, the privileged and powerful neither wish nor seek to share their privilege or their power. No—as Frederick Douglass painfully reminds us, "Power concedes nothing without demand."

Xavier and his X-Men love America—they'd have to. Every day they face oppression by the U.S. government and yet amazingly run toward the guns in defense of the very same people who oppress them. As such, the X-Men and those mutants aligned with Magneto represent real-world injustices faced by the marginalized, discriminated, and oppressed, so particularly pertinent to modern-day political and social climates in the world in general (and most visibly in the United States).

Life Mirrors Art: Reflections on a House Deliberately Divided

There is no better example of minority oppression than the events leading up to, and following, the 2016 U.S. presidential election. Regardless of where one falls on the political spectrum, most Americans agree that up until that election year, the United States had not been so profoundly polarized since the 1960s civil rights movement (if not the Civil War of 1861–1865).

Note: This author is not a political analyst, a disclaimer proffered both in advance and in the spirit of full disclosure so as to make it clear that the following observations and perceptions of the state of partisan divide within the United States are predicated upon a considered clinical evaluation of how this election and its unanticipated results emotionally affected marginalized groups.

If one were to speak to the vast majority of these minorities, they would tell you that they love America, or at least the *idea* of America, even when America does not love them back. Despite tolerating centuries of harassment and hatred, minorities as an aggregate struggle to find a place of acceptance and respect in society, even with the full expectation that complete and total equality in America will never be possible for them.

Like this author's parents, many Asian, black, religious, Latino, European, Irish, Slavic, Middle Eastern and other minority members (back to the origins of time) have had to work two or three jobs in dangerous neighborhoods, under horrific conditions, in hostile working environments, and (as often as not) at prejudicially reduced wages in the attempt to obtain better lives for their families. Many members of the LGBTQ population have been rejected, even assaulted, by their own family members and have experienced loathing and violence from a society intent upon defaming them as "freaks," "fags," "queers" and other belittling monikers based on naught but the speakers' own preferences (not to mention their own ignorance, hatred, and baseless fears).

Every day, societal lip service is given to the plight of minorities to the effect that they are "no different" and have "the exact same opportunities" as any Caucasian, heterosexual, male American. And every day, minorities wake up *hoping beyond hope* to be able to cash this verbal egalitarian check—even though the stares and sneers around them, and the physical violence against them, say all too clearly that this check is written in politically expedient disappearing ink.

This is the day-to-day reality of minority groups. They are victimized—and then blamed for their victimization. When black people are attacked without provocation, the privileged shrug and say, "They must have done *something* to deserve it." When refused a job or a home due to their ethnicity, accent, or appearance, the marginalized are told, "If only you would just try a little bit harder," or "You have to understand...." When women are groped (or worse) and report it, too often their claims are dismissed, challenged, or dismissively ignored; they dressed too provocatively, and the rape kits are rarely processed.

Privileged individuals who are usually immune to such invasions of privacy and person reject horrible accounts like these because they simply don't (or, in willful ignorance, choose not to) believe that such atrocities occur—but they *do*.

The chasm between the haves and the have nots is not a new phenomenon, and, sadly, too many minorities have become inured to "no-win" scenarios. Yet, every day, they take another run at it. They try once again to make a difference, to change things in their own small way. And so they go out to work, and so they go out to vote (if and when allowed to do either).

Following the 2016 election, many minorities, in moments of uncharacteristic candor, confessed to being terrified of President Donald Trump and his administration, given that so many (now collectively "out of the closet," so to speak) felt empowered to "finally" make their long-dissembled bigotries a matter for public utterance.

To be clear, not everyone who voted for this president is a racist or a homophobe. Indeed, some voted for him *despite* glaring character flaws. Many who voted for Trump identified themselves as part of an afflicted *majority*—economically disenfranchised, intellectually denigrated, disparaged by an elitist liberal opposition and besieged by bureaucratic regulations viewed as having been artificially gerrymandered to benefit the multiple minorities around them. Others said they voted for this president because they chose what they perceived to be "the lesser of two evils," choosing to tacitly endorse their candidate's public disparagement and oppression of multiple marginalized groups in order to avoid the opposing candidate's ascendency.

What does all this tell us about America? It should tell us that after decades of increasing exasperation with "the other side," we, to our own peril, have reached a breaking point. We are now possessed of neither the time nor the patience for (much less interest in) alternate opinions or varied approaches. We have met the enemy and have had our fill of "those people."

At the very minimum, the 2016 election and its aftereffects should tell us that, regardless of how far we have come since Civil War Reconstruction or the race riots of the 1960s, Americans remain fundamentally, if not irreconcilably, polarized. The current situation should open our minds to the regrettable reality that this country, while supposedly founded on the rule of law and the belief that *all* men are created equal, has dismissed brutalities—toward Native Americans, African Americans, Latin Americans, Asian Americans, the disabled, (fill-in-the-blank) Americans, small European ethnicities of all types, LGBTQ Americans and millions of immigrants seeking to *be* Americans.

Our country has continuously been a Darwinian thrash (a battle to survive in an environment where one's genes, along with certain traits are currently rewarded by society while other traits, such as dark skin pigmentation or homosexuality, are not) of who receives an invitation to join the "We the People" club. George Orwell's Snowball had it right: "All Animals Are Equal, But Some Animals Are More Equal Than Others."[23]

The pace of separation between those on top of the social ladder and those at the bottom has been escalating for decades, and, in and of its own accord, in 2016 America fell upon its own sword, its political and emotional positions ossifying into a fragile, brittle, and dangerous state. Many continue to promulgate a dark "zero-sum" message of hatred and disdain for the minority. And why is this?

It can be logically argued that such negative messages are seditious; certainly they are *de*structive rather than *con*structive. Yet those who oppose these paradigms are told that they should work toward inclusion, to capitulate, to be reasonable, to give the government a chance, to "get in the boat" and support programs and proposals. Such psycho-babble is sheer folly.

Bludgeoning the oppressed into supporting oppression is something all but the most demented will resist. Without question, most minorities will reject these messages of hatred, oppression, and second-class citizenship, because once any group is oppressed, no one is truly free.

In the mutant world of Marvel Comics, Professor X takes on the responsibility of attempting to liberate the minds around him from tendencies toward aggressive oppression, moving toward a future where humans and mutants can live in peace. In the real world, however, liberating our minds from such inclinations is our own responsibility. Such liberation is only possible through insight into what has happened (and continues to happen) to marginalized groups in America.

Many activists fight against long odds to end discrimination and make this world a better place for all its residents. We don't have to be X-Men or social activists, but we can still be heroes—even if only in our own zip codes or on our own blocks. We are all equipped to make a difference through our voices and our actions, one syllable or one step or one safety pin at a time.

The Moral of the Chapter

It is just such dehumanizing experiences, persecuted histories, hope-sapping prejudice and rage-infusing bigotry that the X-Men mutant chronicles attempt to expose. A reader (who, by definition, is one step removed from the emotional trauma of such experiences) will find it far easier to absorb the societal unfairness of something so psychologically burdensome when it's placed in the form of a fable or myth, rather than accepting the reality of such discrimination being the true way of things in their daily lives. It is also far easier to internalize the lessons of such fables and begin in our own grassroots ways to promote a fairer and more egalitarian world—not to mention that absorbing such lessons and acting in accordance with them is a lot more productive in the long run.

This is what the X-Men mutant chronicles are really all about. This is why their stories beguile us, and ring so true, because they *are* true. They are born of life, drawn from life, and by extension are the lives we lead and have about us, if we are only aware enough to see it. And this is why these stories consistently prod us to explore the misguided tendencies of our society, so that one day we might escape the avaricious tar pit to which a self-serving society aggressively runs to immerse itself.

The brilliance of syndicated columnist Charles Blow is best quoted here to conclude this chapter and to ask *the* question posed not just by Marvel's mutant chronicles but also by our collective lives and the societies we create to contain them. Blow asks, "Will the people who can see clearly that there is no such thing as selective, discriminatory, exclusionary outrage and grieving when lives are taken, be heard above those who see every tragedy as a plus or minus for a cumulative argument? Will the people who see the protests over police killings and the killings of police officers as fundamentally about the value of life rise above those who see political opportunity in this arms race of atrocities?"[24]

As the reader might well suspect, the jury is still out on such collective decisions. It is now for the individual to decide how (or if) they will move toward the light.

SEVEN

The One That Got Away

Girls flirt with the dangerous guy, Logan.
They don't take him home. They marry the good guy.
—Jean Grey

When it comes to Logan and his relationships with women, let's just say he's a bit ... indiscriminate. Seriously, with whom *hasn't* this mutant slept (other than this author)? Our Casanova's dance card never seems to sport a vacancy, even for an intermission, and regardless of the circumstances, his personal parade of seduction seems endless.

Women fall for Logan for several reasons: he's a strong, rugged, charming protector; he's an exhilarating risk taker, a rule breaker, a rebel—he rides a motorcycle, smokes cigars, and tolerates no insult or injury.

Logan's appealingly nonconforming "bad boy" arrogance is made abundantly clear in Hugh Jackman's 20-second cameo in the film *X-Men: First Class*: Logan is at a bar drinking and smoking his cigar when Charles Xavier and Erik Lehnsherr approach him. Before they voice so much as one syllable, Logan says, "Go fuck yourself." Practicing good judgment, Charles and Erik turn abruptly on their heels and depart rather than pursue the issue. This forcefully dismissive interaction establishes a permanent identity for Logan in the minds of the audience in general, and in those of his female viewers in particular. Clinician Tehrina Billi adds to this sentiment: "Logan doesn't seek approval. In fact, he's the antithesis of conformity. He's going to do whatever he deems is best regardless of others' opinions."[1]

Other reasons women come to crave Logan include his being a sensitive, chivalrous warrior of fabled proportions, wounded many times over in both love and life, yet still willing to shield the oppressed and the defenseless—especially the red-headed or betrothed. And while often unpredictable or out of control, it's this very "wild card" willingness that augments his charm.

So, if Logan lacks a permanent intimate relationship with another human being, the reason(s) must lie within Logan. It's not that the boy can't get a date for the prom—far from it. He is physically and emotionally compelling ... at least from a discreet distance or in a relationship's hormonally infused incipient stages. It is Logan who "kills off" the relationship, either literally in several cases or figuratively in that he is afraid of commitment or, worse, afraid of what will happen to his selected partner once he *has* made a commitment, with that fear extending not only to his partner's emotional or physical life but also to his own emotional status.

So, with this in mind, let's have a look at the women in Logan's history, what they brought to the party that Logan found compelling, and the how's and why's of those relationships' demises.

The Women

Each of Logan's relationships cannot possibly be recounted here, but a few are worth mentioning. His first love (and first romantic casualty) was the lovely Rose O'Hara. Appearing in the *Origin* series (covered in chapter two), Rose was the gracious red-haired beauty hired to be Logan's companion who grew up at the Howlett estate and later escaped with Logan following the murders of Thomas Logan and John Howlett.

Rose loved Logan, but not romantically, falling instead for Logan's logging-camp boss Smitty during Logan's extended emotional detachment. And while Logan comes to endorse the union, he later grievously becomes the instrument of Rose's death when she falls on his claws during his first battle with Dog. Stricken by grief, Logan retreats into the wilderness to live among wolves to heal and to forget.

Another of Logan's ill-starred love affairs occurs after he returns to civilization, when he has started a new life for himself in a cabin within the Canadian Rockies, living with a beautiful Native American woman named Silver Fox (storyline introduced in *Wolverine* #10, written by Chris Claremont and John Buscema). For the first time in his life that he can remember, Logan is happy, living a simple life with his young love. Then, on Logan's birthday, Silver Fox is raped and killed by Dog/Sabretooth, the first of what will become a series of annual attacks on Logan.

Logan returns home to the horrible scene and is sickened by the sight of Silver Fox's violated body and enraged by the note reading, "Happy

Birthday." He carries her body into town and demands to know who killed her. There, knowingly awaiting Logan's arrival, is the scathingly grinning perpetrator of the killing, Sabretooth. What follows is one of the greatest fight scenes between the long-time foes.

Another of Logan's lovers who seemingly dies at the hands of Sabretooth is Seraph. Owner of the Princess Bar in Madripoor circa 1920, Seraph is an accomplished spy and a ruthless assassin who seduces Logan and proceeds to instruct him in the art of killing with subtlety and panache.[2]

Another of Wolverine's more memorable concubines is encountered in Japan. While living in a small Japanese village and expanding upon his combat training, Logan meets and falls in love with Itsu. However, during a celebration ritual to prove his worth as a ninja master, Logan accidentally stabs another ninja with his claws. Disgraced by his lack of control and the damage he has done to a revered warrior, Wolverine promises to return to Itsu once he deems himself worthy as a husband and father. When he arrives at her cabin, however, he discovers Itsu's dead body, their unborn son (Daken) having been cut out of her womb.

Burning Love

Other noteworthy mentions among Logan's great love affairs are Mariko Yashida, a wealthy businesswoman from Japan with ties to organized crime, and Jean Grey (a.k.a. the Phoenix), a fellow crime-fighting mutant. Involvement with either of these women would be nothing short of dangerous, complicated, and highly unpredictable, so naturally Wolverine dives in head first, smitten by both.

First among any of the aforementioned involvements is arguably the most famous and controversial X-Men pairing of Wolverine and Jean Grey. As an abbreviated recap, Jean Grey is a powerful mutant with telepathic powers enabling her to read minds, move objects, project her thoughts into the minds of others, embark on astral travel and mentally stagger her opponents with pure psionic energy. Her powers were magnified to near-infinite levels while she served as an avatar for the cosmic Phoenix Force. While growing up under the care of Charles Xavier, she fell in love with fellow student and mutant Scott Summers (a.k.a. Cyclops). Later, she develops a strong attraction toward one of the team's new recruits: the untamed Wolverine.

The nature of the Logan–Jean Grey relationship is a source of great contention in the comic book world. As noted above, Jean's heart has belonged to Scott Summers/Cyclops since her earliest days in Charles Xavier's care. And yet she is also strongly attracted to Logan, fascinated by his feistiness.

When Logan is introduced to the team, he is as immediately attracted to Jean as she is to him. The chemistry between the fiery redhead (again, a redhead) and the clawed berserker is undeniable, with the love triangle becoming a recurring subplot in the *X-Men* films. Still, for the most part, Logan defers to the strong long-standing relationship between Jean and Scott—that is, until temptation gets the best of him.

With different escapades, varying manifestations of the team and even Jean dying a couple of times—she's a Phoenix, and resurrection is one of her mutant powers—Jean and Logan never have a chance to develop anything between them. But throughout the years, both hold a special place in their hearts for one another. Witness Logan and Jean sharing moments of platonic (if deeply involved) emotional intimacy, such as in a famous 1993 issue, *Wolverine* #75 (famously known as *Fatal Attractions*), by Larry Hama, Adam Kubert, and Mark Farmer, in which Logan demonstrates the depth of his love for Jean.

In this series of panels, Magneto mercilessly rips the adamantium from Logan's skeleton. Logan screams in agony while the X-Men scramble to board him onto their Blackbird spy plane. Professor X and Jean Grey then attempt to save Logan's life telepathically by forcibly invading the layers of his mind, wherein they extensionally experience the torture that Logan endured in the Weapon X program.

While in flight the Blackbird encounters a horrible storm, the turbulence causing severe structural and mechanical problems to the plane itself and hurtling Logan around in the plane's interior, crashing him into its walls. At this moment, Logan's healing factor is failing him. Emotionally exhausted and physically defeated, Logan relinquishes his life and heads toward the light.

Among other damage to the Blackbird caused by the storm, the plane's hatch is ripped open. Jean uses her powers to temporarily force the hatch closed, but she loses her concentration and the hatch again flies open, causing her to cling desperately for her life to the plane's fuselage.

In the fog of semi-consciousness, Logan reaches out for a hand, presumably meant to guide him to the afterlife, but then he realizes that the hand belongs to Jean. He forces himself awake, fights through his physical misery and pulls Jean to safety, consciously foregoing his hope for death in order to save Jean.

Another similarly memorable encounter between Jean and Logan is found in the 2001 miniseries *New X-Men* #148, created by Grant Morrison, Phil Jimenez, and Andy Lanning. In it Magneto traps Wolverine and Jean on Asteroid M as it travels into the sun. Their deaths are imminent:

> JEAN: I'm dying ... don't leave me...
> LOGAN: Never. I'm right beside ya. I'd die to save yer life, Darlin'. I'd take all yer pain on myself. But I can't. I can only take it away. [Logan pops out his claws and stabs Jean through the abdomen.]
> LOGAN: Ah God, Ah God!
> [Carrying Jean in his arms, Logan walks out into the sun.]
> LOGAN: You and me Jeannie. You and me in a blaze of glory.[3]

In a moment when all hope is lost, Wolverine selflessly and honorably kills Jean before they are incinerated. However, once again, Jean doesn't die. The heat of the sun activates the Phoenix force within her, and she ends up saving herself and Logan.

These examples emphasize that when it comes to Jeannie (as Logan affectionately calls her), Logan is doomed to either kill her or witness her continuing affections for Scott. Regardless of the tenderness between them, and at times her own confusion vis-à-vis her divided affections, Jean *always* chooses Scott. No matter the chemistry between Jean and Logan, Jean is practical about her relationships.

Matching Hypothesis

When it comes to choosing partners, most people tend to lean toward those who best align with their values, temperament, attractiveness, and other characteristics. Social psychologist Elaine Hatfield and her colleagues proposed the *matching hypothesis* in 1966 to explain the mystery behind human attraction.[4] According to this theory, we are more likely to form attachments and succeed in committed relationships with someone who is equally socially desirable. Physical allure, although certainly a major component of attraction, is not the sole determining factor in choosing a partner. For example, some people overlook physical attractiveness in favor of other compensatory traits, such as a sense of humor, intelligence, wealth, status, or a similar temperament.

Jean knows all too well Logan is not a safe bet for a long-term commitment. He may be ruggedly handsome, witty, physically commanding and downright irresistible, but he is *not* husband material. Logan is stubborn, impetuous, and seemingly more than a bit deranged at times. These characteristics alone can impede a relationship from lasting in the long term. Ultimately, Jean chooses to marry Scott, who is her better match.

Facing a future without the love he desires leads Logan to bury his feelings in a number of other ways, such as drinking, pursuing meaningless sexual relationships, or (his favorite coping skill) running away. Paradoxically, Logan's impulsive drifter disposition, which makes him so alluring, is likely the reason why Jean could never seriously entertain the idea of accepting him as a husband.

Logan, however, does not perceive the validity of these assessments. His affections for Jean remained undiminished by either reason or alternate attractions, and so his heart silently aches for her. Wolverine's longing for Jean reflects the same emotional distress many of us feel when we desire someone or some condition beyond our ability to attain.

Longing and Losing: Repetition Compulsion

Psychologically, one's inability to attain someone or something so captivating to us makes the goal of attaining that object disproportionately more valuable. And in the case of human relationships, we tend to long for that important "someone" or "something" when we are apart from our partners, we feel unfulfilled in our current relationships, the feelings of desire are not reciprocated, or the relationship ends.

Longing for someone also causes a person to experience vulnerability, which is especially problematic for Logan. We all know that Logan does not generally tolerate emotional exposure well, let alone hopeless vulnerability at any juncture. Certainly the defenses that we know to be his will surface to keep him safe when his conflicts become perilous. But at a lower level of emotional irritation, anxiety, or angst, why would he knowingly indulge such self-induced disruption by pursuing a goal that he has every reason and experience to believe is unattainable?

One possible explanation is that we have come to know Logan to have a vein of deep humanistic emotion buried beneath all his emotional scar tissue. In short, hope springs eternal, even for someone as hardboiled as Logan and even in the teeth of an excessively high expectation of failure and heartache.

Another possible explanation for Logan's entrenched attachment to Jean stems from his childhood experiences. As a child, he endured a lifetime of emotional absence from his mother, as Elizabeth Howlett never reciprocated his affections. The longing created by such an unreciprocated emotional exchange might well explain Logan's repeated attraction to potential partners just beyond his grasp. Jean's repeated denials of Logan's pursuit cut him deeply because Jean's rejection subconsciously reminds him of his mother's dismissal.

According to analytical psychology, while the specific reasons vary from person to person, there is a tendency to unconsciously repeat past patterns in future relationships, a penchant that Sigmund Freud called *repetition compulsion.*[5] This defense mechanism occurs when we unconsciously try to resolve, through repeated experiences, a past dysfunctional aspect of a primary or central past relationship.

When one experiences trauma, loss, or mistreatment (Logan is only too familiar with all three) at the hands of a parent or primary caregiver, one subconsciously searches for a partner who possesses traits similar to those of the more problematic parent. For example, if we grow up with a parent who belittles us or demeans our accomplishments, we tend to seek a partner who continues that invalidation. In doing so, we seek to heal old wounds, to achieve the heretofore unachieved, to accomplish the yet-to-be realized. In this respect, an unattainable woman is psychologically the perfect object of desire for Logan. Jean's refusal of Logan's advances reinforces Logan's *core belief* about himself formed by his mother's rejection— namely, that he is not deserving of love and should therefore be denied it.

Studies have found a link between emotional abuse during childhood and self-criticism, as well as a further link between childhood maltreatment, self-criticism and dissatisfaction in romantic relationships.[6] When a child longs for the withheld emotional affections of a parent (such as Logan did), that child, as an adult, will tend to seek the satisfaction of those long-unfulfilled longings via projecting the desire for those approvals upon the romanticized image of another person.[7] This relationship pattern is based on repeated fantasies, emotional defenses and feelings of longing that one experienced during childhood. Thus, a lost childhood attachment (such as those we covered in chapter two) can appear as a love fixation in later adult life.

Within this cycle, feelings of the rejection experienced during childhood are triggered when the affections of that idealized partner remain unrequited, leading to familiar emotions of distress, frustration, and anger (and thus beginning the pattern of seeking the missing approval once again). A victim thus traumatized remains fixated on their yearnings even as the predictable rejections cause them prolonged, unnecessary, and indeed self-induced suffering.

Following the trail of such an unfulfilled illusionary fantasy to its deflationary conclusion, were the relationship between Logan and Jean actually to be realized, there exists the very real potential for the partners to not feel fulfilled or, worse, to even be disappointed by the reality of who they each truly are. However, Logan's inability to fulfill his desire for Jean causes him to idolize her and create in her an image of unrealistic perfection.

Repetition compulsion explains why, for the most part, Logan does well with women who are more like himself, such as Yukio, Domino, or Mystique. Similar to Logan in their independence, rebelliousness, and sense of adventure (and thus dissimilar from Jean in her balanced rationality, planning, and cognitive assessment), these vagabond women do not place emphases on a long-term commitment.

Logan certainly loves Jean, but, since they have never actually been in a relationship, he likely is more in love with the *idea* of Jean. According to Adam Kubert, famed illustrator of the *Fatal Attractions* issue, "Jean is the love of Logan's life. This is the feeling I got when I drew this issue. Whether in his dream and his reality, she is the most important thing to him.... He loved Mariko, but he has a true connection to Jean."[8]

The connection Logan feels for Jean is unyielding and heartbreaking. Witness the events leading to Jean's death in the film *X-Men: The Last Stand*: After Jean returns from the dead as the resurrected Dark Phoenix, Logan is forced into a heart-wrenching decision—in order to stop the Phoenix from killing humans and mutants, he will have to kill her. The Phoenix asks Logan, "You would die for them?" He responds, "No, not for them. For you.... For you." Before he unleashes his claws, he looks at Jean with pure heartbreak in his eyes and says, "I love you." Logan then stabs Jean in the stomach. Having just killed the woman he loves, Logan screams in agony.

Logan has grieved the death of Jean before. Her subsequent resurrections then gave him hope to love her once more. Having to watch her die (again), this time by his own claws, causes him unspeakable anguish. Many X-Men fans believe this singular event is what ultimately "broke" Logan emotionally.

Through his extended life, Logan has endured torture, was turned into a killing machine, fought in many wars, and lost many friends. But losing Jean—the woman Logan equates with the perfection of love—means a strain of death from which he never fully recovers.

And so, never having been subjected to the acid test of an intimate affair, or the commitment of marriage, Logan's boundless infatuation with Jean lingers unresolved long after her death. In the 2013 film *The*

Wolverine, the film opens with Logan in the wilderness, retreating once more from his emotions. Logan being haunted by the guilt of slaying Jean, his exchange with Yukio says it all:

> YUKIO: You're a soldier, and you seek what all soldiers do.
> LOGAN: And what's that?
> YUKIO: An honorable death. An end to your pain.
> LOGAN: Who says I'm in pain?
> YUKIO: A man who has nightmares every night of his life is in pain.[9]

PTSD and Relationships

While covered at some length in chapter four, Logan's symptomology and diagnosis of post-traumatic stress disorder (PTSD) now merits closer inspection. Aside from causing the victim emotional anguish, symptoms associated with PTSD have the capacity to radiate outward from the victim, adversely affecting not only the people around them but also their environments. This potential for extended damage will be investigated in this section.

As with other survivors of trauma, Logan often feels emotionally numb, frustrated, and anxious about his relationships; he's many things, both positive and negative, but he is neither ignorant nor imperceptive. Thus, when he emerges from the quieter, more introspective moments spent with his soul, perusing fragmented memories and disjointed recollections of berserker rages, he comes up feeling "broken" beyond repair.

Problematic behaviors such as these, along with impulsivity, reactivity, and lack of focus, often cause a traumatized person to be misunderstood, further fueling their feelings of loneliness and desperation. Individuals experiencing such trauma then slide ever further into their own darkness, choosing to suffer in silence rather than add to their burden the inability to explain how they feel. In such states, traumatized individuals can experience further losses of interest in social or sexual activities, all the while feeling an intense need to protect their loved ones, which may result in their being rebuffed even more for being controlling or demanding.

Such behavior is not necessarily acquired via trauma as an adult. Indeed, a trauma such as what Logan experienced in childhood affects how one communicates and relates to other people throughout one's life. Often the victim is unaware of this impairment until later in life, when they find themselves incapable of properly expressing their emotions to their partners. Because of this frustration and inability, individuals with such concerns often prefer to remain socially reclusive and detached.

Logan may be reserved and aloof, but having a sexual problem is a bullet he seems to have dodged. Yes, an inability to sleep soundly, nightmares, and his cutting of his nocturnal sex-mates all do trouble Logan's sleep. But his libido and interpersonal performance would seem to have been spared.

Witness a scene from the film *The Wolverine*, where Jean "visits" Logan in the form of nightmares and flashbacks, causing him further distress:

> LOGAN: I'll never hurt you or anyone ever again. I made a vow.
> JEAN GREY: A solemn vow?
> LOGAN: You're making fun of me.
> JEAN GREY: It's too late.
> [Logan looks down. He screams in horror at the sight of his claws buried in Jean's abdomen.]
> LOGAN: No! No, Jean! No, no, no! Please!
> JEAN GREY: You can't hide.
> LOGAN: No, no, no! Please![10]

Anxiety, flashbacks, anger, impulsivity, aggression, substance exploitation, physical or emotional abuse—all are peas in the same pod, and all conspire to drown the sparks of any budding relationship. Coping with these issues can exhaust a partner, leading to misunderstandings, false assumptions, a breakdown in communication, and ultimately, in many cases, the full-on dissolution of the relationship. Again, mercifully for Logan, when he's loved, the beast is tame; he is somehow able to channel his lethality on his enemies, while venting only his nonlethal sarcastic cynicism on his teammates. Think of it as lethal light, Logan style.

Rōnin: A Samurai without a Master

Another of Logan's great loves—considered by many to be his greatest love—is Mariko Yashida. Created by Chris Claremont and John Byrne, Mariko first appeared in *Uncanny X-Men* #118. The tragic love of Logan and Mariko is best illustrated through the first four-part eponymous limited series, *Wolverine* (written by Chris Claremont, penciled by Frank Miller and inked by Joe Rubinstein).

This series, as memorable for introducing Wolverine's iconic "I'm the best at what I do, but what I do best isn't very nice" catchphrase as it is replete with romance, intrigue, and pandemonium, covers the besieged berserker's adventures in Japan and illustrates Logan's struggle to prove his honor. In the introduction to the series, Chris Claremont revealed the genesis of his conception of Logan's new role:

> To samurai, duty is all, selfless with grace. Every facet, every moment of their lives, is absolutely under control. Wolverine, however, is almost a primal life force, totally beyond control, as graceless as can be. The one might be considered the ultimate expression of humanity—wherein the will, the intellect, totally overmaster all other aspects of existence—while the other is total animal.... Frank and I began by discussing the central character. Who is Wolverine? ... A mutual image of Wolverine emerged. One we both liked. One we both could relate to and deal with. And deal with him we did, very nastily. And he hasn't been the same since.[11]

By having Logan accept the samurai's neo-Confucian code of Bushido, the creators of this series transformed Wolverine from a feral, uncontrollable animal to a frugal, loyal, honorable fighting machine. Within each panel of this series, a man obsessed by love on a mission of the heart is depicted.

Wolverine travels to Japan when Mariko suddenly stops communicating with him. On orders from her father, Shingen Harada, she has been married. When Logan finds her, he sees that Mariko's face is covered in bruises abusively minted by her husband. Logan begs her to leave, but she is bound by honor to stay in the marriage.

Vowing to fight for Mariko, Logan accepts a challenge of honor from Mariko's father and is defeated when he dares to unleash his claws on Mariko's father. "Behold daughter," Shingen tells Mariko, "the man you profess to love. Except that he is no man at all, but an animal cast in semblance of human form. Gaze upon him Mariko. Witness his true nature, his true self. Here is the ... thing to which you have given your heart."[12]

Mariko and Logan eventually reconcile and marry—after Logan kills Mariko's father, of course. (Love is indeed a many-splintered thing in Marvel-topia.) During the wedding ceremony, Logan reflects on the newfound connection he feels: "Love. Word sounds strange comin' from me. Not my style at all. So I'll change. Everyone does."[13]

Embracing Mariko leads Logan to embrace very real human emotions—love, vulnerability, and selflessness. Logan wants to stop fighting. He wants to plant roots, to form a family, and longs for stability, and it appears (for a brief moment, anyway) that he is about to get all of this and more. However, as fate would have it, Logan's enemies have other plans.

Under the mental control of Mastermind (more brainwashing in the Marvel universe), Mariko suddenly proclaims, "Stop the ceremony! Most imperial majesty, honored guests—there will be no wedding." "Why??" Logan asks. "Because Gaijin—you are not worthy." The *Wolverine* miniseries ends with Logan in tears.[14]

Fast forward a few series: Mariko and Wolverine reunite and are again set to wed, but this time Mariko is poisoned by Matsuo Tsurayaba, leader of an early mid–Edo period Yakuza band called The Hand. Mariko begs Wolverine to kill her and spare her suffering. Unsheathing his claws, Logan mercifully kills Mariko and holds her in his arms as she dies.

This guy just can't get a break.

Given the complex cocktail that makes up Logan's personality, poor coping skills and ferocious temperament, one has to wonder if, given the chance (read: if any love interest lives long enough), he is capable of sustaining a long-term commitment.

A Triangular Theory of Love

The *triangular theory of love*, developed by psychologist Robert Sternberg (not to be confused with a "love triangle"), identifies three components of love in the context of relationships: (1) *passion*, a term commonly used to communicate strong sexual or romantic arousal; (2) *intimacy*, defined as personal or private feelings of attachment or ease toward another person; and (3) *commitment*, a term used to communicate a conscious decision to remain close or loyal to a partner, often determined by a level of satisfaction one feels in a relationship.[15] According to this theory, different combinations of the three components result in different types of love. For example, linking intimacy and passion results in romantic love, while combining passion and commitment leads to fatuous love. Below is found a graph of Sternberg's theory from the psychwonders blog:

Aside from the notion of *nonlove*—or casual interactions such as acquaintances—Sternberg identified seven different kinds of love within the spectrum of the three components. As might be expected, given Logan's preternaturally lengthy life span and exceptionally large pool of interpersonal interactions, he has experienced them all:

1. *Friendship/Liking*: Intimacy is present without the intense feeling of romantic or sexual passion; however, friendship can often lead to the other manifestations of love.

    Example: While admittedly a notion that could be applied to a partner of either birth gender or sexual identification in a relationship with another person, this comment will focus on the female partners of Logan. Rogue and Jubilee were Logan's protégés. Jubilee saved his life in Australia, leading to a close bond between the two. Rogue, however, was at one point a villain who eventually joined the X-Men team. No team member was especially close to Rogue for this reason; however, Logan identified with her as a misunderstood outsider. He took her under his wing and mentored her into becoming an important member of the team.

2. *Infatuated Love*: Couples involved in a purely sexual relationship or "crushes" without commitment fall under this category. Yes, romantic love can develop from infatuation. However, if neither intimacy nor commitment are established, infatuation can fizzle over time.

   Example: Logan's relationship with Jean Grey. Although Logan and Jean have shared occasional intimate moments, Jean has never been committed to Logan outside of friendship. Wit-

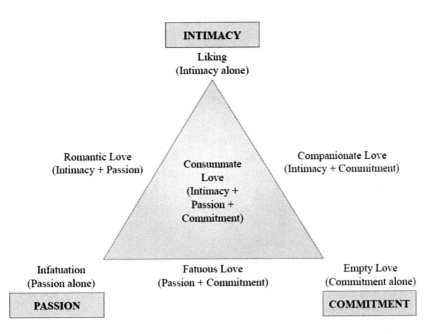

Robert Sternberg's Triangular Theory of Love divides love into three components: intimacy, passion, and commitment. Love can take on many different forms depending on the strength of each component and its relationship to the others.

ness the frustration Logan experiences in the film *X2*, wherein his longing for Jean remains noticeably unrequited:

BOBBY: Have you ever wanted to be with someone so badly, but you can't? … I've seen how you look at Professor Grey.
LOGAN: Excuse me?
BOBBY: Nothing.[16]

3. *Empty Love*: An unhappy marriage or relationship in which commitment is established while lacking respect and/or passion.

   Example: Logan has had a most dysfunctional marriage with Viper. Forcing Logan into marriage was never going to result in anything but resentment.

4. *Romantic Love*: A combination of passion and intimacy but lacking commitment, wherein the couple feels connected physically as well as emotionally but not inextricably bound to one another.

   Example: Logan and Storm have experienced romance from time to time, but the relationship never stuck.

5. *Companionate Love*: A bond stronger than friendship, in which both commitment and intimacy are present, yet passion is absent.

   Example: Logan is known to have felt companionate love for other teammates, such as Rogue or Storm. Although never acting on their mutual attraction beyond sharing an occasional kiss, Logan and Rogue have chemistry. The same applies in *Ultimate Universe*, in which Storm and Logan share a brief romantic relationship terminated by Logan due to their age disparity.

6. *Fatuous Love*: A whirlwind romance containing elements of commitment and passion without intimacy.

   Example: Logan has had purely physical relationships with Domino, Yukio, Snowbird, and Cassie Lathrop, among many, many others. He's even had a brief affair with Brotherhood of Evil Mutants member Mystique.

7. *Consummate Love*: Found at the center of the triangle, consummate love is the ideal type of love containing all three components: intimacy, passion, and commitment. Couples with consummate love cannot imagine life with anyone else. They work toward resolving conflicts gracefully and will likely continue to have a wonderful sex life long into the relationship.

   Consummate love, however, is profoundly more difficult to maintain than to initially achieve and is thus quite rare, with

Sternberg telling us, "The amount of love one experiences depends on the absolute strength of these three components, and the type of love one experiences depends on their strengths relative to each other."[17]

Example: Logan did finally find consummate love with Mariko. Within this relationship he experienced intimacy, passion, and commitment ... until he was compelled to surrender it all—indeed, to be the instrument of its demise, out of (you guessed it) love.

Sexual Desire and Love

Logan is well versed in the pleasures of his female partners. His desires are intense, perhaps attributable physiologically to high testosterone, dopamine or norepinephrine levels, low serotonin, primal urgency, or pure animalistic drive.[18] Psychologically, however, Logan's pursuit of physical contact could just as reasonably be attributed to a latent longing for *connection*. Additionally, his physical desires may be subconsciously linked to arousal, states of fear, and concern for others (see chapter two).

Other factors contributing to Wolverine's carnal cravings might well be his protective nature and his heightened sense of protectiveness toward the objects of his affection. Such defensive inclinations can lead to enhanced physical arousal that, in turn, triggers feelings of ecstasy, excitement, and even intrusive thoughts about his love object. Intense interpersonal arguments with one's partner (witness the movie *Who's Afraid of Virginia Woolf?* or, for that matter, the real-life relationship of Elizabeth Taylor and Richard Burton) likewise demonstrate that the emotional high and endorphin rush of the emotional roller coaster ride (as opposed to its direction) prompts arousal.

As a broad-brush statement, however, sexual desire promotes emotional closeness, although, in this case, Wolverine's strong sense of independence allows him to freely partake of and thoroughly enjoy sex without what he might acknowledge as the extraneous baggage of emotional commitment. But once Logan's time-in-grade with his sex object exceeds a certain point, he leans into emotional intimacy, or *pair-bonding*.[19]

Then there's always the post-coital feeling of a need to "push away" from the intimacy as a function of self-assertion or self-protection. Feelings of fear and exposure may also induce an after-sex sense of anxiety that may prompt emotional retreat, as well as abrupt mood swings.

The digressions and permutations are conceivably endless. But as it's Logan being discussed here, suffice it to say that while sexual desire plays a vital (if variant) role in triggering attraction, motivating communication, inducting contact, and pursuing physical contact that could eventually lead to a romantic commitment, it is not guaranteed to do so. Moreover, and again with Logan as the topic of observation, that which generally contributes to long-term intimacy may just as easily be detoured to short-term physical gratification by the intrusion of larger, more ponderous psychological intervening variables.

A Lesson Learned

Losing the women in his life shapes how Logan perceives loves. A fine example illustrating Logan's concept of love and loss is seen in *Uncanny X-Men* #183. In this issue, written by Chris Claremont and illustrated by John Romita, Jr., Logan teaches fellow X-Man Peter Rasputin (a.k.a. Colossus) a lesson when Peter breaks Kitty Pryde's heart in falling for another. Sitting in a Manhattan bar with Nightcrawler and Peter, Logan speaks to Peter about the difference between love, fear, and commitment:

> LOGAN: You two were goin' beyond playin' games. You were thinkin' marriage, a life together. At the same time, you suddenly had competition—from Doug Ramsey—someone Kitty's age, as smart as her, with th' same upbringin' an' interests. It's easy t' moon over a lost love—t' fantasize over what might have been, secure in the knowledge that it'll never happen—it makes a great excuse for not facin' the risks an' demands o' reality...
> PETER: If I had truly loved Kitty, Wolverine, how then could I have so easily fallen for another?
> LOGAN: Fear makes a boy do stupid things sometimes.[20]

During this conversation, Logan picks up a foe's scent among patrons at the bar. Juggernaut, drink in hand, soon picks a fight with Peter. When the fight is over, Peter is angry at Wolverine and Nightcrawler for not stepping in. Logan reminds him that X-Men are supposed to stand by each other, "go to the wall for each other, pay any price, make any sacrifice" (even their own lives) for one another, illuminating his point via the example of Kitty's commitment to this vow, as illustrated in *Uncanny X-Men* #179, wherein she offered to marry Caliban so that the Morlocks would save Peter's life. Logan tells Peter, "If Caliban hadn't released her from that vow, she'd be there today. You never even said, 'Thank you.'" As Logan walks away, he tells Nightcrawler, "I'm glad he had t' learn the hard way."

It's a taste of what he did to Kitty. From now on ... he'll act from choice not ignorance."[21]

The exchange above demonstrates Logan's growing sense of commitment and his understanding of love's value. For many years, Logan was obsessed with Jean Grey, even after her death. However, now we observe an expanded, more nuanced Logan—one who is prepared to put the past behind him and live, even if living means that he will continue to risk loss and rejection. This point is illustrated through one of Logan's last flashbacks with Jean in the film *The Wolverine*:

> JEAN GREY: Can you stay?
> LOGAN: I can't.
> JEAN GREY: Yes, you can. This is what you wanted.
> LOGAN: Not anymore.
> JEAN GREY: I'm all alone here. You put me here.
> LOGAN: You were hurting people, Jean. I had to. I love you, Jean. I always will.[22]

At the end of the film, Logan chooses to move on with his life, boarding a plane and heading off to his next adventure.

An added example of Logan's romantic maturity is dramatized in the *Wolverine* solo series. After Logan loses a battle with Mariko's father, we witness the fallen hero losing heart, drowning his sorrows in beer, bar fights and the arms of the wild assassin Yukio.

Rejected by Mariko for his berserker rage but accepted as a fellow scrapper by Yukio, Logan wrestles with his feelings for these two women: "No matter how hard I strive for inner serenity, I screw up, so why bother? ... I love 'em both. I failed 'em both. Worse, I failed myself." Still, the maniacal mutant again ponders the existential themes surrounding his identity: "An animal knows what it is, and accepts it. A man may know what he is—but he questions. He dreams. He strives. Changes. Grows."[23] Ultimately Logan chooses his soul mate—the woman who inspires him to want to "change, to grow—to temper the berserker" and be a better man. He chooses Mariko.

Viktor Frankl tells us, "Love is the only way to grasp another human being in the innermost core of his personality ... No one can become fully aware of the very essence of another human being unless he loves them."[24]

Through his love for Mariko, Logan witnesses and is enabled to profit from the traits and features of his beloved, and, even more, he is empowered to see his own potential, "which is not yet actualized but yet ought to be actualized." Logan's true humanity expresses itself through love. And once he realizes his full potential, he can stop hiding behind the masks he wears and embrace the man he truly was meant to be.

As we shall see in the next chapter, we all wear masks, as often to disguise us from ourselves as from others. Mythological stories, such as those illustrated in comic books, can be powerful tools that echo real human experiences of suffering, loss, change, and redemption and, just as important, reveal our capacities and failings to ourselves.

EIGHT

The Myth Behind the Claws

> The key isn't winning—or losing. It's making the attempt. I
> may never be what I ought to be, want to be—but how will I
> know unless I try? Sure it's scary, but what's the alternative?
> Stagnation—a safer, more terrible form of death. Not of the
> body but of the spirit.
>
> —Wolverine

Comic book characters are often referred to as modern-day mythological heroes. Although it may seem strange to compare a Superman or a Jean Grey to a Hercules or a Polyxena, in many ways the comparisons are spot on.

Comic books and graphic novels emphasize timeless aspects of human nature, both good and bad. They are our modern graphic equivalents of the storytelling of the ancients and, in that equivalency, fill the need of communicating societal norms, values, and knowledge from one generation to another.

As with the ancient fables, through their characters our comic books probe the eternal conundrums of good versus evil, personal versus public benefit, and conformity versus dissent. The frictions between antagonist and protagonist mirror the foundational values of their respective societies, where, panel by successive panel, we witness the classic collisions of conflicting human priorities as old as time.

An example of the comic book version of the "man versus god" conflict is depicted in *X-Factor* #5, in which the X-Men must battle a deity—Apocalypse. Created by writer Louise Simonson and artist Jackson Guice, Apocalypse is portrayed as both a deity and the world's first mutant, worshiped as a god since the beginning of civilization.

Originally named En Sabah Nur, the immortal Apocalypse is said to be the earliest and most powerful of the mutants, awakening in the modern age after millennia with the desire to deconstruct the societal and administrative state of humanity. Pursuant to that goal, Apocalypse recruits the disheartened Magneto and other mutants to create a civilization wherein mutants rule and humans are either killed or enslaved.

In the film *X-Men: Apocalypse*, Magneto asks this strange being, "Who are you?" "Elohim ... Shen ... Ra," Apocalypse replies. "I've been called many names over many lifetimes. I am born of death. I was there to spark and fan the flame of man's awakening, to spin the wheel of civilization. And when the forest would grow rank ... and needed clearing for new growth ... I was there to set it ablaze."[1]

Those familiar with religious terminology and references will recognize *Elohim* as the God of Israel, *Shen* as the Chinese word for "god," and *Ra* as the sun deity of ancient Egypt. As is true of ancient mythology or contemporary pulp fables, comic book tales and characters often contain universal symbolic patterns (archetypes) with collective themes such as a lost paradise, heaven and hell, and even an apocalyptic or dystopian parallel universe.

Jung and Archetypes

To reprise an earlier (albeit abbreviated) discussion, psychoanalyst Carl Jung's *collective unconscious* refers to the deepest layers of the unconscious mind present in all of humanity. Often expressed through symbols in mythology, the collective unconscious refers to the most deeply rooted of any given person's fundamental beliefs, emotions, and longings.

Distinguished from the Freudian *personal unconscious*, Jungian analysis involves the examination of a person's relationship to this "all-controlling deposit of ancestral experiences."[2] The collective unconscious contains both instincts and *archetypes*—universal symbols or instinctive patterns such as the wise sage, the earth mother, the tree of life, the trickster, the shadow and others, all of which have a profound influence on our understanding of ourselves and the world.

Perhaps a less clinically accurate but more readily understandable way of holding these personal unconscious and collective unconscious concepts in one's mind is to think of them as a form of universal human genetic memory inherently passed from one generation to the next. In much the same manner, think of *archetypes* as an embodiment, a manifestation—a personification, if you will—of a universal human need for rational order and understanding that "explains" or allows us to "define" (to others and to ourselves) events and situations and observed conditions that defy humanity's current ability to empirically and accurately explain such phenomena.

Among the most important archetypes are the *persona*, the *animus/ anima* and the *shadow*. Let us deal with them in that order.

The *persona* is the metaphorical mask or public face we present to the world. A unique and truly revealing aspect of comic book mythology is the medium's ability to let the reader "know" what the characters are thinking and feeling. Via the expressed verbal "voice bubble" or the often even more revealing "thought bubble," the reader is presented with the opportunity to get into (or even behind) a character's, well ... character— to "see" what a character is thinking and feeling in certain critical (and often revealing) situations.

Put more tangibly by clinician Max Stoltenberg, "Wolverine's brusque remarks and his humor provide a running journal of not only how he is experiencing others and himself but also ... a way of echoing what the reader might be thinking, or think that Wolverine is thinking, along the way. Wolverine's wisecracks are often focused on persona, such as 'If you cage the beast, the beast will get angry,' or, when he observes the Beast fighting in the final battle of *X-Men: Last Stand*, 'I thought you were a diplomat.'"[3] Better yet, behold the hilarious exchange in *X2* between Wolverine and a confused Cyclops, who cannot distinguish Mystique (who has morphed into the image of Logan) from the real Wolverine:

> WOLVERINE: Hey, it's me!
> CYCLOPS: Prove it.
> WOLVERINE: You're a dick.
> CYCLOPS: Okay.[4]

The *amimus* and the *anima* represent the biological and psychological aspects of masculinity and femininity. The anima archetype expresses itself as a feminine personality in men. Equivalently expressed in females, the animus is the masculine personality. According to Jung, no matter how masculine or feminine one may believe oneself to be, both genders retain a certain level of masculine and feminine qualities.

The *shadow* is the most powerful of the archetypes, as it represents the darker side of our personality. Devious thoughts, detestable feelings and unruly behaviors are found lurking within the shadow, and because these elements of our personality are often deemed socially unacceptable, we tend to project them onto others. For example, in the Marvel universe, a character's shadow often gets projected onto their enemy: witness

Sabretooth, for example, who represents all of Logan's ferocity with none of his humanity.

The shadow gets played out through conflicts. In comic books, conflicts are as numerous and as varied as the characters themselves, with the thresholds of criminology becoming indistinguishable and contingent upon for whom or what one is fighting. Thus, when ends justify means, it can be difficult to distinguish the good guys from the bad. For instance, most X-Men storylines depict Magneto as an adversary, but at times he joins forces with former foes to defeat an even more contentious common threat. Comic book heroes and villains personify the paradigms and politics of their audiences.

The main difference between ancient fables and comic book stories appears to be this: archaic mythology does not change much because its histories are stored and sealed in literary form, while the very nature of comic book mythos calls for the stories to be persistently retold and rewritten.

An illustration of the ever-mutable bedrock of comic book origin fables is the lack of a singular narrative in the X-Men tales. Characters are known to switch teams, and some resurrect after death. And even when they die on a more permanent basis, pending the outcries of readership, they may reappear in an alternative universe. Said another way, comic book storylines appear to take on a life of their own and evolve to meet the real-time life experiences of a mutable society. In this respect, comic book myths are more than mere modern-day legends, fixed and forever. They are as enduring, as edifying, and arguably as pertinent today as old myths were to our ancestors because comics illuminate the evolution of our culture's mutable ideals and values.

To illustrate the above point, the X-Men (discussed in detail in chapter six) were created with an eye toward reflecting the era of great racial, gender, and cultural divisions in which the team was born. Through reading their mythos, future generations may understand the injustice of prejudice and, ideally, make different choices than their predecessors. Consequently, comic book mythology, at minimum, continues to reflect and insistently assert an unquestionable effect on modern society in the same way that the earliest fictional stories influenced the societies of their time.

The Evolution of the Superhero

According to Laurence Maslon and Michael Kantor in their book *Superheroes: Capes, Cowls, and the Creation of the Comic Book Culture,* comic books were inspired by the monochromatic reality of the Great Depression, an era when printable news was almost exclusively black and white and those seeking color in print had only the Sunday funnies to which to turn. Printed separately, usually off-site from the newspaper itself, and inserted into the publication either mechanically or by the hand of the route delivery person, the Sunday funnies were a weekly breath of refreshing humor and color satirizing the challenges of daily life in a humorless grey existence. The Adventure Strip, with a more serious storyline, was created around the mid–1920s and often featured a hero who trafficked on his strength and wit to escape one dangerous situation after another. Maslon and Kantor stipulate to the archetype of these heroes being influenced by sagas of military valor and athletic achievement, or else appearing as an extension of the intrepid fiction of the time, such as *Tarzan of the Apes* or *The Curse of Capistrano*.[5]

As the popularity of the genre quickly expanded, readers of the funnies increasingly found themselves mesmerized by the stories of heroes such as Buck Rogers, Secret Agent X-9, Jungle Jim, and Flash Gordon. A bit later, both in the then new *Dick Tracy* strip and in a handful of other concurrent efforts, villains moved from simply being sinisterly drawn (e.g., Ming the Merciless) to being consciously portrayed as scarred, disfigured villains (e.g., the Joker) so as to depict the corroded essence of their criminal souls. And in an effort to add panache and flair and patriotic fervor to the heroes, characters began to appear costumed in tights, masks and even capes, with the first of such "branded" costuming belonging to *The Phantom*.

In their book, Maslon and Kantor recount that the comic writers and artists soon began to receive syndicate contracts, endorsements, and licensing opportunities. "And these characters soon took a life of their own; first in the hearts of young and old throughout the country, then on the radio, where many of them appeared in their own highly rated programs."[6]

Noting that the allure of comics stemmed from the genre's ability to reflect life and times, Maslon and Kantor highlight how the writers and artists began to execute comic art not as simple "one-off" graphic panel add-ons to the written material, such as an illustrated children's book might contain, but rather as a full-on art form unto itself. Soon thereafter, and again driven by public interest in the adventure strips, publishers launched the "pulps," magazines printed on soft, fibrous, spongy pulp paper containing renditions of serialized adventures, which soon found their way onto nearly every newsstand and catered to literally every comic book genre: adventure, mystery, science fiction and horror. An entirely new form of printed fiction was being born.

Heavily inspired by a radio mystery anthology series, the Shadow (a.k.a. the Master of Darkness) made his way into print on April 1, 1931.[7] In this new format, the dodgy character clad in a red-lined cloak and a black hat, with the famous catchphrase "Who knows what evil lurks in the hearts of men? The Shadow knows," visited his personal sense of justice upon criminals.

As with a Wolverine or a Judge Dredd or Hugo Weaving's character "V" in the Guy Fawkes mask in the film *V for Vendetta*, the mysterious Shadow took on the dual roles of judge and executioner. He visited the Far East, worked with "operatives" and was constantly on the move. From this description alone, one could assume the Shadow to be an early influence on *Detective Comics'* nocturnal vigilante Batman and other such officially unendorsed heroes.

People were instantly drawn to the Shadow character despite his lack of the usual American poster superhero qualities. His vicious inclinations, paired with his enigmatic adventurous jaunts, resonated with readers and radio listeners alike. The Shadow's widespread popularity eventually led to his own weekly radio series.

If the Shadow influenced the creation of modern-day antiheroes, then Doc Savage inspired "American Dream" characters (see James Truslow Adams 1931 *The Epic of America*) such as Captain America, a character widely considered equivalent to the modern-day Superman—a creation invested with superior abilities and possessed of a desire to administer justice tempered by adherence to a strict morally elevated ethical code.

While Doc Savage was especially popular during the Great Depression, when disheartened Americans found vicarious release through a superhero who took readers around the world through his adventures, Captain America gave Americans embroiled in World War II the extensional release of an escape into a morality of righteous retribution and payback meted out to the very real tyrannical villains of the day. The popularity of both characters led to several obvious followers, such as the Spider and the Black Bat.[8]

Pulp magazines grew in numbers and readership, now securing their own followers with multiple versions of the "good guy versus bad guy" mythos played out through their own superheroes, antagonists, storylines, and escapades. But none of these comic book hero prototypes ever came close to matching the immense influence of *Detective Comics'* Superman.

Childhood friends Jerry Siegel and Joe Schuster were paradigms— archetypes, if you will—for the modern-day "geek" culture. Both obsessed with cartoon shorts and comic books, they began creating their own versions of pulp magazines. In the summer of 1934, Siegel was "hit" with the idea of the strongest man in the universe—a "pure" superhero with a colorful costume.

The character was not initially well received by comic strip syndicates until one day, in the fall of 1937, when DC Comics began seriously exploring getting an action-oriented book on the stands. Weeding through previously rejected files (no, you don't get to say "Occam's Razor" here—"path of least resistance," perhaps, but not "Occam's Razor"), then managing editor Vin Sullivan came upon the Siegel/Schuster submission of several years prior, and the rest is history. The success of Superman was stunning to DC Comics, as it has become unimaginably profitable, with DC now being home to some of the world's greatest superheroes, including Superman, Wonder Woman and Batman.[9]

But the conceptualization of a superhero, ultimate or not, means nothing without that character being imbued with a sense of purpose. Superheroes exist in *action* comic books, after all, and in order to retain a reader's interest from one publication to the next, those heroes need to be targeted toward some greater overarching good—to fight for the right, to be challenged, to lose faith, to be bested at times by their nemeses, to surmount, and ideally to exit the conflict with the victory won.

Of all the mythical archetypes, the hero's quest is the one that endures the test of time both in its telling and in its capacity to profoundly touch us with its communicated lessons. By definition, the mythological hero is a person or warrior who exemplifies strength, vitality, tenacity, wisdom, and other qualities and ideals most of us aspire to achieve. Citius, Altius, Fortius, and all that.

It is especially noteworthy to point out here that not all heroes are combative, bellicose, testosterone-infused males. After all, the Greek mythological character from whom the term *hero* is derived is female: namely, Hero, a priestess of Aphrodite who lost her lover Leander to a winter storm drowning incident and subsequently her own life when, in despair, she threw herself from atop her tower in Sestos along the Hellespont to be with Leander—even if only in death.

Other noteworthy mythological female characters (yes, indeed, sisters, venerable *females* of mythology) are well documented, if not well renowned. Let's start with Andromeda, Antigone, Aphrodite, Ariadne,

Artemis, Athena—and that's just a first blush on the A's. Happy catching up on one's mythology!

Heroes are venerated as often for their courage, achievements, and abilities as for their tragic flaws, and these characters are by far the most popular mythological figures across cultures. Tales of heroes and anti-heroes possessing superhuman strength and performing unbelievable feats have fascinated the masses through the ages because they represent very real human experiences of calamity, hope lost, and redemption.

American mythologist and author Joseph Campbell's lifelong research has illuminated common literary constructs and formulations running through hero myths and fables from around the world. He referred to this aggregation of common patterns as *the monomyth*.

The Monomyth: The Hero's Journey

In mythology, the monomyth, or *the hero's journey*, is a story of a champion who goes on an adventure or quest, faces a pivotal calamity, achieves victory, and is transformed by the experience. Some examples of the hero myth played out are the mythologies of British King Arthur and Kutoyis, the Native American Blackfoot hero. Other such stories more familiar to the reader may be those of Hercules, Perseus, Beowulf, Gilgamesh, or (more contemporarily) Kahless the Unforgettable of *Star Trek* fame.

Joseph Campbell introduced the concept of the hero's myth in his book *The Hero with a Thousand Faces*. In it Campbell described the basic narrative pattern thus: "A hero ventures forth from the world of common day into a region of supernatural wonder: fabulous forces are there encountered and a decisive victory is won: the hero comes back from this mysterious adventure with the power to bestow boons on his fellow man."[10]

Campbell describes 17 stages of the hero's journey, grouping these stages into three broader "acts": (1) *departure* (or separation)—our hero lives in the ordinary world and, although initially reluctant, affirmatively responds to a call to go on an adventure; (2) *initiation* (sometimes subdivided into *descent* and *initiation*)—the hero crosses a threshold to the unknown, where he faces immense battles or trials (either alone or with the assistance of others); and (3) *return*—he returns to the ordinary world with some sort of treasure, which he may now use for the benefit of his fellow man. In the end, the hero is transformed by his experiences and gains insight or wisdom.

The film *X-Men: Days of Future Past* (also discussed in chapter six) nicely illustrates the Wolverine monomyth. In this film, we witness Logan removed from an apocalyptic future and transported back to the 1970s, where he must convince an emotionally crushed Charles Xavier to return to his guru role in order to stop a future catastrophe of gargantuan proportions. Because of Logan's heroic actions, he returns to an *altered* future in which he finds Xavier, Storm, Jean Grey (alive and breathing), and other professors and students all living and working peacefully within the halls of the Xavier School of Gifted Youngsters.

When it comes to interpreting films such as the *X-Men* franchise, psychologist Dr. Clive Hazell tells us, "One can look at these characters and stories through the lens of Gordon Lawrence's theory of social dreaming. The analyst treats a film as a dream that society, or a cohort of society, has created. Once the film is treated as a dream, then the interpretation can take place. The *X-Men* films reveal unconscious elements operating in a given society. They manifest social symptoms, much as a dream can be read as a compromise between wishes and repressive forces. The films are manifesting a commentary of a society as it is being experienced unconsciously."[11] As such, X-Men hero myths are models for us to follow and provide the assurance of or hope for a better life (or, at the very least, a better afterlife should one choose to live honorably). But unlike fairy tales, myths are not always optimistic and heroes do not always live happily ever after.

True to the nature of humanity, the spirit of myths is often a warning or a lamentation, even an equivocation (as with the witches of *Macbeth*). Taking on themes such as greed or impulsivity, some myths function as instructions and guides to societal norms. One example of such a myth is that of Kuekuatsheu.

The legend of Kuekuatsheu (pronounced KOO A KOO OTT SOO) from the Innu Nation was mentioned in the 2009 movie *X-Men Origins: Wolverine*. As Silver Fox and Logan share an intimate moment by the cabin fire, a hushed wolf howl wafts faintly off the night's distant horizon. So reminded, Silver Fox shares a legend with Logan:

> Why is the Moon so lonely? Because she used to have a lover. His name was Kuekuatsheu, and they lived in the spirit world together. And every night, they would wander the skies together. But one of the other spirits was jealous. Trickster wanted the Moon for himself. So he told Kuekuatsheu that the Moon had asked for flowers; he told him to come to our world and pick her some wild roses. But Kuekuatsheu didn't know that once you leave the spirit world, you can never go back. And every night, he looks up in the sky and sees the Moon and howls her name. But ... he can never touch her again.[12]

Silver Fox explains to Logan that *Kuekuatsheu* translates to "the wolverine" and that to this day the beasts of the earth cry to the moon, baying their sorrows to the lost love who is now forever intangible.

Logan wanted to be Silver Fox's hero, but Victor Creed got to her first; Logan could not save her. His grief over Silver Fox's death, coupled with his many other traumatic experiences, set Logan on a path to become something entirely darker and much more menacing—an anti-hero.

Dr. Hazell reveals, "An analysis of Franco Moretti in his book *Signs Taken for Wonders* reveals an interest in literary 'wonders' such as Dracula and Frankenstein in modern literature. We can take his analysis of these figures and pass it over through to Wolverine. In [*X-Men Origins: Wolverine*] we see an authority figure [Major William Stryker] concerned over the inheritance of wealth and power, who recruits a titanic mutant."[13] (A "titanic" hero, according to Czech philosopher Jan Patočka, is one who, because of the exceptional nature of his actions, can simply detach himself from worldly experiences.[14])

Dr. Hazell's analysis of *X-Men Wolverine* reveals other themes:

> [Stryker] uses this titanic and traumatized mutant to successfully and thanklessly resolve the issue. The viewer understands this is what is happening in the movie, but then one wonders, "Is this also going on in society?" I believe the answer is— yes. We could take a neo-Marxist view that this movie is reflecting class division, workers, class oppression and trauma as irregularly distributed among the classes. For example, Wolverine is depicted as part of the working class who has been mutated further by technology. Similarly, the trauma instilled upon Frankenstein could be taken as a social dream about the dangers of technology…. Just as the technology becomes autonomous, Frankenstein becomes autonomous and wreaks havoc. Technology also causes harm to Wolverine and makes him to lose control. In today's society, we have the belief that we have control over technology, when, in reality, technology controls us. This film expresses this social notion theoretically.[15]

Hero as Distinguished from Antihero

Akin to the archetypal figure of the trickster in mythology and religion, an antihero is a god, spirit, human, or anthropomorphic animal who, among other things, disobeys normal rules and conventional behavior.

An antihero is a protagonist who is often psychologically damaged, simultaneously depicted as superior due to his superhuman abilities and inferior due to his impetuousness, irrationality, or lack of thoughtful evaluation. For these reasons, antiheroes are often unable to maximize their inherent hero talents and potential, and they are thus frequently relegated to lower status than the prototypical heroes.[16]

Antiheroes are rough around the edges, to say the least, but are arguably as endearing as regular heroes. Take characters such as Han Solo from *Star Wars*, Marv from *Sin City*, Spawn from *Image Comics*, Marvel's Deadpool or Wolverine himself. All of them are reckless, persistent, and impetuous, arrogantly asserting a "fuck it" attitude.

The stark distinction between heroes and antiheroes therefore would seem to be that while heroes are generally rock-ribbed purveyors of probity who live by more or less traditional codes of justice, morality, and fairness, antiheroes live by their own utilitarian or pragmatic ethical codes—they never allow laws or restrictions to stop them from doing what they see as needing be done, as often as not "by any means necessary."

Antiheroes often have lamentable origin tales—take, for instance, the origin story of famous *Image Comics* character Albert Francis "Al" Simmons (a.k.a. Spawn). Murdered by his friend and trapped in hell, Simmons sells his soul to Malebolgia, the ruler of hell, in exchange for a chance to see his wife once more. As generally occurs in stories surrounding contracts made with Dark Lords, Malebolgia plays fast and loose with the spirit of the agreement and sends Simmons (now Spawn) back to Earth five years later as a spawn of hell with no memory of what he has done. Once Spawn finally regains his memory, he seeks out his wife only to discover her happily married to his best friend, with whom she shares a child.[17]

Another famous antihero (and, in the spirit of full disclosure, a personal favorite of this author) is Marvel's Punisher. Originally known as Frank Castle, he is a war veteran, a U.S. Marine Corps (Semper Fi) scout sniper, and a vigilante who employs coercion, violence, torture, and murder using all manner of conventional battle weaponry in his war on crime. Motivated by the deaths of his wife and two children, the Punisher wages a one-man war on all criminals.

Similar to Logan, the Punisher is known for his use of ruthless methods and extreme violence in meting out what he views as justice. He is also similar to Logan in that he becomes all the more lethal as he becomes more psychologically unstable. Unlike Logan, however (and unlike other antiheroes created around the same time), the Punisher's personality remains detached and even borders on delusional—at one point he believes himself to be charged by God with castigating evil.

Tragic origins such as those of Spawn and the Punisher typically produce fascinating antiheroes, and Logan is no exception. A vigilante's suffering often results in a blurring of the dividing line between good and evil and a ghoulishly savage approach to dispensing justice. It is here that we see Logan's drinking problem, violent killing methods, sporadic amnesia, and overall rejection of authority defining him more as mutant-rebel than tights-and-cape superhero. *No one* tells Logan what to do (with the exception of Professor X), and he'll assertively share that truism with anyone he encounters.

Doug Kline, author of *The San Diego Comic-Con Survival Guide* (and obsessive X-Men fan since the 1980s), tells us,

> The Wolverine character is an example of how people react to their own mutant metaphor. Wolverine is gruff, angry, and belligerent, but not without good reason. While he has no memory of his past, he understands who he is in the face of danger and fights back. He does not often quibble with the consequences of his actions. This is a guy who could have easily been a villain. What kind of hero has blades in his hands and stabs people, even if they are bad guys? ... On the comic page, Wolverine lashes out in a visceral way that many of us wish we could against injustices. Readers find a release through him, whether unconsciously or not.[18]

Wolverine experiences love, loss, and tragedy (after brutal tragedy) throughout his prolonged life. His is a classic comic book saga—albeit with a serrated edge.

The hero in his story is a misunderstood brute who battles enemies that resemble the darker elements of his own personality. In fact, his main nemesis (Sabretooth) is essentially a clone of Logan in strength, speed, and savagery. But this hero is much more than instinctive brutality, likely as his original creators intended. He is a man who, despite himself, cannot resist the tenderness of a woman's touch or the beseeching cries of those at risk.

Logan's adventures therefore are as innumerable as they are bemusing. Yes, he is a loner antihero with a hostile nature honed by conflict; yet he struggles to control his own inner demons. He reaches the brink of death again and again; yet he rejuvenates to fight another day, both physically and mentally, in search of who he was, who he is and who he is meant to become.

Chris Claremont put it best when he said, "The thing for me about Wolverine is that he is a man forever in primal conflict. There is a part of him that, if you cross him, he will kill you and not even blink. But there's another part of him that is a man. And his entire life is dedicated to overcoming the monster with the man. And he can't. But because he's an X-Man, he's got to keep trying."[19] Logan's ultimate mythos, his archetypal exemplification—our pulling the curtain back from myth behind the claws, if you will—lies in humanity's resilience and search for meaning (and in Logan being the metaphor for it).

Mythological Influences on the Development of Wolverine

The name *wolverine* comes from an English diminution of the word *wolf*; however, the French name for wolverine, *carcajou*, was derived from Algonquian Indian names for the small but powerful creature, such as the Mi'kmaq name *ki'kwaju* or the Innu name *Kuekuatsheu* (mentioned earlier in this chapter).

In Native American folklore, wolverines tend to be portrayed as bullies or antisocial tricksters. However, among the Innu people of Quebec and Labrador the wolverine character is portrayed as a more benevolent modernizer who assists humanity, entertaining them with his often socially inappropriate mishaps as he does so. Wolverines are also considered good luck among some tribes of Northern California. Running into a wolverine is considered fortunate, as they are frequently highlighted in fables as successful tricksters.[20]

Pop culture author-historian J. David Spurlock stated, "Some comic book historians have cited Wallace (Wally) Wood's animalistic antihero character Animan as a prototype for Wolverine."[21] Wood, a founding cartoonist of *Mad Magazine* and Hall of Fame comic book creator, known widely for his work on Marvel's *Daredevil*, rolled out his Animan character in the early issues of his self-published magazine *witzend*, circa 1966.[22] Within the pages of *witzend* the creators were allowed total license to generate whatever they wished without an editorial policy to obstruct their ingenuity. It was perhaps this level of autonomy that led Wood to envision his famous jungle man:

> This is the story of a monster ... neither man, nor beast, but with the attributes of both and superior to both! Picture a being with the strength, reflexes, and senses of a tiger, and the curiosity and ability to reason of a highly intelligent human being and you have—Animan.[23]

In perusing the early depictions and storylines of Animan, it is impossible to deny the character's influence on Wolverine. Animan—part man and part animal—lives in the wild. Like Logan, he possesses incredible strength and speed; yet he combines his reliance on animal instincts with a human's ability to reason. He even sports a pointy coif.

Other mythological influences almost certainly informed the creation of Wolverine, include the Greek demigod Heracles. The last mortal son of Zeus, known as the strongest of mortals (with an equally hard-wearing temperament), Heracles often chose action over assessment. Sporting a lion skin and carrying a club, he was depicted as a chiseled mass of a man. Impulsive and primitive in nature, Heracles frequently got into trouble, even when not consciously tempting fate. A striking similarity between Logan and Heracles is their rages—more specifically, their moments of "serial insanity," which cause the catastrophic deaths of those they love.

While these examples illustrate several of the more salient mythological inspirations for the Logan character, his nature incorporates many more distinguishable antihero qualities, such as his drifter and loner identity, the vicious methods in which he executes justice and his camaraderie with team members.

One quite unique element of Logan's personality, however (and one likely derived from psychology's increasing interest in the "why" of personality to go with its "what"), is his ongoing inner battle with his volatility. Witness his statement: "I'm an X-Man. Mutants like me, band of super heroes, good people, idealists, dreamers—forever looking for the best in others. With them, killing is a last resort. With me, it's second nature. I take the world as it is, an' give better than I get. Come at me with a sword. I'll meet you with a sword. You want mercy. Show a little first."[24]

This level of considered mental conflict makes the Wolverine character unique to the antihero archetype and distinct from all mythological characters upon which he might have been based. He incorporates so many crucial salient character peaks that the variant plausible storylines available to his writers would seem to be without boundaries, and yet, in the end, not at all incongruent with the development of the character. Logan's tendency to experience bouts of traumatically induced amnesia is a good example of such endless possibilities.

Masking the Mutant

Amnesia has a way of making everything new again—and, in the case of Wolverine, new both to the character experiencing the operating milieu being depicted and to readers in their acceptance of the plausibility of the storyline being projected. In a completely new environment, one tends to be fascinated, confused, or terrified. Jung points out that we wear metaphorical masks throughout our lives with different people. The way that one presents oneself to one's partner's family is vastly different from the way one presents to one's biker group. And when it comes to Wolverine, the character can be plausibly inserted in virtually any storyline, no matter how fanciful, and then retrieved for placement in a more mainstream publication with the very next creative execution.

Perhaps this versatility might explain why Logan wears a costume: He wants to escape his loneliness, if only for a while. And although he doesn't trust people, he feels the need to belong to something greater than himself—some sort of cause or purpose. A costume associates Wolverine with team members who sport costumes—something that no doubt required an adjustment period for our favorite loner antihero, but a bonding agent nonetheless. The X-Men uniform also disconnects him from "normal" people.

Mutants know all too well that they are divorced from garden-variety humanity, or, more correctly, that they are the objects of an enforced divorce. Their costumes define and empower their embrace of that estrangement. This is yet another factor that divides the mutants from other superheroes: where mutants wear costumes to distinguish themselves, non-mutant superheroes wear costumes to separate their regular personas from their alter egos. For example, by day Clark Kent (mild-mannered reporter for the *Daily Planet* newspaper) wears a business suit and "squint" eyewear, but at night he dons a bright red cape and garish blue body suit emblazoned with an irregular pentagon-shaped dayglow red-and-yellow "S" on the chest. Likewise, Tony Stark slathers himself in billionaire playboy veneer—that is, until the Ironman suit snaps on.

In this respect, Wolverine is the victim of both edges of the sword. He has neither the luxury nor the necessity of masking his true identity because he doesn't know who he truly is, and he has apparently decided it's nothing about which he needs to care. He doesn't remember much of anything about himself or his origins, anyway, which allows him to be completely himself in every moment.

But behind his mask of indifference to the balance of the world, how terrified must Wolverine be in all of this? How disorienting must it be to be unable to comfortably retreat into one's shielding shell for so much as a moment of reverie or a twinkling of confabulated release—to be unable to skirt a frightening moment made all the more nerve-wracking by having only fleeting awareness of how that moment came to pass?

Logan's murky past and persistent gaps in memory often cause him to go into hiding, assuming aliases such as "Patch" or taking on roles such as cage fighter, assassin, governmental spy, school professor, soldier or predatory killer. Logan is at best unsure of what he is capable, let alone what he's done or how he got where he is (nor are readers much wiser). Such is what makes Logan the quintessential antihero and what makes the endless variety of storylines from the Marvel fantasy machine all the more viable and compelling to its readers.

Readers are intrigued by this character's most prevalent paradox: that even the most berserk of mutants—a government-created walking weapon with the most volatile and violent of potential temperaments—in calmer moments elects to spend his life helping and protecting others. This is Wolverine's fatal flaw. This flaw, this decision, etches in stone his ultimate fate: to suffer in solitary confinement the pain of what he cherishes being consistently ripped away.

While this samurai knows the worth of honor, he also knows its price. He can relish the vibrant brevity of camaraderie and love, but he will never know the lingering serenity of living with them. Time and again he agonizes over being required to unleash his near-unbeatable ferocity while struggling to unearth his humanity. And yet, in repeatedly doing so, he has come to know the frustrated depression that accompanies knowing that all his searching for a way out will likely never deliver the doorway to that release.

Logan's fight for his humanity was exemplified in the *Weapon X* series (discussed in chapter three), but we witness this fight once more—and on a much more existential level—in the famed miniseries *Old Man Logan*.

Old Man Logan: A Last Shot at Humanity

The 2008 *Old Man Logan* miniseries, created by Mark Millar and Steven McNiven, unfolds in an alternative future universe designated as Earth-807128 and replaces the brute muscle of the X-Men gang with an aged and somber (if not sober) Logan.

Exhausted from witnessing and causing so much death during his lifetime, Logan seeks to engender new meaning from that life—or at least what's left of it. As with Ebenezer Scrooge, he knows that the past is the past; it cannot be undone—the fallout of past errors remains inviolate. But he also knows that those errors need not be repeated. And so he strives to be more ... human.

In this alternate universe, the now aged Wolverine exists in a world run by the supervillains. Nearly all gifted mutant superheroes have been killed or have been overthrown and gone to ground.

Hawkeye tries to recruit Logan for a job but finds him enervated, disabled, sick of killing, and inhabiting a quiet life in his post-crime-fighting days. Sharing a drink at a bar, these old friends talk about their lives and past regrets.

At one point Hawkeye tells Logan, "At least you seem a little more like your old self."

"That's what I'm afraid of," Logan responds. "I ain't that guy anymore, Hawkeye. I love my wife. I love my kids. And I love that little life we've carved out for ourselves ... I ain't excited about death anymore."[25]

Logan goes on to explain why he hasn't popped his claws in fifty years: Mind controlled by the Mystero, Logan believed that he and the other mutants in the X-mansion were under attack by an onslaught of supervillains. Viciously, Logan attacked and killed every one of them—that is, until Bullseye shrieked, "Logan, stop. Please ... Why are you doing this? You're supposed to be our friend."

In that instant, Logan snapped to, appalled to discover what had truly transpired: *he* had killed every member of his extended family; *he* had killed all the X-Men, stabbing them all through the heart. Looking around the room, Logan saw the bloodbath he had created: his best friends' lifeless bodies stacked like cordwood, one upon the last!

Logan loved the X-Men, far more than he loved himself. The X-Men represented Logan's brighter side, the part of him that strove to be good, while his enemies reflected the darker elements of his persona. In sum, the human part of Logan died with the X-Men that day—worst of all, they all died at Logan's own hand.

Seeking refuge once more, the emotionally devastated Logan, walking alone with the taste of blood in his mouth, retreated into the woods. But where once he felt connected to the wild and to its creatures, the forested solitude provided no succor; the animals now ran from him in fear.

Logan sought to hurt himself—to kill himself. He laid down on train tracks and allowed the train to run over his neck. Although the train didn't kill him because of his healing factor, Logan was physically deeply wounded, and so he explains to Hawkeye, "Sometimes that's enough." At the very least, Logan was able to bury "the Wolverine."[26]

Allegorically, Wolverine committed suicide. Upon healing from his injuries, Logan considered the berserker part of his life dead and buried. He stopped going by the name "Wolverine" altogether and swore an oath to never kill again.

In telling all this to Hawkeye, burying his head in his hands, Logan says, "Now you just try tellin' me Wolverine didn't deserve to die. You just try tellin' me I been a fool to hide these claws for fifty years." Acknowledging his friend's suffering, Hawkeye responds simply, "I wouldn't dare."[27]

True to form, this being a Wolverine series, Logan returns home to discover his wife and children murdered. It is now not refuge but revenge that Logan seeks! He breaks his vow, unsheathes his claws once more and sets out to secure his revenge. He has nothing left to lose; he vows to hunt down and kill every one of the new world's villains.

In the 2016 version of *Old Man Logan* written by Jeff Lemire and penciled by Andrea Sorrentino, the apocalypse never takes place, but the storyline retains Logan's loner/drifter personality. He's still the Logan of old, but now much more an old Logan, aged to a debilitated shadow of the once formidable Wolverine, yet still in search of meaning in a meaningless world.

Mythology's Ability to Inform—Yesterday, Today and Tomorrow

In the Marvel mythos we witness human-like creatures whose conflicts with personal and societal acceptance challenge our concepts of beauty, sanity, and normality. In this universe, millions of mutant faces (including Logan's own venerable, if scarred, visage) reflect *sacred* elements of human life: uniqueness, rebelliousness, resistance to a hostile world, and ultimately the unavoidable demise and decay that awaits all, whether animal, vegetable, mineral, mutant, or human.

The chronicles of superheroes (anti or otherwise) such as Logan connect us to properties of human life larger than the ones we employ in parceling out our own allotted life spans. Whether someone is a comic book "geek" or a casual dilettante taking in the occasional *X-Men* film, we witness real-time representations of what Jung referred to as his collective unconscious.

Logan's struggles reflect our struggles. His trauma reminds us of our trauma. As Logan continues to grieve over his many losses, we empathize with him, sympathize with him and mourn the lack of the better existence that could have been his—or ours. Through the Wolverine mythos we are reminded that regardless of whatever life challenges we have or will yet endure, we, too, must put the past behind us and persevere.

The appeal of the *Old Man Logan* character to its audience was as immediate as it was opportune; it resonated profoundly with the next generation of Wolverine fans. The *Old Man Logan* series inspired the 2017 film *Logan*, in which Hugh Jackman gives his final and (as fans around the world argue) most compelling performance as Wolverine. As we shall see in the final chapter of this work of character analysis, Laura Kinney (a.k.a. X-23) takes on the mantle of Wolverine, but not before Logan fights his last battle. Yet, in his passing, Logan not only "passes" to the next life (or so it is implied) but also "passes" the baton of his centuries of experience, value assessment, and the power of (and proper perspective on) human interaction that in and of themselves become legends, modern-day mythology, and stories that convey the morals, standards, and hopes of this generation.

NINE

Wolverine's Last Stand

Nature made me a freak. Man made me a weapon. And God
made me last too long.

—Logan

Through a lifetime numbered in centuries as much as years, Logan
has endured torments, privations, and indignities galore. He's survived
wars, natural disasters, brainwashing, beheadings, and torture. He's been
torn apart by the Hulk, had his skeleton infused with adamantium, and
had the molecules of that same indestructible metal pulled from him
through his pores by the mutant master Magneto.

True to his innate capacity for barbarity, and with minimal provocation, Logan has savagely retaliated against his adversaries. But under the
mentorship of Charles Xavier, and via his extensive samurai training,
Logan has also learned to love, acquired a sense of loyalty and defended
his mutant tribe at all costs.

The explanations for the multidimensional nature of this character
are as complex and as personal as his background story. These explanations are intended to echo the chaotic and unpredictable coalescence of
specifics that forge a human nature—any human nature, whether Logan's
or someone else's.

No thinking person, Wolverine included, would operate in the world
as if that world were governed by a set of irreproachable absolutes. Yes,
sometimes we will legitimize, we will justify, we will bend the boundaries,
we will rationalize—all in an effort to deliver what, on the surface, will
appear to be a thoughtful, unemotional, and lucid decision. Humans are,
after all, not so much rational beings as they are rational*izing* beings.

However, defining our operating universe in absolute terms—black
or white, up or down, left or right, good or bad, right or wrong—does not
work, save for those who prefer to be unaware or uninformed.

Put another way, and from a much broader prospective, no one is all "good" or all "bad." Given a motivation to learn from past mistakes and an opportunity to recover from past injuries, an individual can and will change. This aspect of human nature is echoed in the Wolverine saga through one of Wolverine's core powers—his ability to heal and rejuvenate.

Wolverine's healing factor, at times pushed well past its crush depth, extends his life far beyond those of his mutant counterparts. This ability—to heal physically and recover mentally—has been tested time and again throughout his long lifetime. It would seem that his extended life span relies mightily on his ability to endure protracted suffering.

Ironically, the immortality that has shielded Logan so often is deemed "a curse" by Logan himself, and one that eventually visits its own unique vengeance on this otherwise vigorous mutant. While Logan's healing factor has for centuries kept him alive and functional, it deprives him of the luxury of a peaceful and natural death. Growing tired of outliving his friends and feeling as if he is losing his own mind, yet trapped in a body that will not set him free, Logan experiences profound hopelessness and sadness.

Logan reevaluates the meaning of his existence in several venues: (a) amid the panels of the *Old Man Logan* series (discussed in the previous chapter); (b) in the *Death of Wolverine* series; and (c) in the 2017 film *Logan*, which was inspired by the *Death of Wolverine* series. We will address the meaning and the lessons to be gleaned from both the series and the *Logan* film in a bit, but first we must explore the significance of the events integral to Wolverine's demise.

Logan finally meets his end among the panels of the 2014 series appropriately titled *Death of Wolverine*, written by Charles Soule and illustrated by Steve McNiven. Unique to this much-anticipated series is a broad assortment of variant cover designs included within its back pages. In an interview with Chandler Rice, CEO of Desert Wind Enterprises and manager of comic book legends such as the late Len Wein, John Romita, Jr., Joe Rubinstein and the late Herb Trimpe, this author was privileged to learn the story of how Wolverine's co-creator Herb Trimpe based his variant cover for the work upon the character's commencement:

> In early 2014 I was on a trip with Herb and his wife Patricia for a collectors' show in Hawaii. While on this trip, I had read Marvel was going to kill off the character Wolverine. Later that evening, while at dinner, I mentioned to Herb I read that Marvel planned on killing off Wolverine. Herb's response was "How do you kill someone that can't die?" ... I said to Herb, "I was thinking it would be appropriate

for the man who created the very first cover with Wolverine on it (which was *The Incredible Hulk* #181 cover) to create one of the very last covers of Wolverine...." I asked Herb, "When you created the *Incredible Hulk* cover, if that cover had been an interior page, and you turned the page, what would have been the next frame?" He said, "That would've had to have been 'HULK SMASH!'" Hence the cover was born.[1]

Herb Trimpe's variant cover reflects a battle between two of the most indefatigable fighters in the Marvel universe. Trimpe drew flayed slashes in Hulk's skin where Wolverine had landed several well-placed claw strikes, and, in a last gesture of Wolverine's vulgarity, Trimpe illustrated Logan's middle claw erect—expressing his contempt at being killed off.

The Death of Wolverine

The series opens with Logan sitting alone in British Columbia staring off into a sunset. In his eyes we see that poignant familiarity known only to those mindful of their own time winding down.

Wolverine has been infected with a mysterious virus. While he maintains his indestructible adamantium skeleton, some of his enhanced strength, heightened tracking abilities, and innate healing factor have vanished.

Facing this newfound vulnerability, Logan's ability to manage his berserker rages remains a matter of life or death—only now it's a matter of his *own* life or death. He cannot risk deploying his claws for fear of developing an infection from unsheathing them out of and reabsorbing them back into his body—an especially problematic prospect for a combatant who has accumulated a long list of enemies. And now, at his weakest moment, a price has been placed on Logan's head. In single file, his enemies come knocking.

Still a force to be reckoned with, Wolverine turns offensive; the hunted becomes the hunter. One by one he captures, interrogates, and eliminates his attackers. If he must die, Logan surmises, he will depart this life in the same way he has lived it: contentious and combative to the bitter end.

Former Logan protégé Kitty Pryde, now a powerful mutant in her own right, appears on the scene to defend Logan against his ex-wife Viper, who, as he has discovered through his interrogations, has subcontracted mercenaries to track him down.

Logan and Kitty have a deep connection based on friendship and trust, so he discloses to her his current conflict:

LOGAN: I wonder if it'll ever stop. Just one fight after another, tearing me apart in slow-motion. You won't always be here with some magic potion, either, Kitty, or McCoy, or Reed, or Tony. One day, I'll be too slow and then ... done. Sometimes I wonder if it might be better to find some place where I can watch the sun set, then just...
KITTY: Don't ever say that Logan.
LOGAN: Don't worry, Kitty. I got plans. I lost my healing factor, sure, but there's a good side to that. It means I can get old.
KITTY: Why would you want that?
LOGAN: Because no more chances. No more doing something horrible and telling myself I've got until the end of damn time to make up for it. No, just one lifetime, where every choice matters.[2]

Here we witness another aspect of Logan's expanded moral compass. Up to this point, his body's ability to rejuvenate allowed him unlimited time and opportunities to learn from his mistakes and atone for his wrongs. (Whether he took advantage of those opportunities is another discussion entirely.) Now, however, with his expiration date looming large, Logan confronts the universal mortality faced by all. No more time to make amends. No more mulligans. No more dismissive self-indulgent rationalizations of repulsive carnage. Just as he has held his adversaries accountable for their actions, from here on out, whenever he crosses the line, Logan lives (or dies) fully cognizant of the permanence of his actions.

Self-reproach, although painful, has its benefits. Sincere regret can inspire future corrective action that precludes regret. Logan is now keenly aware of his increasingly reduced immunity from the results of any berserker rage and ill-considered impulsivity.

Redemption and Resignation

Fast forward in the storyline a bit, and the reader discovers that it is Dr. Abraham Cornelius—the very same scientist responsible for bonding adamantium to Logan's skeleton—who has set the bounty for Logan's capture.

A certain strain of cosmic justice might consider Wolverine's creator delivering his demise to be righteous, a long-overdue cleansing of a past error, however ill intended. But such a successful intervention would deprive Logan of some equally honorable retribution—and retribution is precisely what Logan has in mind.

Thus, regeneration serum secured, Logan sets off for a remote base in Nevada where Cornelius is busy trying to replicate the Weapon X program with other subjects. Cornelius acknowledges that he wants to be memorialized for creating the ultimate "super soldier," and all is going well save for one problem: Cornelius's current victims lack Wolverine's healing factor. His subjects cannot survive the adamantium bonding process without it, so Cornelius disingenuously attempts to convince Logan to sacrifice himself in order to become something "better" than the brute that he is.

Unbeknownst to Cornelius, however, Wolverine has evolved since the Weapon X program. He is no longer the cold-blooded killer Cornelius and his colleagues created all those years ago. Logan laughs at Cornelius as he shares his healing-factor deficiency. In a rage, Cornelius attempts to escape by activating the adamantium bonding on the test subjects, only to be fatally injured in the process.

Logan then unsheathes his claws for the final time. He slashes the tank holding the heated adamantium before the bonding process can begin, causing the liquid to engulf his body. The hardening liquid metal begins to suffocate Wolverine, but in his final moments he remains true to his X-Men calling, saving the test subjects by injecting them with the regeneration serum.

Begging for his life, Cornelius pleads, "I tried to change the world! What did you ever do but kill people? What did you ever do?"[3]

Many lifetimes of memories flash through Wolverine's mind: the centuries of war, the good life, the travels, the adventures, the women, Xavier's school. Through it all, he has lived his life to the fullest.

Staggering out into the sunset, Logan falls to his knees as the adamantium coating his body solidifies. He voices his final word—"Enough"—and dies.

At the end, Logan sacrificed his life one last time. Given his long history as a practically unbeatable lethal force aimed at carrying out justice on his own terms, one would expect Wolverine's death to be nothing short of a blood-splattering save-the-world finale. Not so in the case of the evolved Logan, and therefore not so in *Death of Wolverine*.

Logan's death was both private and personal, and he became once more what John Romita, Jr., referred to as "judge, jury, and executioner."[4] Wolverine was set on killing Cornelius for multiple reasons that were not entirely self-sacrificing, though he certainly intended to kill Cornelius before he could do to others what he did to Logan. However, Logan also expected that he likely would not survive the encounter. That being said (and regeneration in Marvel-topia being what it is), the *Death of Wolverine* series leaves an opportunity for Wolverine's return. The 2017 movie *Logan*, however, would not seem to provide that same wiggle room.

Logan *(the Movie)*

Borrowing prominently from Mark Millar and Steve McNiven's *Old Man Logan* series, the 2017 noir film *Logan*, cowritten by famed director James Mangold, along with Scott Frank and Michael Green, has the feel of a classic western and takes place in a semi-apocalyptic world.

The year is 2029; the location is El Paso, Texas. Logan is a drunken scrapper who struggles to make ends meet as a limo chauffeur. He remains a renegade, but he's much older: he wears glasses, coughs frequently, and walks with a limp. The once insurmountable hero's claws are now slow on the draw. His healing factor is finally failing him. He is slowly dying.

No new mutants have been born in the past 25 years. Logan, along with Caliban, cares for an aged Charles Xavier—founder of the School for Gifted Youngsters, leader of the X-Men and himself a Class 4 mutant with profound telepathic powers. Charles has been diagnosed with a neurodegenerative disease that causes him to have seizures. However, Charles's seizures fog his telepathic mind and gravely wound anyone within a radius of a few miles.

All three live a bleak existence on the desert site of a defunct and desolate smelting plant, seemingly to suppress the range of Charles's psychic seizures. In his suffering, Logan has shut everyone out emotionally. He does not speak about his frustrations. The bitterness and brutalities of life are no longer tolerable.

Alone in his room, Logan holds a gun and an adamantium bullet—the only thing that can kill him. The once unconquerable Wolverine, deemed a lethal adversary by his enemies and a relentless protector by his friends, now contemplates suicide. As it turns out, even a mutant as resilient as Wolverine can lose faith.

Ego Integrity versus Despair

According to psychologist Erik Erickson's theory of psychosocial development, we experience eight stages of development from infancy to late adulthood. As we grow older and slower both mentally and physically, we concern ourselves less with productivity and much more with the personal gratifications to be found in exploring our new world of relatively unencumbered retirement age. We contemplate whether we were successful at developing integrity and purpose in our younger years.

The main challenge posed by Erickson in this last developmental stage, known as *ego integrity versus despair*, is our affirmative take on that ongoing retrospective review of our past. If we believe that our life was without meaning or that we missed out on life goals, we become discontented and develop a sense of desolation, depression, and hopelessness. Wolverine proves no less susceptible to such conflicts, as we encounter him continuing to battle his inner demons right up to the end.

In the film, Johnny Cash's rendition of the Nine Inch Nails song "Hurt" is heard playing in the background. Of all the comic book superheroes, if anyone deserves to be associated to Johnny Cash's rendition of "Hurt," it is Logan, because the lyrics seamlessly mirror Logan's sorrow and forlornness.

Given Logan's tortured past, fragmented memories, and profound losses, as well as the stark consequences of aging, the consideration of suicide is not at all remarkable—even for Wolverine.

Without so much as a whiff of hyperbole, it's safe to say that there is a lot of misery in this world. Desolation, resentment, prejudice, desperation, poverty, hunger, disability, disease … you name it. And in absorbing those blows, many of us have experienced the same crippling sense of hopelessness that afflicts Logan at the beginning of the movie.

Heroes are not always defined by what is good, chaste, moral, or constructive. Sometimes one's strength lies in staring at one's own reflection in a cracked mirror and realizing that things are really *not* okay. Just like Logan, we've all had moments in life when we've felt like giving up, but during these taxing times, it is especially important to seek help whenever possible because isolation on any level precludes our access to the better angels of alternate unburdened input.

According to the American Association of Suicidality, risk factors of suicide include the following: (1) biological factors—medical concerns, substance abuse and mental disorders; (2) psychological factors—certain personality types, a person's state of mind and developmental history; (3) social factors—stressful life events and exposure to suicide through either family history or social influence; (4) cultural or social beliefs—the notion that suicide is an acceptable or noble resolution to a personal dilemma or dishonorable situation; (5) environmental barriers—an unwillingness or inability to seek help paired with the accessibility of lethal weapons; and (6) demographic factors—teens, LGBTQ populations, Native Americans, the elderly and, as a discrete group, individuals who compile a list of aggregate potential factors inclusive of being single, male, socially isolated, and living alone are at greater risk than other groups.[5]

Logan's risk factors for suicide dovetail all too well with those broadly outlined above. His current mental state is one of futility, given his deteriorating health and lack of purpose. He does not talk about his problems—not even to Caliban. He has been consumed by the stress of caring for a chronically ill Charles Xavier, to whom he feels as emotionally attached as anyone on the planet. And, worse, Logan has not only motive and opportunity but also the wherewithal: gun at the ready, adamantium bullet in hand, and samurai sword on the wall.

Logan has always prided himself on his ability to shield from harm the precious few others about whom he cares—and now he can't even do that effectively. Recently he was unable to save his fellow X-Men (the only family he has ever known) and can now barely provide the medicines that Charles desperately needs. In short, Wolverine is not only losing his friends; he is also losing his identity.

Compounded, these factors make Logan a high risk for suicide. Logan's only protective factor is his commitment to care for and defend Charles, and once Charles dies even that overtaxed stopgap measure will be breached.

Logan has grown tired of running. He wants the unrelenting curse of immortality to end. In the words of clinician Joel Terry, "Logan's never had a lot of control over his life. He has been stripped of his family, his memories and, on some level, his humanity. But now he has lost everyone that ever meant anything to him. The only thing left within his power is the ability to take his own life."[6]

But just as the curtain seems to be dropping on Logan's final act, his risk factors all but disappear with the appearance of Laura—a young girl with deadly adamantium claws of her own.

Laura (X-23)

Laura is based on the comic book character Laura Kinney (a.k.a. X-23), the clone daughter of Logan who was raised within the laboratories of Transigen—a scientific project with the aim of creating living weapons out of mutants. As such, she epitomizes the definitions of "lab rat" and "living weapon" to an even greater degree than Logan.

The movie *Logan* exposes the viewer to perhaps the most unpredictable and uncontrollable superheroine ever. Director James Mangold states regarding Laura, "She's an 11-year-old girl equipped with all the volatility, instability, mood swings, shadows, and potential violence of our hero."[7]

Laura is an almost perfect reflection of Wolverine's power, agility, and unchecked temper. She is cunning, ferocious, merciless, and, like Logan, capable of eviscerating anyone who stands between her and her goal. A humorous moment in the film that illustrates Laura's temperament occurs when, during an argument, she punches Logan in the face. Laura is certainly her father's daughter.

Laura seeks Logan's help in escaping capture by the Reavers, mercenary killers vowing to return her to Transigen Laboratories. She convinces Logan and Charles to head to North Dakota, to what many consider a mythical location called "Eden," a refuge for the young mutants. What ensues during that quest are likely the most violent, head-to-head battles seen in the *X-Men* film series, the script assuaging the depicted barbarism with an attestation to the power of love.

Depressive Realism

Charles Xavier, ever the mutant beacon of hopefulness in a hazardous world, never ceases to believe in Wolverine's humanity. Charles endeavors to inspire Logan to plant roots, to create a family with Laura. Charles tells Logan, "This is what life looks like—people who love each other. A home. You should take a moment. Feel it. Logan, you still have time."[8]

Charles wants Logan to accept Laura as his daughter; however, Logan is disheartened with life and has become deeply embittered by humankind. Additionally, he fears emotional closeness—whenever he gets close to someone, he loses them to a violent death. Therefore, he has no intention of forming any more relationships.

The sense of contentedness that Charles tries to instill in Logan is short-lived when Charles recalls a heartbreaking truth—his own brilliant mind betrayed him and led to the torture and death of mutantkind. "I did something ... something unspeakable," he says. "I remembered what happened in Westchester. This is not the first time that I've hurt people. Until today, I didn't know. You didn't tell me, so we kept on running away from it. I think.... I finally understand you."[9]

Charles, at long last, grasps the abysmal depths of Logan's inner torment. Logan is a loner and a drifter, yes, but not so much by nature as out of a conscious need for emotional self-preservation. Charles and Wolverine are now connected in their devastation at having killed the very people they swore to protect. However, despite losing everything, Wolverine's sense of loyalty remains intact. The quintessential mutant drifter, Logan could have easily abandoned Charles, but, even in the face of grave personal, emotional, and physical peril, he stays to care for his mentor.

Depressive realism is a theory developed by Lauren Alloy and Lyn

Yvonne Abramson, which states that depressed individuals may have a more accurate perception of reality than non-depressed individuals. Although people suffering from depression are believed to have a negative cognitive bias that results in recurrent and dysfunctional worldviews, depressive realism argues that this negativity may in fact reflect a more accurate appraisal of the world. In Logan's case, he knows all too well that anyone he cares for dies by his own hands, at his will, or through the actions of those in power who oppress mutants.

Logan has, at times, bought into the conciliatory and mutually beneficial ideological beliefs of Charles Xavier, but now he realizes that the zero-sum truth behind Magneto's prophecy has proven to be unwaveringly accurate—the government continues to persecute mutants well into the future, even going so far as experimenting on children.

Emphasizing the point of minority subjugation, when casting Laura, James Mangold insisted on finding a Hispanic actress to play the part in order to use the film's mutant struggle to mirror the real-life struggle of Hispanics affected by U.S. political attempts to build a wall along the Mexican/U.S. border. In a *Rolling Stone* interview, Mangold shared his perspective on Trump-era moments and ideas from the film:

> As we were working on how these [mutant] children were being developed, the idea that it could happen south of the border seemed really realistic to how nasty things like that happen in our world. And the idea of Laura being Hispanic was really interesting for both the obvious reasons—again, of reflecting our world and the sense of otherness that we apply to people—but also because I was very conscious that I didn't want to get into this kind of cloy father-daughter cutesy banter between Logan and Laura [played by Daphne Keen].[10]

Logan has grown tired of fighting oppression, fighting his enemies, and fighting himself. He has given up on humanity—and, worse, on his own ability to make any headway against the unthinking xenophobic enemies by whom he is so gravely outnumbered. Logan's fear of connection is demonstrated through his rejection of Laura. "I am not whatever it is you think I am," he tells her. And yet Laura vies for Logan's affection, as she desperately wants a family.

Humanity Discovered

Flash forward to the Reavers catching up with the mutant children as they strive to reach Eden. Logan chases after them in the desperation of a father fighting to save his child. It is at this moment that Logan becomes a parent. He will walk through walls, face machine-gun fire, and accept certain death in any form if doing so will spare his daughter. Logan does not hesitate to sacrifice himself in order to give her a chance to have a life he's never known—a life free from persecution.

In a last-ditch attempt to defeat Wolverine and to halt the children's advance toward the Canadian border and freedom, Donald Pierce, leader of the Reavers, unleashes a new and improved Wolverine clone, X-24—one possessing all of Logan's mutant strengths and none of his humanity.

No one expected that Logan would be fighting a younger version of himself in his final battle in the X-Men universe. In many ways, however, Wolverine contesting the embodiment of his younger, more unprincipled and belligerent self is the ultimate expression of conquering what remains of his bestial nature. Metaphorically, Logan fights his old demons—the part of himself that existed before he gained a sense of morality and duty.

The mutant clone X-24 barbarically impales Logan on a tree branch before Laura is able to kill him with Logan's one remaining adamantium bullet. Fatally wounded and gasping for breath, Logan tells Laura, "Don't become what they wanted you to be." His last message to her is clear—he instructs Laura to avoid at all costs the life sentence he served.

Holding Logan's hand, and with tears in her eyes, Laura refers to Logan as "Daddy." He smiles and proclaims, "So this is what it feels like," breathes his last and dies.

Wolverine's death, as demonstrated through the vision of James Mangold, reminds the movie audience of the poignant prediction by Yukio in 2013's *The Wolverine*: "I see you on your back, there's blood everywhere. You're holding your own heart in your hand."[11] In the film, Logan dies on his back holding his metaphorical "heart"—the hand of his daughter.

Psychologist Viktor Frankl teaches us, "In accepting this challenge to suffer bravely, life has a meaning up to the last moment, and it retains this meaning literally to the end."[12] Logan has learned that value lies not in one's evaluation of oneself in one's own mirror but in the reflections of oneself in others. Here Logan's long-sought humanity surfaces. He chooses self-sacrifice in order to spare others his fate, finding his life's purpose through his ultimate sacrifice. In his last moments, Logan has embraced the advice given him by Charles—he accepts the joy and heartbreak of life through his acceptance of Laura and, in so doing, embraces his true purpose.

His tragic story has come to an end. At long last, Wolverine has found peace.

The children safely cross the Canadian border shortly after they bury

Logan's body. Before leaving his grave, Laura tips the marker from being an upright cross to an "X" in honor her father's identity as the last X-Man.

All human drama is, to a great extent, a story of how well we have lived and what it is of ourselves and our morality that we bring to the rim of the grave. Throughout his life, Logan was the defender and avenger of those in need. His last act on earth was embracing his role as a father and the preserver of his daughter's life. And now Logan's legacy will live on through Laura, as she represents not only Xavier's communicated beliefs in a brighter future forged in mutual benefit, negotiation, compromise, and sacrifice but also Logan's depth of commitment to those goals.

Epilogue

Wolverine.

James Howlett by birth, Logan to his friends, Wolverine to the X-Men, Patch and Weapon X to his enemies. This character—conceptualized by Roy Thomas, created by Len Wein, designed by John Romita, Sr., first drawn for publication by Herb Trimpe, and brought to life by actor Hugh Jackman—has come a long way since first marking his territory as an unknown and unheralded Canadian superhero.

Initially the product of creative resourcefulness, and ever propelled by a desire to outstrip the established restraints of the genre, *Marvel Comics* in 1974 rolled out a new breed of superhero—an antihero, if you will: a wounded loner, a restless nomad, a flawed renegade plagued by recurring bouts of rage and forgetfulness. In so doing, Wolverine's malevolently smoldering personality, coupled with his maniacal killing tendencies, bent the established archetype of "superhero" into a previously unexplored and far more relevant character.

Originally the unwelcome residential badass of Charles Xavier's mutant crew, Logan was neither designed nor destined to be some kind of rusted redeemer. Yes, Logan was all along acknowledged to be a beast, but he was *your* beast: the damaged-goods mutant you relied upon to do the necessary (if unthinkable) bloodbath jobs no one else dared.

But what are the necessary aspects of a personality that creates such a soldier, such an antihero so ironically necessary to preserve the functioning framework of an orderly, if inconsistently humane, world? This was the question posed at the outset of this book and explored in each chapter through careful analysis of the life and struggles of Marvel's most internally conflicted character.

Wolverine is neither the most consciously alive character Marvel has ever created nor the most deranged and conflicted. He's simply the one best able to balance the unbalanced contradictions of life.

Rejected by society and burdened with the inability to piece together elements of his own history, Wolverine did "what he did best," pretty though it wasn't. Yet all the while he transcended the animal within and, in the process, sought answers to life's most complex questions.

For this reason, many Wolverine fans do not consider him a mere comic book hero. Wolverine is "real" in the sense that he anthropomorphizes all-too-real inner human conflicts. His struggles, faults, failures, and aspirations smack of our own, and his complexities and conflicts make him—and us—human. As such, the mythological tales of Wolverine empower us, inspire us, *compel* us to look *more* deeply into *ourselves* in search of the resolve to endure, to persevere, to get up again, to live that next painful first day of the rest of our lives, daunting prospects be damned.

Wolverine reminds us that Barry Goldwater had a point when, in his acceptance speech as the 1964 Republican presidential candidate, he said, "I would remind you that extremism in the defense of liberty is no vice! And let me remind you also that moderation in the pursuit of justice is no virtue." Wolverine indicates to us that scars incurred in the furious pursuit of dignity are less disfigurations and more acceptable collateral damage because humans are fallible and systems are corruptible.

Logan's bouts of unhinged savagery mirror our own righteously enraged psyches as we absorb the injustice and prejudice around us. And, just as with Logan, that adrenaline-infused rage girds us to resist that which we can no longer tolerate or ignore, to battle for what we believe to be right, and, as a result, to weave the cloth of who we really are and of which we are made.

But perseverance in pursuit of legitimacy is hardly the only lesson to be derived from Wolverine's saga. Aside from the above points, there is much more in the mythology of Wolverine to inform our lives.

1. **Embrace diversity**—Wolverine was a mutant and thus personified what it means to be "different." Yet, in the disparagement he received, he relished his distinctiveness. He staunchly remained true to this calling, to his own self, on his *own* terms. He refused to be defined by others—*any* others, mutant or not.

   Wolverine and the X-Men tales teach us that right behind awareness as a first step toward unification is understanding. Under the tutelage of Charles Xavier and other mentors, in time

Wolverine sought his rightful place in a world unaccepting of his like. Never forgetting his values, he sought to understand his oppressors in an effort to form a more tolerant and accepting society of inclusion and respect.

2. **Learn and evolve**—The scientists of the Weapon X program tortured and brainwashed Wolverine with the purpose of eradicating his humanity. They wanted him to fully succumb to his feral nature—to be the "animal" *they* saw him as being meant to be.

   But Wolverine knew he was much more than that. He defined himself through his choices. His relative immortality allowed him to search the world for mentors. He embraced alternate cultures, learned different languages, and immersed himself in Bushido, which provided him with an unflinching sense of discipline and honor.

   Wolverine accepted his imperfections but moved to consistently observe and evolve. He learned from his mistakes (even if challenged to remember them) and strove to improve, to rise above his beginnings and into the powerful mutant he was meant to become.

3. **Life is not a destination but a journey**—Ranked as one of the 10 greatest physicists of all time, Dr. Richard Feynman has said, "I would rather have questions that can't be answered than answers that can't be questioned." As powerful as that statement was when first uttered, it is all the more poignant and powerful in tumultuous political environments.

   Wolverine's mind was fragmented after years of enduring countless traumatic events. Therefore, he was far less able to acquire a sense of purpose from an evaluation of past experiences, instead seeking insight from the split-second decisions he made in the present moment.

   Nevertheless, Logan was relentless in pursuing information about his past and in his search for his life purpose. He didn't have the answers to his questions, but he did question what he was told were the answers. And in that questioning, he gave what he found in himself as an answer: he gave of himself.

4. **We must impart our knowledge**—Logan, in his last moments of life, remained dedicated to his vow to protect others. As he lay dying, the best that he could do (now that he couldn't fight anymore) was to pass his knowledge on to his daughter Laura.

In his darkest moment, he was able to elevate Laura to a higher place even when he could no longer get there himself. He instilled within her the belief that, regardless of circumstance or whatever crushing obstacles she might endure, she alone would determine her destiny. "Don't be what they made you," he told her. Logan wanted Laura to become her own kind of hero.

A hero is an ordinary person who discovers within themselves the courage and fortitude to suffer defeats and nevertheless persevere. After all, it is often an extraordinarily challenging situation that provides us with the chance to develop beyond our expectations of our own capacities and, at times, in spite of ourselves.

5. **It is not that we die; it is how we live**—Mohandas Gandhi often gets credit for this saying, but it was not he who said it; it was Wilhem Stekel. Nonetheless, both would have loved the Wolverine saga.

    Stekel is also credited with saying, "The mark of the immature man is that he wants to die nobly for a cause, while the mark of the mature man is that he wants to live humbly for one."

    Although he was not in the slightest humble, no matter how many times Logan's spirit was fractured, he pressed on. Similarly, we need to believe that no matter what kind of challenges we face, or what kind of trauma we endure, there is hope for us—both singular and plural.

6. **What goes around**—As it turns out, even the formerly deceased Wolverine gets another chance in *Marvel Legacy #1*, written in 2017 by Jason Aaron, illustrated by Esad Ribic and Steve McNiven, and inked by Matthew Wilson. After three years of Wolverine-free existence in Marvel-topia, Logan, now in possession of an Infinity Stone, returns from the dead—claws unsheathed, physically rejuvenated, and as surly as ever—to fight another day. Not even death could hold this mutant down forever.

    While it's unclear what Logan's return means to his daughter Laura, the X-Men, and his millions of fans the world over, one thing is clear: he is *still* "the best he is at what he does."

After surviving a battle, we leave with a sense of grace, of accomplishment (if only because we survived), of knowing that because of this experience, however painful, we are forever changed (and perhaps a bit stronger than before). We may be defeated many times more in our lives, but not today! And, just like Logan, we may bend, but we are not broken.

Relentless. Indestructible. Unyielding. "Adamantium," the metal that makes up Wolverine's skeleton, is derived from the Greek word *adamas* or *adamantos*, meaning "untamable." Thus, Logan's skeletal structure—or, more to the point, his disposition, his essence, his life force—is *untamed*.

We wouldn't have it any other way.

Chapter Notes

Chapter One

1. Interview with Paul Jenkins (2016).
2. Interview with Roy Thomas (2017).
3. Interview with Len Wein (2017).
4. Interview with John Romita, Sr. (2017).
5. Interview with Elliott Serrano (2016).
6. M.K. Manning (2009), *Wolverine: Inside the World of the Living Weapon* (London, UK: Dorling Kindersley), p. 124.
7. J. Aaron (2010), *Wolverine: Road to Hell*, Vol. 1, #1 (New York, NY: Marvel Publishing).
8. Interview with John Romita, Jr. (2016).
9. Raven Software (2005, September), *X-Men Legends II: Rise of Apocalypse* [Video Game].
10. B. Singer (Director) (2000), *X-Men* [Motion Picture] (United States: Twentieth Century–Fox).
11. Manning (2009), *Wolverine: Inside the World of the Living Weapon*, p. 35.
12. L. Hamma (1996), "Fade to Black," *Wolverine*, Vol. 2, #98 [Graphic Novel] (New York, NY: Marvel Publishing).
13. Interview with Tom DeFalco (2017).
14. Manning (2009), *Wolverine: Inside the World of the Living Weapon*, p. 33.

Chapter Two

1. P. Jenkins & B. Jemas (2009), *Wolverine: Origin*, Vols. 1–6 [Graphic Novel] (New York, NY: Marvel Publishing).
2. Interview with Paul Jenkins (2016).
3. Jenkins & Jemas (2009), *Wolverine: Origin*.
4. http://taboo.news/most-common-human-genetic-mutations-and-disorders/.
5. Interview with Eric Snyder (2017).
6. R. S. Rosenberg (2013, August 6), "The Psychology of Wolverine," *Psychology Today*, retrieved from https://www.psychologytoday.com/blog/the-super heroes/201308/the-psychology-wolverine.
7. D. Howe (2011), *Attachment Across the Lifecourse* (Basingstoke, UK: Palgrave Macmillan), p. 13.
8. R. Kobak & S. Madsen (2008), "Disruption in Attachment Bonds," in J. Cassidy and P.R. Shaver (Eds.), *Handbook of Attachment: Theory, Research and Clinical Applications* (New York, NY: Guilford Press), pp. 23–47.
9. P. Crittenden (1999), "Danger and Development: The Organisation of Self-Protective Strategies," in J.I. Vondra & D. Barnett (Eds.), *Atypical Attachment in Infancy and Early Childhood Among Children at Developmental Risk* (Malden, MA: Society for Research in Child Development), pp. 145–171.
10. C. Murray Parkes (2006), *Love and Loss* (London, UK, and New York, NY: Routledge), p. 13.
11. A. Miller & R. Ward (1979), *The Drama of the Gifted Child* (New York, NY: Basic Books).
12. E. Kübler-Ross & D. Kessler (2007), *On Grief and Grieving: Finding the Meaning of Grief Through the Five Stages of Loss* (Reprint ed.) (New York, NY: Scribner).

13. Jenkins & Jemas (2009), *Wolverine: Origin*.

14. Jenkins & Jemas (2009), *Wolverine: Origin*.

Chapter Three

1. B. Innes (2016), *The History of Torture* (Rev. Upd. ed.) (London, UK: Amber Books).

2. J.P. Wilson, Z. Harel, & B. Kahana (1988), *Human Adaptation to Extreme Stress: From the Holocaust to Vietnam* (New York, NY: Plenum Press).

3. B. Windsor-Smith (1993), *Marvel Comics Presents Weapon X* #72–84 [Graphic Novel] (New York, NY: Marvel Publishing).

4. M. Nussbaum (1995, Autumn), "Objectification," *Philosophy and Public Affairs*, 24(4), 249–291.

5. Center for Sex Offender Management (n.d.), "Section 1: Lecture Content & Teaching Notes—Supervision of Sex Offenders in the Community: An Overview," retrieved May 25, 2008, from http://www.csom.org/train/supervision/medium/01_02_04.html.

6. Windsor-Smith (1993), *Weapon X*.

7. J.P. Sartre (1958), "Preface," in H. Alleg, *The Question* (J. Calder, Trans.) (London, UK: John Calder).

8. S. Milgram (1974), *Obedience to Authority: An Experimental View* (New York, NY: HarperCollins).

9. S.A. McLeod (2007), "The Milgram Experiment," retrieved from www.simplypsychology.org/milgram.html.

10. Milgram (1974), *Obedience to Authority*.

11. E.A. Caspar, J.F. Christensen, A. Cleeremans, & P. Haggard (2016), "Coercion Changes the Sense of Agency in the Human Brain," *Current Biology*, 26(5), 585–592.

12. C.G. Jung (1938), "Psychology and Religion," in *The Collected Works of C.G. Jung* (Vol. 11: *Psychology and Religion: West and East*) (London, UK: Routledge), p. 131.

13. C.G. Jung (1952), "Answer to Job," in *The Collected Works of C.G. Jung* (Vol. 11: *Psychology and Religion: West and East*) (London, UK: Routledge), p. 12.

14. Windsor-Smith (1993), *Weapon X*.
15. Windsor-Smith (1993), *Weapon X*.
16. Windsor-Smith (1993), *Weapon X*.

Chapter Four

1. L.A. Pearlman & K.W. Saakvitne (1995) *Trauma and the Therapist: Countertransference and Vicarious Traumatization in Psychotherapy with Incest Survivors* (New York, NY: Norton).

2. American Psychiatric Association (2013), *Diagnostic and Statistical Manual of Mental Disorders* (5th ed.) (Washington, D.C.: American Psychiatric Publishing).

3. S. Landa & R. Duschinsky (2013), "Crittenden's Dynamic-Maturational Model of Attachment and Adaptation," *Review of General Psychology*, 17(3), 326.

4. M.E. Seligman (1975), *Helplessness: On Depression, Development, and Death* (New York, NY: Freeman).

5. M. Seligman (1972), "Learned Helplessness," *Annual Review of Medicine*, 23(1), 407–412.

6. Seligman (1975), *Helplessness*.

7. P. Jenkins & B. Jemas (2009), *Wolverine: Origin*, Vols. 1–6 [Graphic Novel] (New York, NY: Marvel Publishing).

8. D.G. Kilpatrick, L.J. Vernon, & C.L. Best (1985), "Factors Predicting Psychological Distress in Rape Victims," in C.R. Figley (Ed.), *Trauma and Its Wake* (New York, NY: Brunner/Mazel).

9. Interview with Ed Ottesen (2017).

10. Interview with Larry Yarbrough (2017).

11. I.L. Janis (1982), "Decision Making Under Stress," in L. Goldberger & S. Breznitz (Eds.), *Handbook of Stress: Theoretical and Clinical Aspects* (New York, NY: Free Press), pp. 69–87.

12. Interview with Gerald Newport (2017).

13. Interview with Joseph de la Rosa (2017).

14. L.C. Kolb (1987), "Neurophysiological Hypothesis Explaining Posttraumatic Stress Disorder," *American Journal of Psychiatry*, 144, 989–995.

15. Interview with Gerald Newport (2017).

16. Interview with Joe Garcia (2017).

17. B.A. Van der Kolk & C.P. Ducey (1989), "The Psychological Processing of Traumatic Experience: Rorschach Patterns in PTSD," *Journal of Traumatic Stress*, 2(3), 259–274.

18. B.A. Van der Kolk & M.S. Greenberg (1987), "The Psychobiology of the Trauma Response: Hyperarousal, Constriction, and Addiction to Traumatic Reexposure," in B.A. Van der Kolk (Ed.), *Psychological Trauma* (Washington, D.C.: American Psychiatric Press), pp. 66–88.

19. Interview with Roumen Bezergianov (2017).

20. P. Jenkins & C. Castellini (2004), *Wolverine: The End*, Vols. 1–6 [Graphic Novel] (New York, NY: Marvel Publishing).

21. V. Frankl (1997), *Man's Search for Meaning* (London, UK: Pocket Books).

22. B.M. Bendis (2005), *House of M*, Vol. 8 [Graphic Novel] (New York, NY: Marvel Publishing).

23. Interview with Lisa Gaudet (2017).

Chapter Five

1. J.J. Macionis & L. Gerber (2010), *Sociology* (7th Canadian ed.) (Toronto: Pearson Canada).

2. F. Vitaro, M. Brendgen, & E.D. Barker (2006), "Subtypes of Aggressive Behaviors: A Developmental Perspective," *International Journal of Behavioral Development*, 30, 12–19.

3. D.M. Buss & J.D. Duntley (2006), "The Evolution of Aggression," in M. Schaller, J.A. Simpson, & D.T. Kenrick (Eds.), *Evolution and Social Learning* (New York, NY: Psychology Press).

4. D.M. Buss & J.D. Duntley (2006). "The Evolution of Aggression." In M. Schaller, J.A. Simpson, & D.T. Kenrick (Eds.) *Evolution and Social Learning*. New York: Psychology Press.

5. J.D. Duntley (2005), "Adaptations to Dangers from Humans," in D.M. Buss (Ed.), *The Handbook of Evolutionary Psychology* (Hoboken, NJ: John Wiley & Sons), pp. 224–254.

6. "Wolverine's 18 Greatest Enemies in Comic History" (2016), *ScreenRant*, retrieved from https://screenrant.com/wolverine-greatest-enemies/.

7. M. Daley & M. Wilson (1988), "Evolutionary Social Psychology and Family Homicide," *Science*, 242, 519–524.

8. T. DeFalco (2003), *Hulk: The Incredible Guide* (London, UK: Dorling Kindersley), p. 200.

9. DeFalco (2003), *Hulk*.

10. Interview with Patricia Trimpe (2016).

11. G. Hood (Director) (2009), *X-Men Origins: Wolverine* [Motion Picture] (United States: Twentieth Century–Fox).

12. Interview with Vijay Jain (2016).

13. J. Tiihonen, M-R. Rautiainen, H.M. Ollila, E. Repo-Tiihonen, M. Virkkunen, A. Palotie, O. Pietiläinen, K. Kristiansson, M. Joukamaa, H. Lauerma, J. Saarela, S. Tyni, H. Vartiainen, J. Paananen, D. Goldman, & T. Paunio (2015), "Genetic Background of Extreme Violent Behavior," *Molecular Psychiatry*, 20, 786–792.

14. T.M. Moore, A. Scarpa, & A. Raine (2002), "A Meta-Analysis of Serotonin Metabolite 5-HIAA and Antisocial Behavior," *Aggressive Behavior*, 28(4), 299–316.

15. "Antisocial Personality Disorder" (2013), Mayo Foundation for Medical Education and Research, retrieved from https://www.mayoclinic.org/diseases-conditions/antisocial-personality-disorder/symptoms-causes/syc-20353928.

16. J. McCaine (2016), "Ties That Bind: Understanding Intimate Partner Violence," Workshop Presentation.

17. McCaine (2016), "Ties that Bind."

18. American Psychiatric Association (2013), *Diagnostic and Statistical Manual of Mental Disorders* (5th ed.) (Washington, D.C.: American Psychiatric Publishing).

19. C. Claremont & J. Byrne (2012), *The Uncanny X-Men: The Dark Phoenix Saga* #129–138 [Graphic Novel] (New York, NY: Marvel Publishing).

20. American Psychiatric Association (2013), *Diagnostic and Statistical Manual of Mental Disorders*.

21. M. Gruenwald (1993), *Captain America*, Vol. 1, #419 [Graphic Novel] (New York, NY: Marvel Publishing).

22. C. Claremont (1998), *Wolverine*, Vol. 2, #125 [Graphic Novel] (New York, NY: Marvel Publishing).

23. M.K. Manning (2009), *Wolverine:*

Inside the World of the Living Weapon (London, UK: Dorling Kindersley), p. 44.

24. American Psychiatric Association (2013), *Diagnostic and Statistical Manual of Mental Disorders*.

25. J. Loeb, S. Bianchi, M. Morales, & A. Deschesne (2013), *Wolverine: Sabretooth Reborn* #310–313 [Graphic Novel] (New York, NY: Marvel Publishing).

Chapter Six

1. "Nazi Germany 1933–1939: Early Stages of Persecution; How Hitler Laid the Groundwork for Genocide" (2012), *My Jewish Learning*, retrieved from https://www.myjewishlearning.com/article/1933–1939-early-stages-of-persecution/.

2. Interview with Joe Rubinstein (2016).

3. C. Claremont (1982), *X-Men: God Loves, Man Kills* [Graphic Novel] (New York, NY: Marvel Publishing).

4. B. Ratner (Director) (2006), *X-Men: The Last Stand* [Motion Picture] (United States: Twentieth Century–Fox).

5. J.J. Darowski (2014), *X-Men and the Mutant Metaphor: Race and Gender in the Comic Book* (Lanham, MD: Rowman & Littlefield).

6. B. Singer (Director) (2003), *X2* [Motion Picture] (United States: Twentieth Century–Fox).

7. Editorial Board (2016, June 15), "The Corrosive Politics That Threaten L.G.B.T. Americans," *New York Times*, retrieved from https://www.nytimes.com/2016/06/15/opinion/the-corrosive-politics-that-threaten-lgbt-americans.html.

8. P. Jonsson (2011), "Annual Report Cites Rise in Hate Groups, But Some Ask: What Is Hate?" *Christian Science Monitor*, retrieved June 29, 2015, from https://www.csmonitor.com/USA/Society/2011/0223/Annual-report-cites-rise-in-hate-groups-but-some-ask-What-is-hate.

9. "Hate Map" (n.d.), Southern Poverty Law Center, retrieved December 7, 2015, from https://www.splcenter.org/hate-map.

10. Interview with Jon McCaine (2017).

11. S. Humphries (2013), *Avengers A.I.* #2 [Graphic Novel] (New York, NY: Marvel Publishing).

12. M. Vaughn (Director) (2011), *X-Men: First Class* [Motion Picture] (United States: Twentieth Century–Fox).

13. F. Nicieza & S. Lobdell (1993), *X-Men: Fatal Attractions* [Graphic Novel] (New York, NY: Marvel Publishing).

14. Interview with Max Stoltenberg (2017).

15. J. Aaron (2014), *Amazing X-Men #4* [Graphic Novel] (New York, NY: Marvel Publishing).

16. R. Lamble (2014, February 25), "Hugh Jackman Interview: X-Men: Days of Future Past and Playing Wolverine," *Den of Geek!*, retrieved from http://www.denofgeek.com/us/movies/hugh-jackman/233301/hugh-jackman-interview-x-men-days-of-future-past-and-playing-wolverine.

17. D. Fingeroth (2004), *Superman on the Couch: What Superheroes Really Tell Us About Ourselves and Society* (New York, NY: Continuum).

18. "Maslow's Hierarchy of Needs" (2012, June 16), *Research History*, retrieved from www.researchhistory.org/2012/06/16/maslows-hierarchy-of-needs/.

19. A.H. Maslow (1943), "A Theory of Human Motivation," *Psychological Review*, 50(4), 370–396.

20. C. Claremont (2008), *X-Men: Kitty Pryde & Wolverine* [Graphic Novel] (New York, NY: Marvel Publishing).

21. Singer (2003), *X2*.

22. A. Lorde (1983), "The Master's Tools Will Never Dismantle the Master's House," in C. Moraga & G. Anzaldúa (Eds.), *This Bridge Called My Back: Writing by Radical Women of Color* (New York: Kitchen Table Press), pp. 94–101.

23. G. Orwell (1945), *Animal Farm* (London, UK: Secker and Warburg).

24. C.M. Blow (2016, July 8), "A Week in Hell," *New York Times*.

Chapter Seven

1. Interview with Tehrina Billi (2017).

2. C. Claremont (1998), *Wolverine*, Vol. 2, #126 [Graphic Novel] (New York, NY: Marvel Publishing).

3. G. Morrison (2003), *New X-Men*, Vol. 1, #148 [Graphic Novel] (New York, NY: Marvel Publishing).

4. D.G. Myers (2009), *Social Psychol-*

ogy (10th ed.) (New York, NY: McGraw-Hill Higher Education).

5. G. Karlson (2010), *Psychoanalysis in a New Light* (Cambridge, UK: Cambridge University Press), p. 147.

6. D. Lassri & G. Shahar (2012), "Self-Criticism Mediates the Link Between Childhood Emotional Maltreatment and Young Adults' Romantic Relationships," *Journal of Social & Clinical Psychology, 31*(3), 289–311.

7. D. Levy (1937), "Primary Affect Hunger," *American Journal of Psychiatry, 94*, 643–652.

8. Interview with Adam Kubert (2017).

9. J. Mangold (Director) (2013), *The Wolverine* [Motion Picture] (United States: Twentieth Century–Fox).

10. Mangold (2013), *The Wolverine.*

11. C. Claremont (1982), *Wolverine #1–4* [Graphic Novel] (New York, NY: Marvel Publishing).

12. Claremont (1982), *Wolverine #1–4.*

13. Claremont (1982), *Wolverine #1–4.*

14. Claremont (1982), *Wolverine #1–4.*

15. R.J. Sternberg (2007), "Triangulating Love," in T.J. Oord (Ed.), *The Altruism Reader: Selections from Writings on Love, Religion, and Science* (West Conshohocken, PA: Templeton Foundation), p. 332.

16. B. Singer (Director) (2003), *X2* [Motion Picture] (United States: Twentieth Century–Fox).

17. R.J. Sternberg (2004), "A Triangular Theory of Love," in H.T. Reis & C.E. Rusbult (Eds.), *Close Relationships* (New York, NY: Psychology Press), p. 258.

18. H.E. Fisher, A. Aron, D.M. Mashek, H. Li, & L.L. Brown (2002), "Defining the Brain Systems of Lust, Romantic Attraction, and Attachment," *Archives of Sexual Behavior, 31*(5), 413–419.

19. L.M. Diamond (2003), "What Does Sexual Orientation Orient? A Biobehavioral Model Distinguishing Romantic Love and Sexual Desire," *Psychology Review, 110*(1), 173–192.

20. C. Claremont (1984), *Uncanny X-Men*, Vol. 1, #183 [Graphic Novel] (New York, NY: Marvel Publishing).

21. Claremont (1984), *Uncanny X-Men* #183.

22. Mangold (2013), *The Wolverine.*

23. Claremont (1982), *Wolverine #1–4.*

24. V. Frankl (1997), *Man's Search for Meaning* (London, UK: Pocket Books).

Chapter Eight

1. B. Singer (Director) (2016), *X-Men: Apocalypse* [Motion Picture] (United States: Twentieth Century–Fox).

2. D.P. Schultz & S.E. Schultz (2016), *Theories of Personality* (11th ed.) (Melbourne, VIC: Wadsworth).

3. Interview with Max Stoltenberg (2017).

4. B. Singer (Director) (2003), *X2* [Motion Picture] (United States: Twentieth Century–Fox).

5. L. Maslon & M. Kantor (2013), *Superheroes! Capes, Cowls, and the Creation of the Comic Book Culture* (New York, NY: Crown Archetype).

6. Maslon & Kantor (2013), *Superheroes!*

7. R.W. Stedman (1977), *Serials: Suspense and Drama by Installment* (Norman, OK: University of Oklahoma Press), p. 154.

8. Maslon & Kantor (2013), *Superheroes!*

9. Maslon & Kantor (2013), *Superheroes!*

10. J. Campbell (1949), *The Hero with a Thousand Faces* (Princeton, NJ: Princeton University Press), p. 23.

11. Interview with Clive Hazell (2017).

12. G. Hood (Director) (2009), *X-Men Origins: Wolverine* [Motion Picture] (United States: Twentieth Century–Fox).

13. Interview with Clive Hazell (2017).

14. J. Patočka (1988), "Europa und Nach-Europa," in K. Nellen & J. Nemec (Eds.), *Ketzerische Essais zur Philosophie der Geschichte und ergänzende Schriften* (Stuttgart, BD: Klett-Cotta), p. 207–287.

15. Interview with Clive Hazell (2017).

16. P.K. Jonason, G.D. Webster, D.P. Schmitt, N.P. Li, & L. Crysel (2012), "The Antihero in Popular Culture: Life History Theory and the Dark Triad Personality Traits," *Review of General Psychology, 16*(2), 192–199.

17. M.K. Booker (Ed.) (2010), *Encyclopedia of Comic Books and Graphic Novels*, Vol. 2 (Santa Barbara, CA: Greenwood Press), pp. 583–585.

18. Interview with Doug Kline (2017).

19. Maslon & Kantor (2013), *Superheroes!*

20. "Native American Wolverine Mythology" (2015), http://www.native-languages.org/legends-wolverine.htm.

21. Interview with David Spurlock (2017).

22. "Wally Wood Jungle Adventures with Jim King & Animan Deluxe HC" (n.d.), Forbidden Planet International, retrieved from http://www.forbiddenplanet.co.uk/wally-wood-jungle-adventures-with-jim-king-animan-deluxe-hc.

23. W. Wood (2016), *Wally Wood Jungle Adventures—Animan* (D. Spurlock, Ed.) (Lakewood, NJ: Vanguard).

24. C. Claremont (1982), *Wolverine* #1 [Graphic Novel] (New York, NY: Marvel Publishing).

25. M. Millar, S. McNiven, & D. Vines (2008), *Old Man Logan* [Graphic Novel] (New York, NY: Marvel Publishing).

26. Millar, McNiven, & Vines (2008), *Old Man Logan.*

27. Millar, McNiven, & Vines (2008), *Old Man Logan.*

Chapter Nine

1. Interview with Chandler Rice (2017).

2. C. Soule & S. McNiven (2014), *Death of Wolverine*, Vol. 1 [Graphic Novel] (New York, NY: Marvel Publishing).

3. Soule & McNiven (2014), *Death of Wolverine.*

4. Interview with John Romita, Jr. (2016).

5. Recognizing and Responding to Suicide Risk: Essential Skills for Clinicians (2008), American Association of Suicidology.

6. Interview with Joel Terry (2017).

7. R. Fletcher (2017, January 19), "Exclusive: Logan Director James Mangold Gives Us a Scene-by-Scene Breakdown of His Explosive New Trailer" [Video File], *Digital Spy*, retrieved from http://www.digitalspy.com/movies/wolverine/feature/a819368/logan-director-james-mangold-breaks-down-violent-new-trailer-wolverine-x-men-movie/.

8. J. Mangold (Director) (2017), *Logan* [Motion Picture] (United States: Twentieth Century–Fox).

9. Mangold (2017), *Logan.*

10. B. Hiatt (2017), "How 'Logan' Director James Mangold Made the Most Violent Wolverine Movie Yet," *Rolling Stone*, retrieved March 2, 2017, from https://www.rollingstone.com/movies/features/logan-director-on-making-a-wolverine-movie-for-the-fans-w469808.

11. J. Mangold (Director) (2013), *The Wolverine* [Motion Picture] (United States: Twentieth Century–Fox).

12. V. Frankl (1997), *Man's Search for Meaning* (London, UK: Pocket Books).

Bibliography

Aaron, J. (2010). *Wolverine: Road to Hell*, Vol. 1, #1 [Graphic Novel]. New York, NY: Marvel Publishing.

Aaron, J. (2014). *Amazing X-Men* #4 [Graphic Novel]. New York, NY: Marvel Publishing.

American Psychiatric Association. (2013). *Diagnostic and Statistical Manual of Mental Disorders* (5th ed.). Washington, D.C.: American Psychiatric Publishing.

"Antisocial Personality Disorder." (2013). Mayo Foundation for Medical Education and Research. Retrieved from https://www.mayoclinic.org/diseases-conditions/antisocial-personality-disorder/symptoms-causes/syc-20353928.

Bendis, B.M. (2005). *House of M*, Vol. 8 [Graphic Novel]. New York, NY: Marvel Publishing.

Blow, C.M. (2016, July 8). "A Week in Hell." *New York Times*.

Booker, M.K. (Ed.). (2010). *Encyclopedia of Comic Books and Graphic Novels*, Vol. 2. Santa Barbara, CA: Greenwood Press.

Burton, N. (2012, May 23). "Our Hierarchy of Needs." *Psychology Today*. Retrieved from https://www.psychologytoday.com/blog/hide-and-seek/201205/our-hierarchy-needs.

Buss, D.M., & Duntley, J.D. (2006). "The Evolution of Aggression." In M. Schaller, J.A. Simpson, & D.T. Kenrick (Eds.), *Evolution and Social Learning*. New York, NY: Psychology Press.

Campbell, J. (1949). *The Hero with a Thousand Faces*. Princeton, NJ: Princeton University Press.

Caspar, E.A., Christensen, J F., Cleeremans, A., & Haggard, P. (2016). "Coercion Changes the Sense of Agency in the Human Brain." *Current Biology, 26*(5), 585–592.

Center for Sex Offender Management. (n.d.). "Section 1: Lecture Content & Teaching Notes—Supervision of Sex Offenders in the Community: An Overview." Retrieved May 25, 2008, from http://www.csom.org/train/supervision/medium/01_02_04.html.

Claremont, C. (1982). *Wolverine* #1–4 [Graphic Novel]. New York, NY: Marvel Publishing.

Claremont, C. (1982). *X-Men: God Loves, Man Kills* [Graphic Novel]. New York, NY: Marvel Publishing.

Claremont, C. (1984). *Uncanny X-Men*, Vol. 1, #183 [Graphic Novel]. New York, NY: Marvel Publishing.

Claremont, C. (1998). *Wolverine*, Vol. 2, #125 [Graphic Novel]. New York, NY: Marvel Publishing.

Claremont, C. (1998). *Wolverine*, Vol. 2, #126 [Graphic Novel]. New York, NY: Marvel Publishing.

Claremont, C. (2008). *X-Men: Kitty Pryde & Wolverine* [Graphic Novel]. New York, NY: Marvel Publishing.

Claremont, C., & Byrne, J. (2012). *The Uncanny X-Men: The Dark Phoenix Saga* #129–138 [Graphic Novel]. New York, NY: Marvel Publishing.

Crittenden, P. (1999). "Danger and Development: The Organisation of Self-Protective Strategies." In J.I. Vondra & D. Barnett (Eds.), *Atypical Attachment in Infancy and Early Childhood Among Children at Developmental Risk* (pp. 145–171). Malden, MA: Society for Research in Child Development.

Daley, M., & Wilson, M. (1988). "Evolutionary Social Psychology and Family Homicide." *Science, 242,* 519–524.

Darowski, J.J. (2014). *X-Men and the Mutant Metaphor: Race and Gender in the Comic Book.* Lanham, MD: Rowman & Littlefield.

DeFalco, T. (2003). *Hulk: The Incredible Guide.* London, UK: Dorling Kindersley.

Diamond, L.M. (2003). "What Does Sexual Orientation Orient? A Biobehavioral Model Distinguishing Romantic Love and Sexual Desire." *Psychology Review, 110*(1), 173–192.

Duntley, J.D. (2005). "Adaptations to Dangers from Humans." In D.M. Buss (Ed.), *The Handbook of Evolutionary Psychology* (pp. 224–254). Hoboken, NJ: John Wiley & Sons.

Editorial Board. (2016, June 15). "The Corrosive Politics That Threaten L.G.B.T. Americans." *New York Times.* Retrieved from https://www.nytimes.com/2016/06/15/opinion/the-corrosive-politics-that-threaten-lgbt-americans.html.

Fingeroth, D. (2004). *Superman on the Couch: What Superheroes Really Tell Us About Ourselves and Society.* New York, NY: Continuum.

Fisher, H.E., Aron, A., Mashek, D.M., Li, H., & Brown, L.L. (2002). "Defining the Brain Systems of Lust, Romantic Attraction, and Attachment." *Archives of Sexual Behavior, 31*(5), 413–419.

Fletcher, R. (2017, January 19). "Exclusive: Logan Director James Mangold Gives Us a Scene-by-Scene Breakdown of His Explosive New Trailer" [Video File]. *Digital Spy.* Retrieved from http://www.digitalspy.com/movies/wolverine/feature/a819368/logan-director-james-mangold-breaks-down-violent-new-trailer-wolverine-x-men-movie/.

Frankl, V. (1997). *Man's Search for Meaning.* London, UK: Pocket Books.

Gruenwald, M. (1993). *Captain America,* Vol. 1, #419 [Graphic Novel]. New York, NY: Marvel Publishing.

Hamma, L. (1996). "Fade to Black." *Wolverine,* Vol. 2, #98 [Graphic Novel]. New York, NY: Marvel Publishing.

"Hate Map." (n.d.). Southern Poverty Law Center. Retrieved December 7, 2015, from https://www.splcenter.org/hate-map.

Hiatt, B. (2017). "How 'Logan' Director James Mangold Made the Most Violent Wolverine Movie Yet." *Rolling Stone.* Retrieved March 2, 2017, from https://www.rollingstone.com/movies/features/logan-director-on-making-a-wolverine-movie-for-the-fans-w469808.

Hood, G. (Director). (2009). *X-Men Origins: Wolverine* [Motion Picture]. United States: Twentieth Century–Fox.

Howe, D. (2011). *Attachment Across the Lifecourse.* Basingstoke, UK: Palgrave Macmillan.

Humphries, S. (2013). *Avengers A.I.* #2 [Graphic Novel]. New York, NY: Marvel Publishing.

Innes, B. (2016). *The History of Torture* (Rev. Upd. ed.). London, UK: Amber Books.

Interview with Adam Kubert, via telephone (2017, April 11).

Interview with Chandler Rice, via telephone (2017, May 22).

Interview with Clive Hazell, via telephone (2017, April 21).

Interview with David Spurlock, via telephone (2017, March 12).

Interview with Doug Kline, via telephone (2017, September 26).

Interview with Ed Ottesen, via telephone (2017, October 7).

Interview with Elliott Serrano, via telephone (2016, December 27).

Interview with Eric Snyder (2017, February 22).

Interview with Gerald Newport (2017, March 3).

Interview with Joe Garcia (2017, January 8).
Interview with Joe Rubinstein (2016, September 9).
Interview with Joel Terry (2016, November 12).
Interview with John Romita, Jr. (2016, September 9).
Interview with John Romita, Sr. (2017, May 2).
Interview with Jon McCaine, via telephone (2017, June 14).
Interview with Joseph de la Rosa, via telephone (2017, June 13).
Interview with Larry Yarborough, via telephone (2017, October 28).
Interview with Len Wein (2017, February 18).
Interview with Lisa Gaudet (2017, November 12).
Interview with Max Stoltenberg, via telephone (2017, January 10).
Interview with Patricia Trimpe (2016, September 9).
Interview with Paul Jenkins, via telephone (2016, February 4).
Interview with Roumen Bezergianov (2017, April 12).
Interview with Roy Thomas, via Facebook Messenger (2017, May 19).
Interview with Tehrina Billi (2017, November 12).
Interview with Tom DeFalco (2017, May 31).
Interview with Vijay Jain (2016, November 14).
Janis, I.L. (1982). "Decision Making Under Stress." In L. Goldberger & S. Breznitz (Eds.), *Handbook of Stress: Theoretical and Clinical Aspects* (pp. 69–87). New York, NY: Free Press.
Jenkins, P., & Castellini, C. (2004). *Wolverine: The End*, Vols. 1–6 [Graphic Novel]. New York, NY: Marvel Publishing.
Jenkins, P., & Jemas, B. (2009). *Wolverine: Origin*, Vols. 1–6 [Graphic Novel]. New York, NY: Marvel Publishing.
Jonason, P.K., Webster, G.D., Schmitt, D.P., Li, N.P., & Crysel, L. (2012). "The Antihero in Popular Culture: Life History Theory and the Dark Triad Personality Traits." *Review of General Psychology, 16*(2), 192–199.
Jonsson, P. (2011). "Annual Report Cites Rise in Hate Groups, But Some Ask: What Is Hate?" *Christian Science Monitor*. Retrieved June 29, 2015, from https://www.csmonitor.com/USA/Society/2011/0223/Annual-report-cites-rise-in-hate-groups-but-some-ask-What-is-hate.
Jung, C.G., & Hull, R. F. (1938). "Psychology and Religion." In *The Collected Works of C.G. Jung* (Vol. 11: *Psychology and Religion: West and East*). London, UK: Routledge.
Jung, C.G., & Hull, R.F. (1952). "Answer to Job." In *The Collected Works of C.G. Jung* (Vol. 11: *Psychology and Religion: West and East*). London, UK: Routledge.
Karlsson, G. (2010). *Psychoanalysis in a New Light*. Cambridge, UK: Cambridge University Press.
Kilpatrick, D.G., Vernon, L.J., & Best, C.L. (1985). "Factors Predicting Psychological Distress in Rape Victims." In C.R. Figley (Ed.), *Trauma and Its Wake*. New York, NY: Brunner/Mazel.
Kobak, R., & Madsen, S. (2008). "Disruption in Attachment Bonds." In J. Cassidy & P.R. Shaver (Eds.), *Handbook of Attachment: Theory, Research, and Clinical Applications* (pp. 23–47). New York, NY: Guilford Press.
Kolb, L.C. (1987). "Neurophysiological Hypothesis Explaining Posttraumatic Stress Disorder." *American Journal of Psychiatry, 144*, 989–995.
Kübler-Ross, E., & Kessler, D. (2007). *On Grief and Grieving: Finding the Meaning of Grief Through the Five Stages of Loss* (Reprint ed.). New York, NY: Scribner.
Lamble, R. (2014, February 25). "Hugh Jackman Interview: X-Men: Days of Future Past and Playing Wolverine." *Den of Geek!* Retrieved from http://www.denofgeek.com/us/movies/hugh-jackman/233301/hugh-jackman-interview-x-men-days-of-future-past-and-playing-wolverine.
Landa, S., & Duschinsky, R. (2013). "Crittenden's Dynamic-Maturational Model of Attachment and Adaptation." *Review of General Psychology, 17*(3), 326.

Lassri, D., & Shahar, G. (2012). "Self-Criticism Mediates the Link Between Childhood Emotional Maltreatment and Young Adults' Romantic Relationships." *Journal of Social & Clinical Psychology, 31*(3), 289–311.

Levy, D. (1937). "Primary Affect Hunger." *American Journal of Psychiatry, 94,* 643–652.

Loeb, J., Bianchi, S., Morales, M., & Deschesne, A. (2013). *Wolverine: Sabretooth Reborn* #310–313 [Graphic Novel]. New York, NY: Marvel Publishing.

Lorde, A. (1983). "The Master's Tools Will Never Dismantle the Master's House." In C. Moraga & G. Anzaldúa (Eds.), *This Bridge Called My Back: Writing by Radical Women of Color* (pp. 94–101). New York: Kitchen Table Press.

Macionis, J.J., & Gerber, L. (2010). *Sociology* (7th Canadian ed.). Toronto, ON: Pearson Canada.

Mangold, J. (Director). (2013). *The Wolverine* [Motion Picture]. United States: Twentieth Century–Fox.

Mangold, J. (Director). (2017). *Logan* [Motion Picture]. United States: Twentieth Century–Fox.

Manning, M.K. (2009). *Wolverine: Inside the World of the Living Weapon.* London, UK: Dorling Kindersley.

Maslon, L., & Kantor, M. (2013). *Superheroes! Capes, Cowls, and the Creation of the Comic Book Culture.* New York, NY: Crown Archetype.

Maslow, A.H. (1943). "A Theory of Human Motivation." *Psychological Review, 50*(4), 370–396.

McCaine, J. (2016). "Ties That Bind: Understanding Intimate Partner Violence." Workshop Presentation.

McLeod, S. (1970). "The Milgram Experiment." Retrieved from https://simplypsychology.org/milgram.html.

Milgram, S. (1974). *Obedience to Authority: An Experimental View.* New York, NY: HarperCollins.

Millar, M., McNiven, S., & Vines, D. (2008). *Old Man Logan* [Graphic Novel]. New York, NY: Marvel Publishing.

Miller, A., & Ward, R. (1979). *The Drama of the Gifted Child.* New York, NY: Basic Books.

Moore, T.M., Scarpa, A., & Raine, A. (2002). "A Meta-Analysis of Serotonin Metabolite 5-HIAA and Antisocial Behavior." *Aggressive Behavior, 28*(4), 299–316.

Morrison, G. (2003). *New X-Men,* Vol. 1, #148 [Graphic Novel]. New York, NY: Marvel Publishing.

Murray Parkes, C. (2006). *Love and Loss.* London, UK, and New York, NY: Routledge.

Myers, D.G. (2009). *Social Psychology* (10th ed.). New York, NY: McGraw-Hill Higher Education.

"Native American Wolverine Mythology." (2015). Retrieved from http://www.native-languages.org/legends-wolverine.htm.

"Nazi Germany 1933–1939: Early Stages of Persecution; How Hitler Laid the Groundwork for Genocide." (2012). *My Jewish Learning.* Retrieved from https://www.myjewish learning.com/article/1933–1939-early-stages-of-persecution/.

Nicieza, F., & Lobdell, S. (1993). *X-Men: Fatal Attractions* [Graphic Novel]. New York, NY: Marvel Publishing.

Nussbaum, M. (1995, Autumn). "Objectification." *Philosophy and Public Affairs, 24*(4), 249–291.

Orwell, G. (1945). *Animal Farm.* London, UK: Secker and Warburg.

Patočka, J. (1988). "Europa und Nach-Europa." In K. Nellen & J. Nemec (Eds.), *Ketzerische Essais zur Philosophie der Geschichte und ergänzende Schriften* (pp. 207–287). Stuttgart, BD: Klett-Cotta.

Pearlman, L.A., & Saakvitne, K.W. (1995). *Trauma and the Therapist: Countertransference and Vicarious Traumatization in Psychotherapy with Incest Survivors.* New York, NY: Norton.

Ratner, B. (Director). (2006). *X-Men: The Last Stand* [Motion Picture]. United States: Twentieth Century–Fox.

Raven Software. (2005, September). *X-Men Legends II: Rise of Apocalypse* [Video Game].

Recognizing and Responding to Suicide Risk: Essential Skills for Clinicians. (2008). Retrieved from http://www.suicidology.org/.

Rosenberg, R.S. (2013, August 6). "The Psychology of Wolverine." *Psychology Today*. Retrieved from https://www.psychologytoday.com/blog/the-superheroes/201308/the-psychology-wolverine

Sartre, J.P. (1958). "Preface." In H. Alleg, *The Question* (J. Calder, Trans.). London, UK: John Calder.

Schultz, D.P., & Schultz, S.E. (2016). *Theories of Personality* (11th ed.). Melbourne, VIC: Wadsworth.

Seligman, M. (1972). "Learned Helplessness." *Annual Review of Medicine, 23*(1), 407–412.

Seligman, M.E. (1975). *Helplessness: On Depression, Development, and Death*. New York, NY: Freeman.

Singer, B. (Director). (2000). *X-Men* [Motion Picture]. United States: Twentieth Century–Fox.

Singer, B. (Director). (2003). *X2* [Motion Picture]. United States: Twentieth Century–Fox.

Singer, B. (Director). (2016). *X-Men: Apocalypse* [Motion Picture]. United States: Twentieth Century–Fox.

Soule, C., & McNiven, S. (2014). *Death of Wolverine*, Vol. 1 [Graphic Novel]. New York, NY: Marvel Publishing.

Stedman, R. W. (1977). *Serials: Suspense and Drama by Installment*. Norman, OK: University of Oklahoma Press.

Sternberg, R.J. (2004). "A Triangular Theory of Love." In H.T. Reis & C.E. Rusbult (Eds.), *Close Relationships*. New York, NY: Psychology Press.

Sternberg, R.J. (2007). "Triangulating Love." In T.J. Oord (Ed.), *The Altruism Reader: Selections from Writings on Love, Religion, and Science*. West Conshohocken, PA: Templeton Foundation.

Tiihonen, J., Rautiainen, M.R., Ollila, H.M., Repo-Tiihonen, E., Virkkunen, M., Palotie, A., Pietiläinen, O., Kristiansson, K., Joukamaa, M., Lauerma, H., Saarela, J., Tyni, S., Vartiainen, H., Paananen, J., Goldman, D., & Paunio, T. (2015). "Genetic Background of Extreme Violent Behavior." *Molecular Psychiatry, 20*, 786–792.

Van der Kolk, B.A., & Ducey, C.P. (1989). "The Psychological Processing of Traumatic Experience: Rorschach Patterns in PTSD." *Journal of Traumatic Stress, 2*(3), 259–274.

Van der Kolk, B.A., & Greenberg, M.S. (1987). "The Psychobiology of the Trauma Response: Hyperarousal, Constriction, and Addiction to Traumatic Reexposure." In B.A. Van der Kolk (Ed.), *Psychological Trauma* (pp. 66–88). Washington, D.C.: American Psychiatric Press.

Vaughn, M. (Director). (2011). *X-Men: First Class* [Motion Picture]. United States: Twentieth Century–Fox.

Vitaro, F., Brendgen, M., & Barker, E.D. (2006). "Subtypes of Aggressive Behaviors: A Developmental Perspective." *International Journal of Behavioral Development, 30*, 12–19.

"Wally Wood Jungle Adventures with Jim King & Animan Deluxe HC." (n.d.). Forbidden Planet International. Retrieved from http://www.forbiddenplanet.co.uk/wally-wood-jungle-adventures-with-jim-king-animan-deluxe-hc

Wilson, J.P., Harel, Z., & Kahana, B. (1988). *Human Adaptation to Extreme Stress: From the Holocaust to Vietnam*. New York, NY: Plenum Press.

Windsor-Smith, B. (1993). *Marvel Comics Presents Weapon X* #72–84 [Graphic Novel]. New York, NY: Marvel Publishing.

"Wizard's Top 200 Comic Book Characters." (n.d.). *Comic Vine.* Retrieved January 29, 2015, from https://comicvine.gamespot.com/profile/johnnie619/lists/wizards-top-200-comic-book-characters/16937/.

Wood, W. (2016). *Wally Wood Jungle Adventures—Animan* (D. Spurlock, Ed.). Lakewood, NJ: Vanguard.

Index